SEVEN SEAS ENTERTAINMENT PRESENTS

Siúil, a Rún
The Girl from the Other Side

story and art by **NAGABE**   vol. 7

P9-DXM-627

TRANSLATION
Adrienne Beck

ADAPTATION
Ysabet MacFarlane

LETTERING AND RETOUCH
Lys Blakeslee

COVER DESIGN
Nicky Lim

PROOFREADER
Jocelyne Allen

ASSISTANT EDITOR
Shanti Whitesides

PRODUCTION MANAGER
Lissa Pattillo

MANAGING EDITOR
Julie Davis

EDITOR-IN-CHIEF
Adam Arnold

PUBLISHER
Jason DeAngelis

THE GIRL FROM THE OTHER SIDE: SIUIL, A RUN VOL. 7
©nagabe 2019
Originally published in Japan in 2019 by MAG Garden Corporation, Tokyo.
English translation rights arranged through TOHAN CORPORATION, Tokyo.

Seven Seas press and purchase enquiries can be sent to Marketing Manager
Lianne Sentar at press@gomanga.com. Information regarding the distribution
and purchase of digital editions is available from Digital Manager CK Russell
at digital@gomanga.com.

Seven Seas and the Seven Seas logo are trademarks of
Seven Seas Entertainment. All rights reserved.

ISBN: 978-1-64275-116-1

Printed in Canada

First Printing: August 2019

10 9 8 7 6 5 4 3 2 1

FOLLOW US ONLINE: *www.sevenseasentertainment.com*

READING DIRECTIONS

This book reads from *right to left*, Japanese style.
If this is your first time reading manga, you start
reading from the top right panel on each page and
take it from there. If you get lost, just follow the
numbered diagram here. It may seem backwards at
first, but you'll get the hang of it! Have fun!!

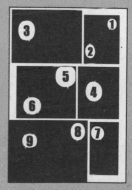

A Bonus from the Outside

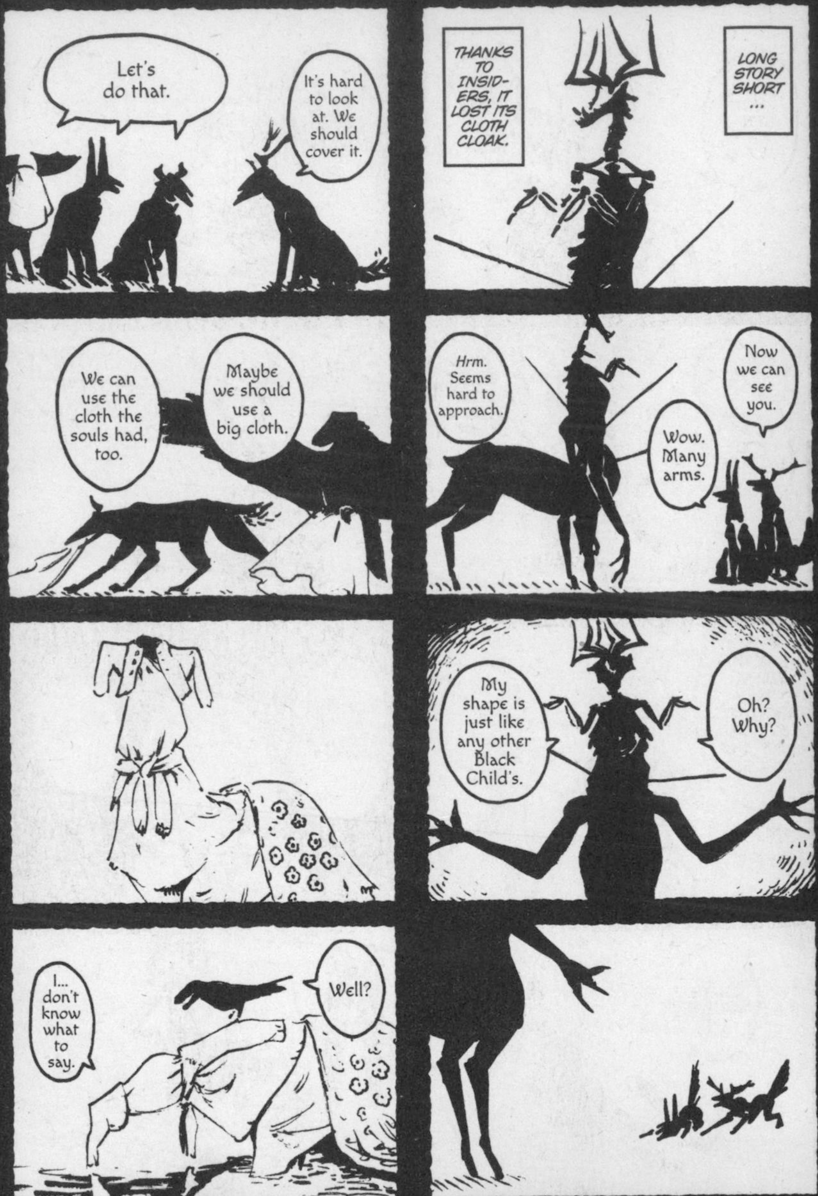

LONG STORY SHORT ...
THANKS TO INSIDERS, IT LOST ITS CLOTH CLOAK.
It's hard to look at. We should cover it.
Let's do that.
Now we can see you.
Wow. Many arms.
Hrm. Seems hard to approach.
Maybe we should use a big cloth.
We can use the cloth the souls had, too.
Oh? Why?
My shape is just like any other Black Child's.
Well?
I... don't know what to say.

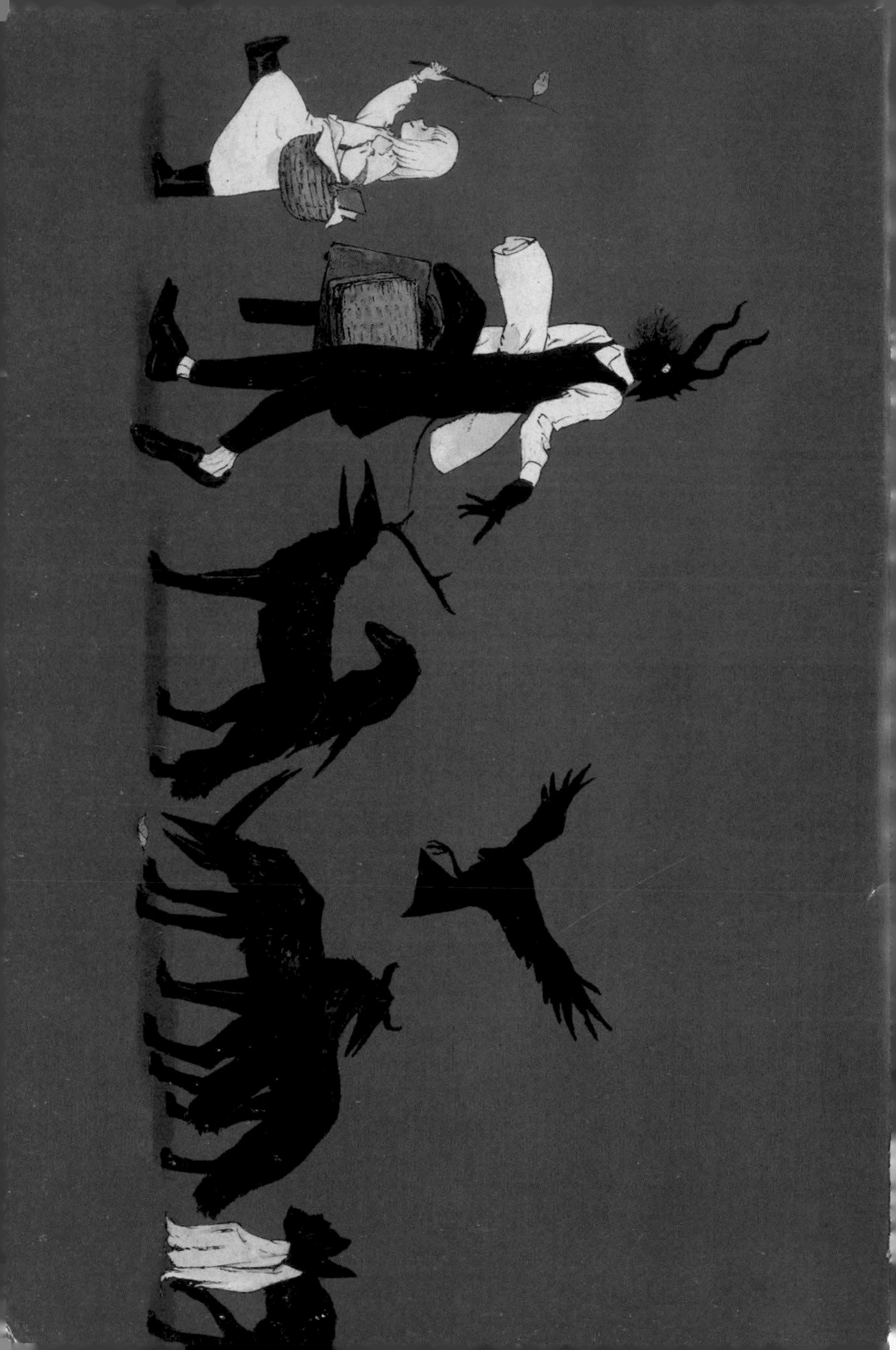

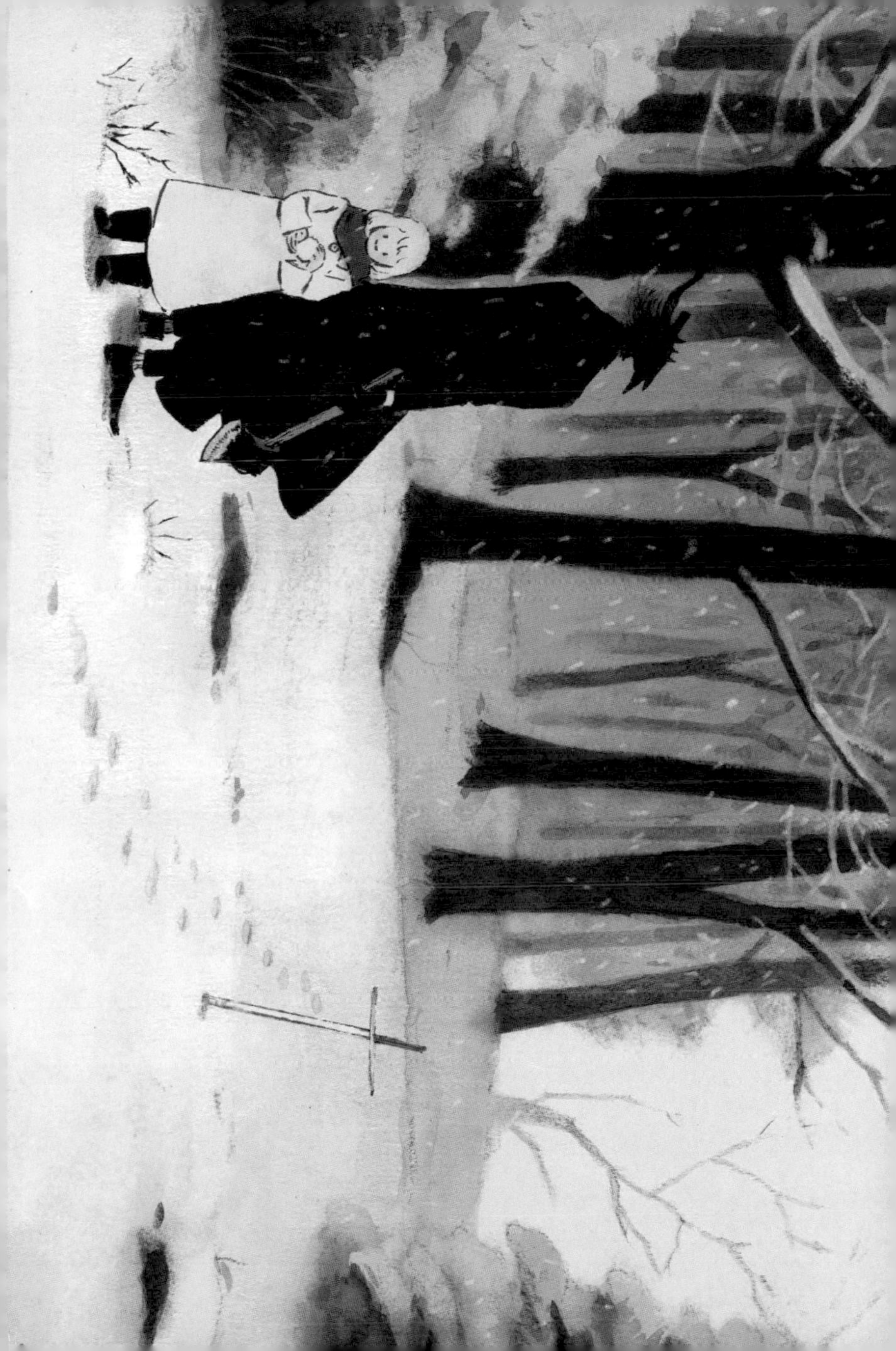

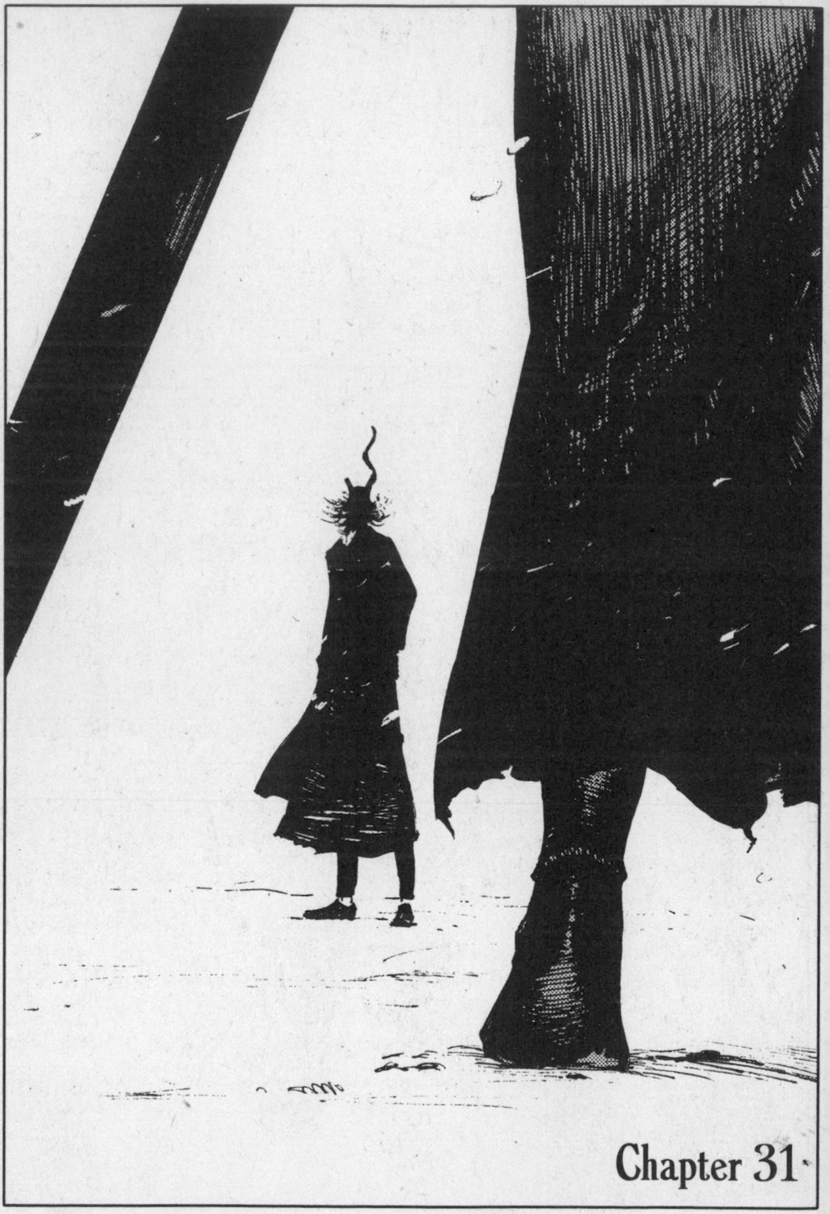
Chapter 31

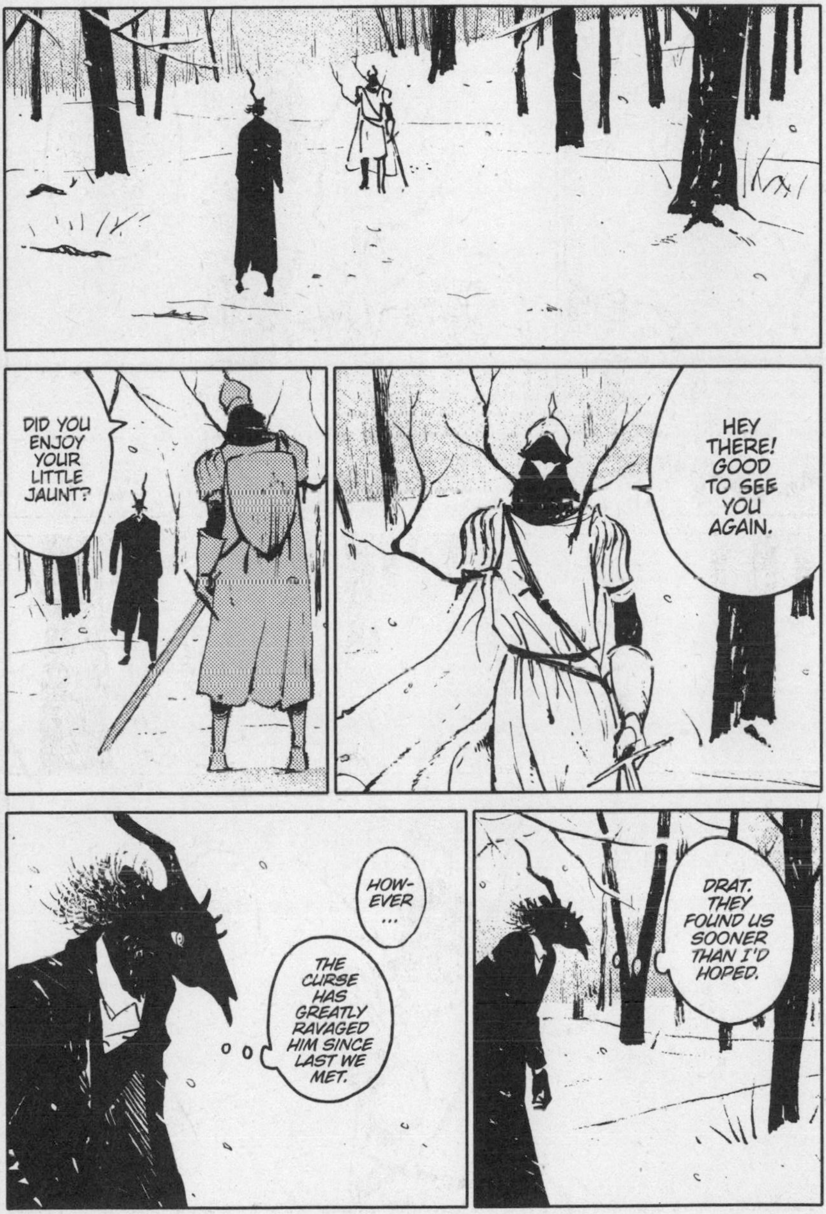
HEY THERE! GOOD TO SEE YOU AGAIN.
DID YOU ENJOY YOUR LITTLE JAUNT?
DRAT. THEY FOUND US SOONER THAN I'D HOPED.
HOW-EVER...
THE CURSE HAS GREATLY RAVAGED HIM SINCE LAST WE MET.

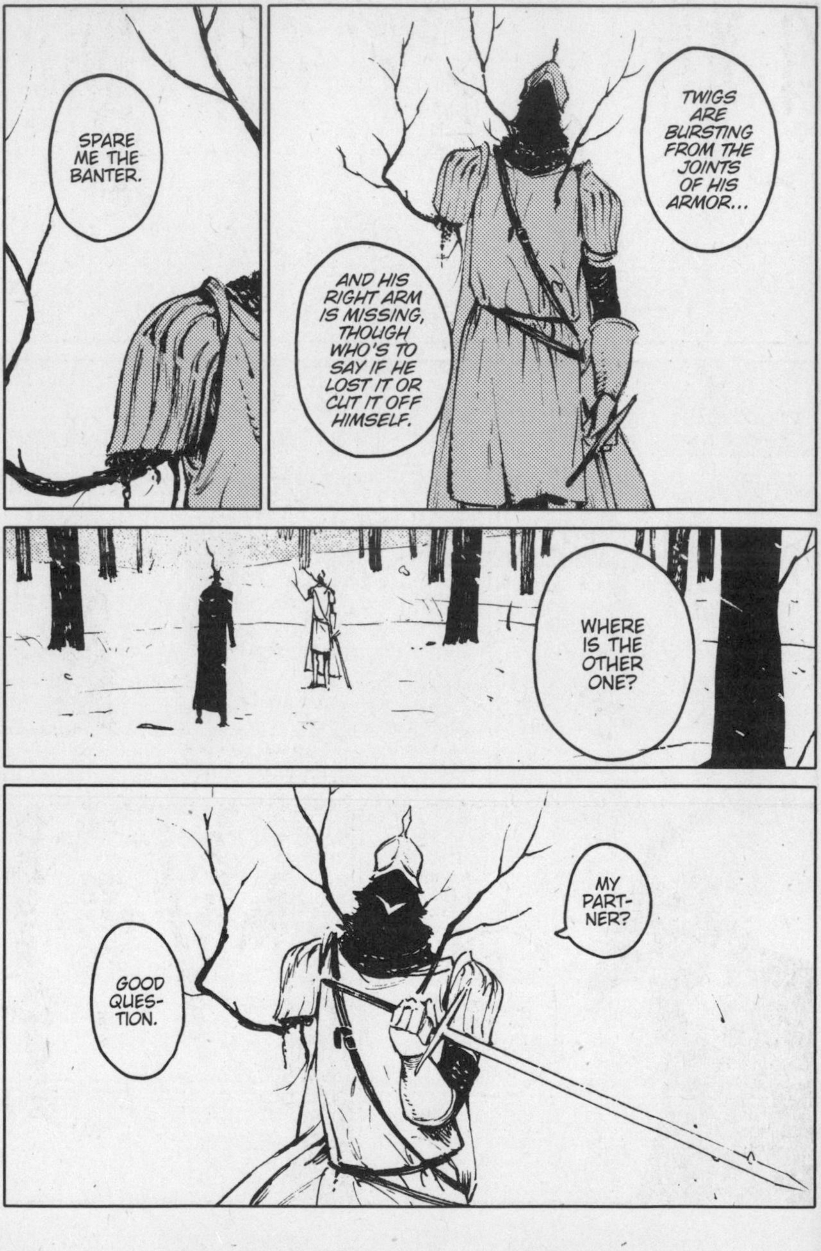
TWIGS ARE BURSTING FROM THE JOINTS OF HIS ARMOR...
AND HIS RIGHT ARM IS MISSING, THOUGH WHO'S TO SAY IF HE LOST IT OR CUT IT OFF HIMSELF.
SPARE ME THE BANTER.
WHERE IS THE OTHER ONE?
MY PART-NER?
GOOD QUES-TION.

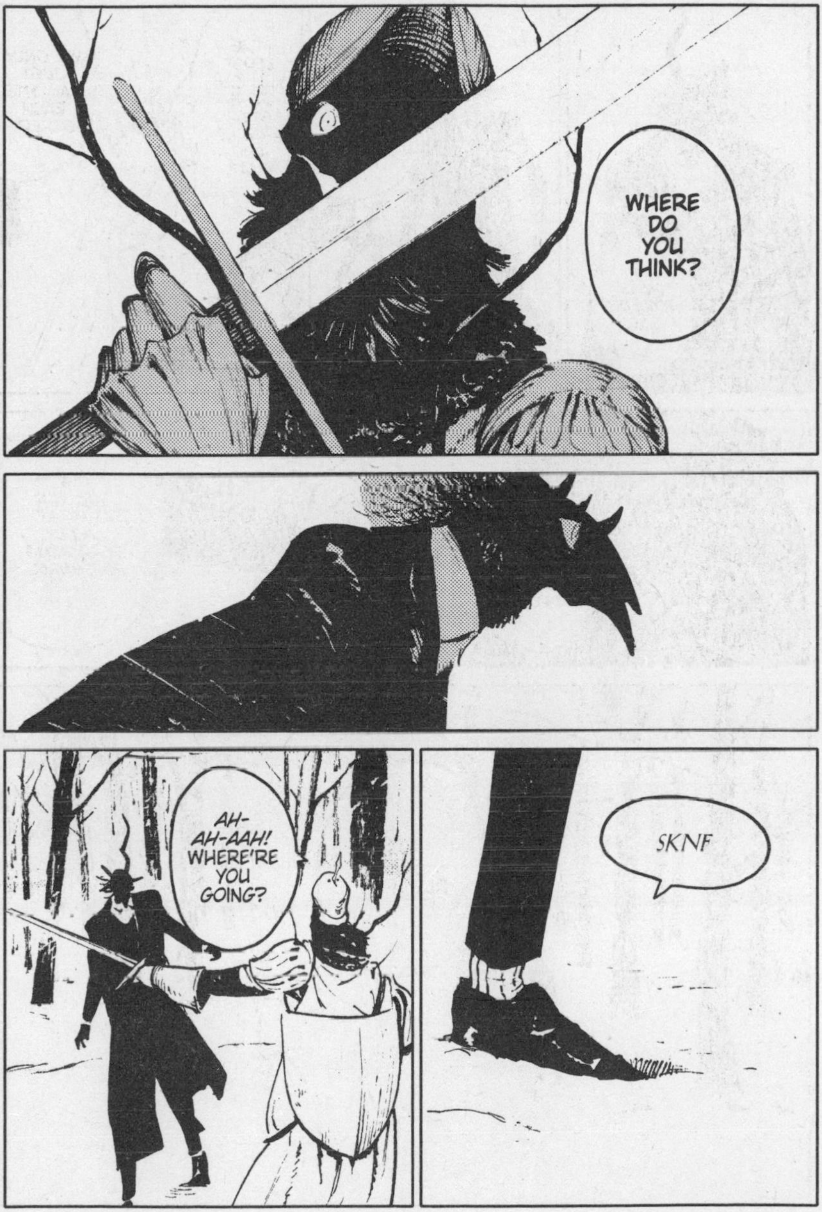
WHERE DO YOU THINK?
SKNF
AH-AH-AAH! WHERE'RE YOU GOING?

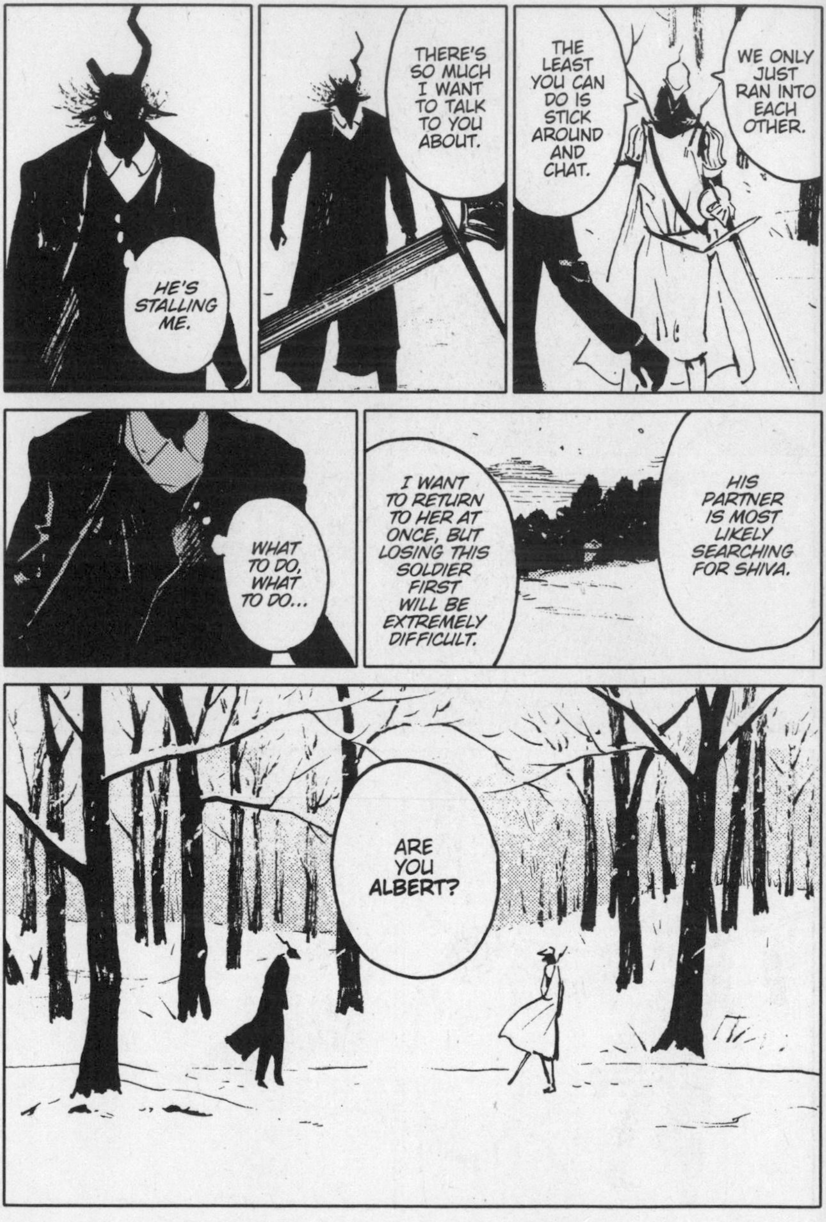
WE ONLY JUST RAN INTO EACH OTHER.
THE LEAST YOU CAN DO IS STICK AROUND AND CHAT.
THERE'S SO MUCH I WANT TO TALK TO YOU ABOUT.
HE'S STALLING ME.
HIS PARTNER IS MOST LIKELY SEARCHING FOR SHIVA.
I WANT TO RETURN TO HER AT ONCE, BUT LOSING THIS SOLDIER FIRST WILL BE EXTREMELY DIFFICULT.
WHAT TO DO, WHAT TO DO...
ARE YOU ALBERT?

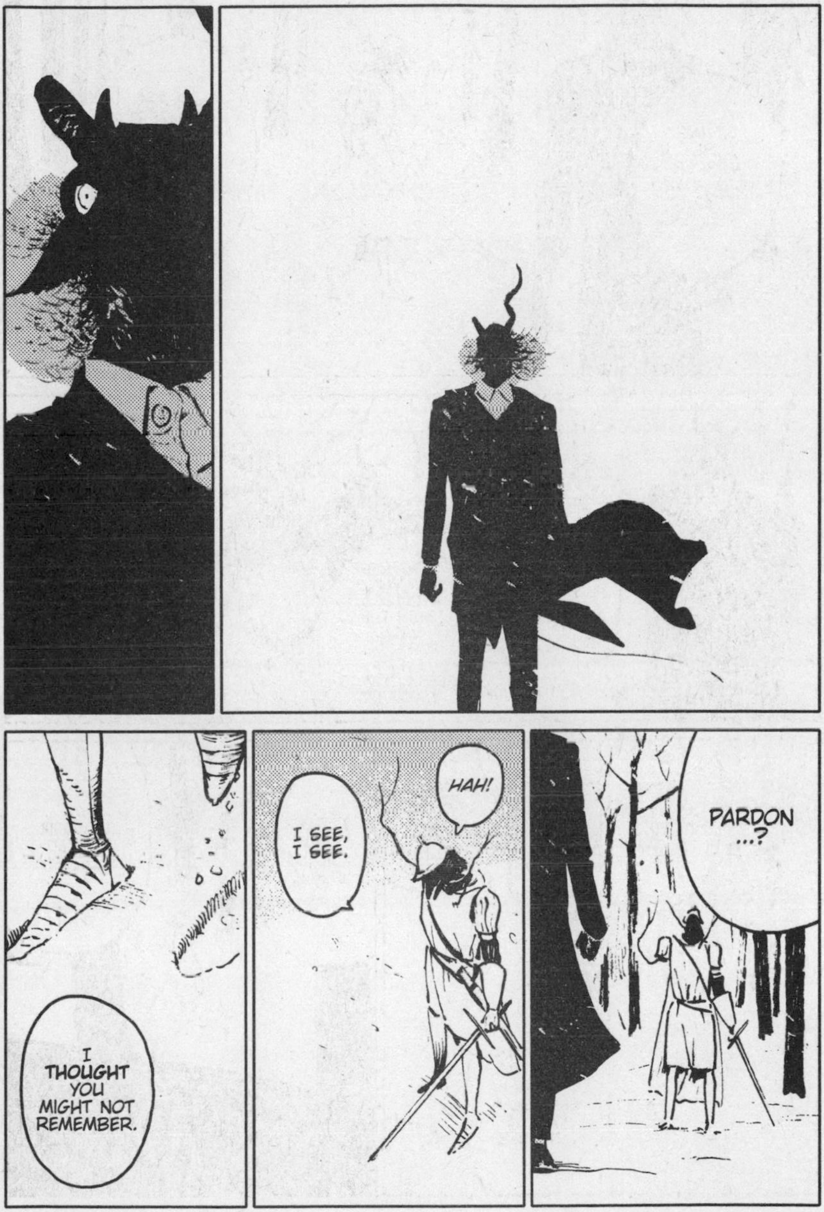
PARDON ...?
HAH!
I SEE, I SEE.
I THOUGHT YOU MIGHT NOT REMEMBER.

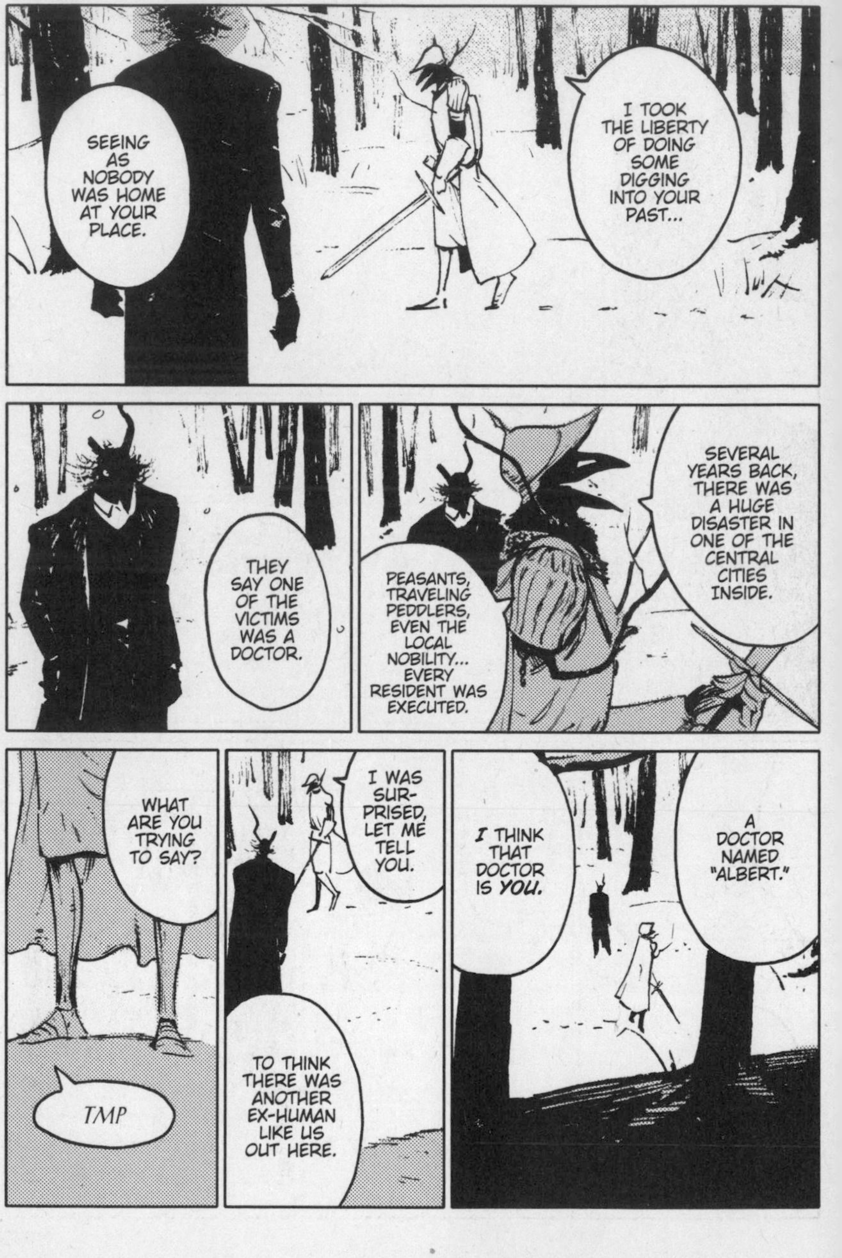
I TOOK THE LIBERTY OF DOING SOME DIGGING INTO YOUR PAST...
SEEING AS NOBODY WAS HOME AT YOUR PLACE.
SEVERAL YEARS BACK, THERE WAS A HUGE DISASTER IN ONE OF THE CENTRAL CITIES INSIDE.
PEASANTS, TRAVELING PEDDLERS, EVEN THE LOCAL NOBILITY... EVERY RESIDENT WAS EXECUTED.
THEY SAY ONE OF THE VICTIMS WAS A DOCTOR.
A DOCTOR NAMED "ALBERT."
I THINK THAT DOCTOR IS ***YOU.***
I WAS SUR-PRISED, LET ME TELL YOU.
TO THINK THERE WAS ANOTHER EX-HUMAN LIKE US OUT HERE.
WHAT ARE YOU TRYING TO SAY?
TMP

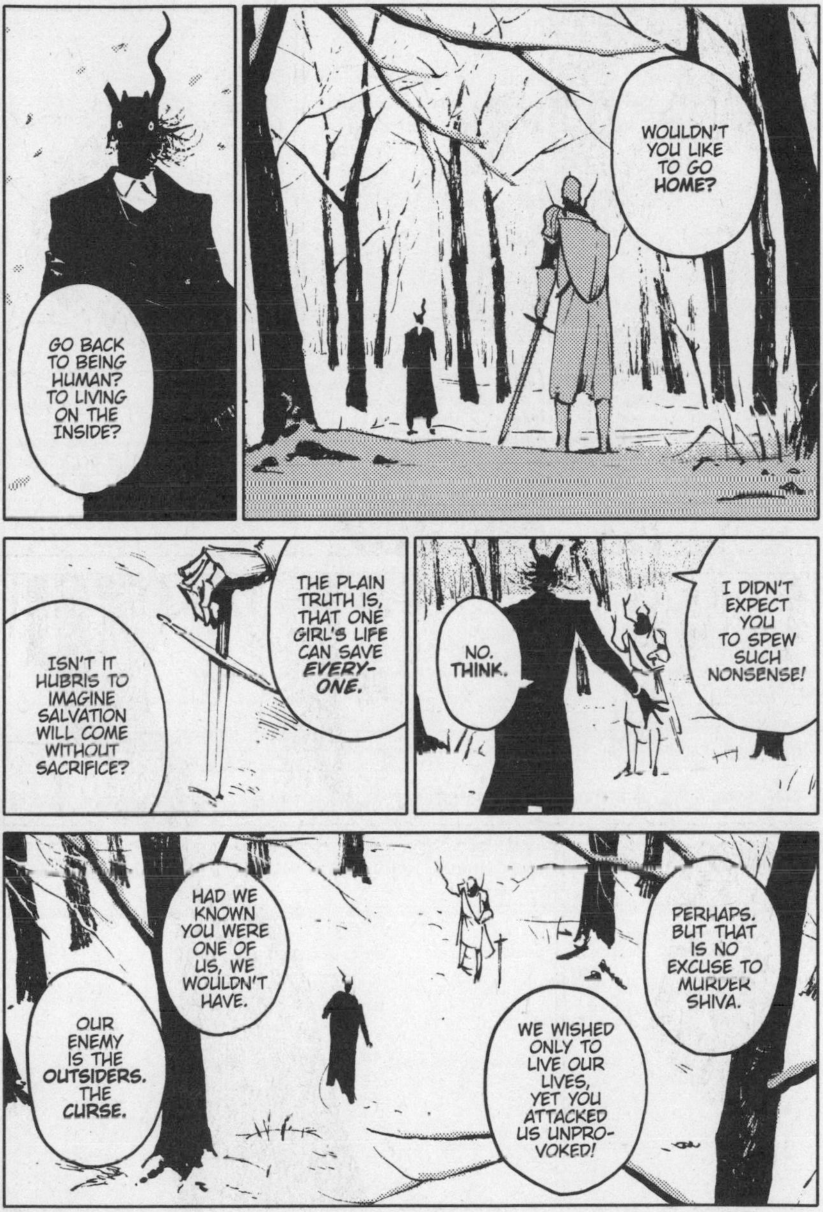
WOULDN'T YOU LIKE TO GO HOME?
GO BACK TO BEING HUMAN? TO LIVING ON THE INSIDE?
I DIDN'T EXPECT YOU TO SPEW SUCH NONSENSE!
NO. THINK.
THE PLAIN TRUTH IS, THAT ONE GIRL'S LIFE CAN SAVE EVERY-ONE.
ISN'T IT HUBRIS TO IMAGINE SALVATION WILL COME WITHOUT SACRIFICE?
PERHAPS. BUT THAT IS NO EXCUSE TO MURDER SHIVA.
WE WISHED ONLY TO LIVE OUR LIVES, YET YOU ATTACKED US UNPROVOKED!
HAD WE KNOWN YOU WERE ONE OF US, WE WOULDN'T HAVE.
OUR ENEMY IS THE OUTSIDERS. THE CURSE.

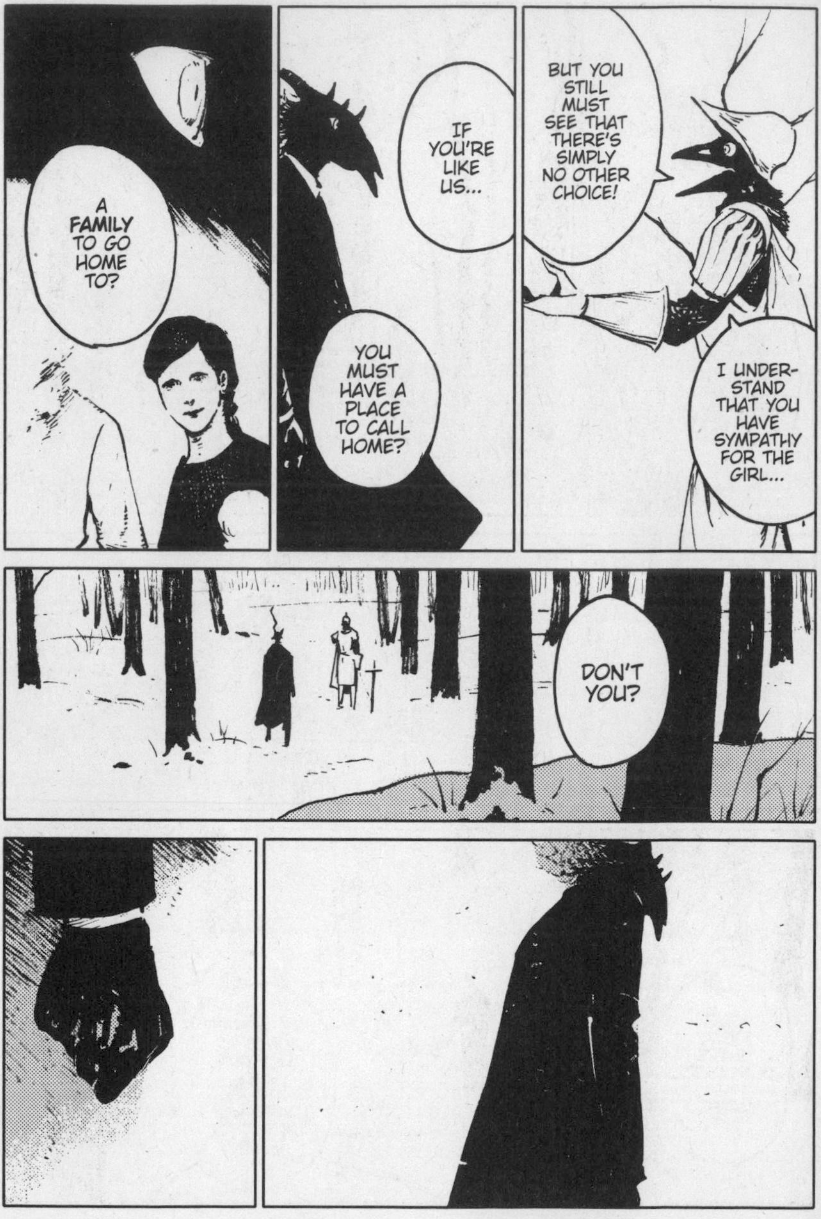
I UNDERSTAND THAT YOU HAVE SYMPATHY FOR THE GIRL...
BUT YOU STILL MUST SEE THAT THERE'S SIMPLY NO OTHER CHOICE!
IF YOU'RE LIKE US...
YOU MUST HAVE A PLACE TO CALL HOME?
A FAMILY TO GO HOME TO?
DON'T YOU?

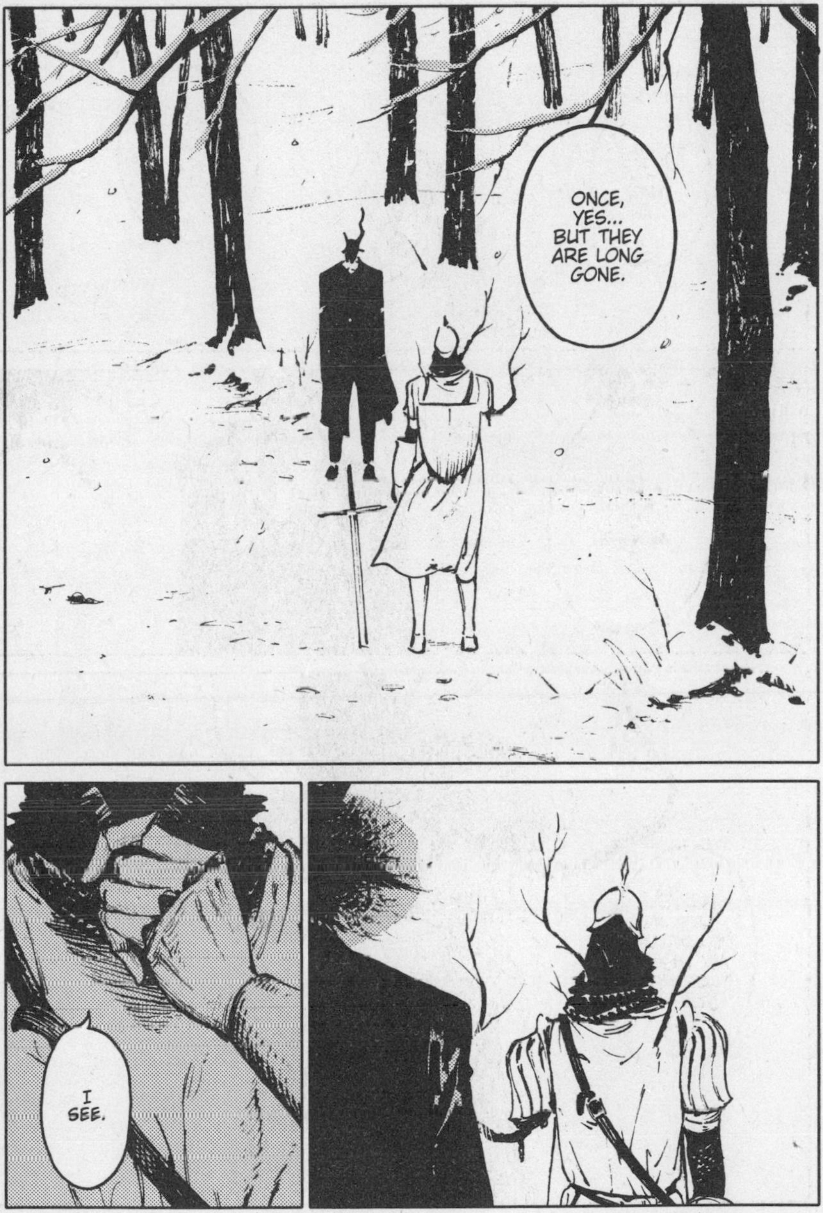
ONCE, YES... BUT THEY ARE LONG GONE.
I SEE.

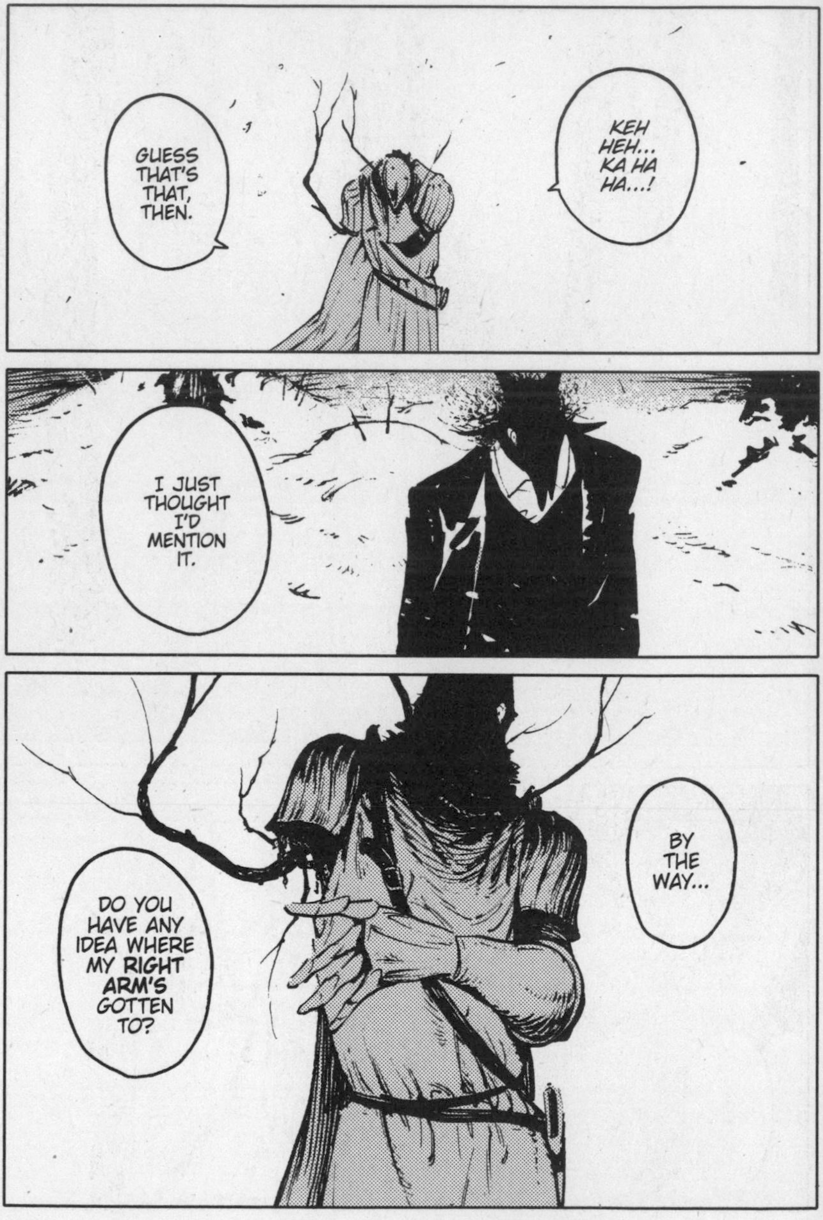
KEH HEH... KA HA HA...!
GUESS THAT'S THAT, THEN.
I JUST THOUGHT I'D MENTION IT.
BY THE WAY...
DO YOU HAVE ANY IDEA WHERE MY **RIGHT ARM'S** GOTTEN TO?

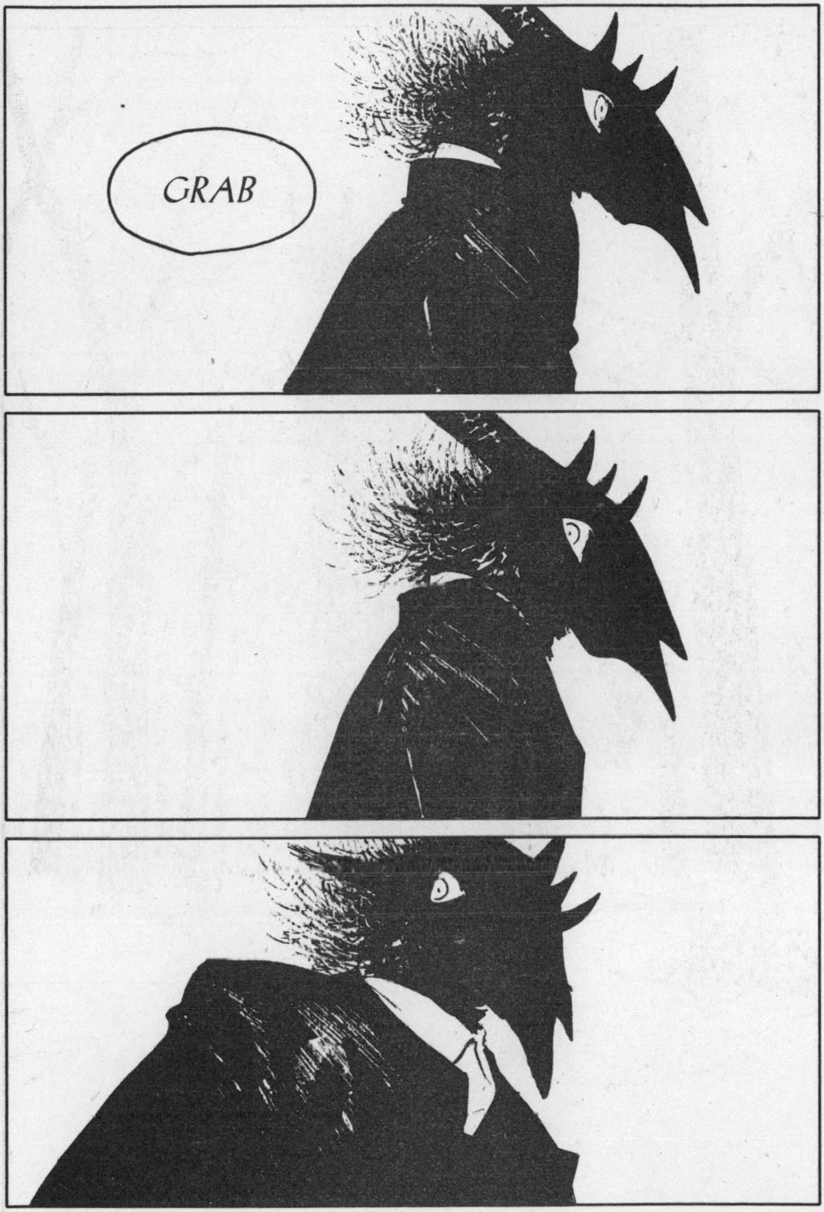
GRAB

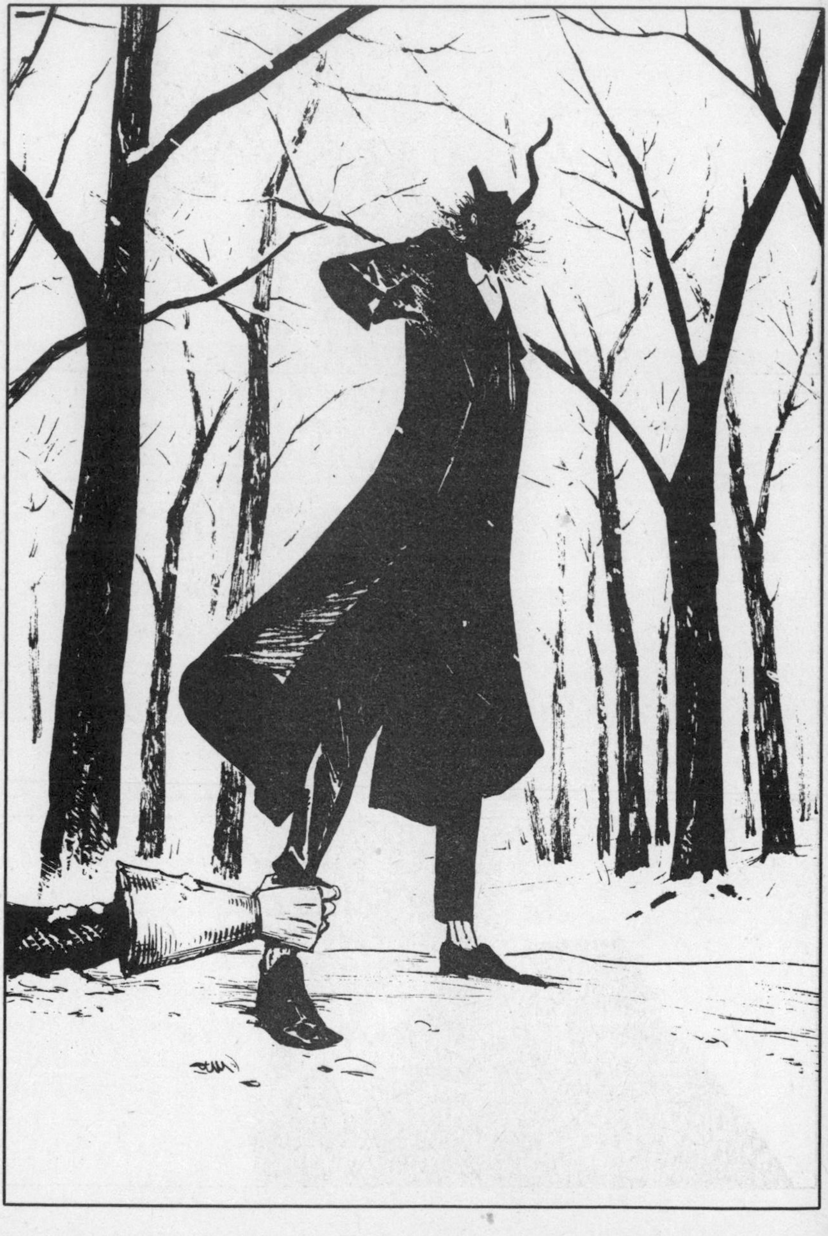

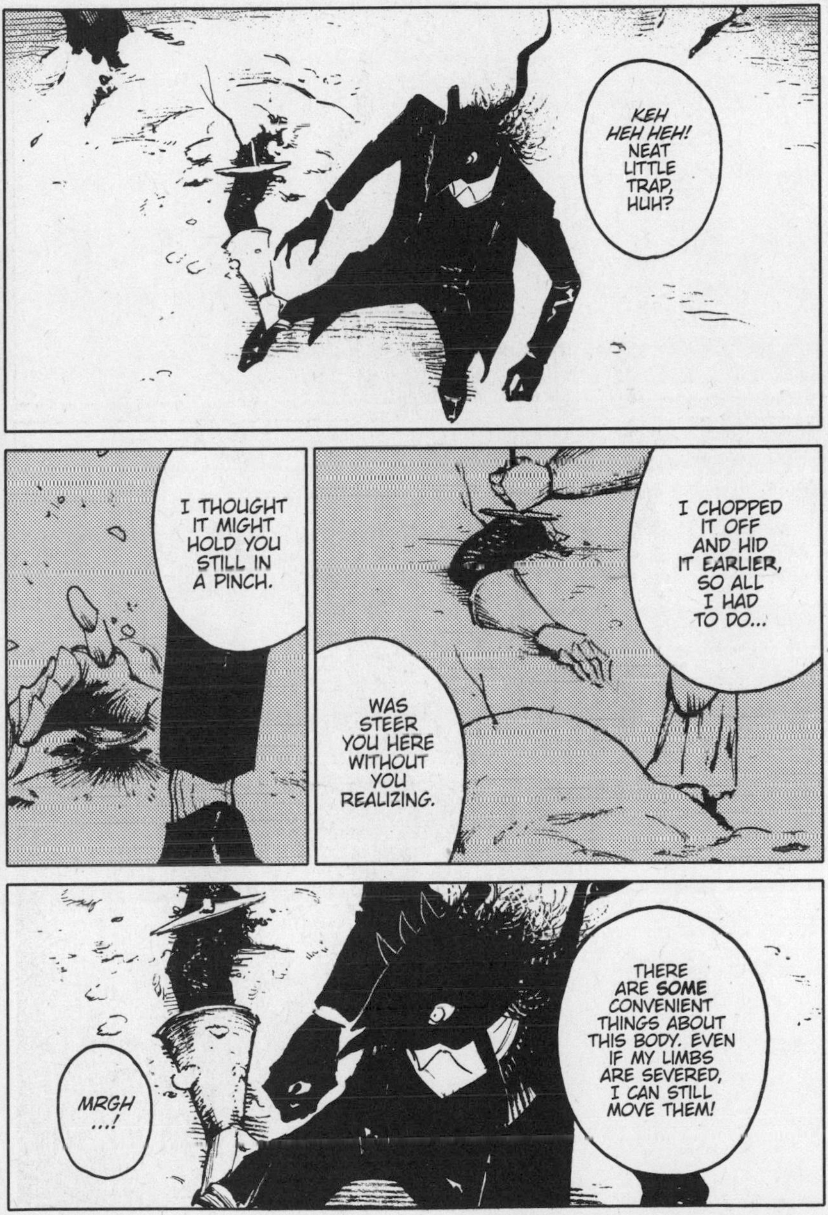
KEH HEH HEH! NEAT LITTLE TRAP, HUH?
I CHOPPED IT OFF AND HID IT EARLIER, SO ALL I HAD TO DO...
WAS STEER YOU HERE WITHOUT YOU REALIZING.
I THOUGHT IT MIGHT HOLD YOU STILL IN A PINCH.
THERE ARE SOME CONVENIENT THINGS ABOUT THIS BODY. EVEN IF MY LIMBS ARE SEVERED, I CAN STILL MOVE THEM!
MRGH ...!

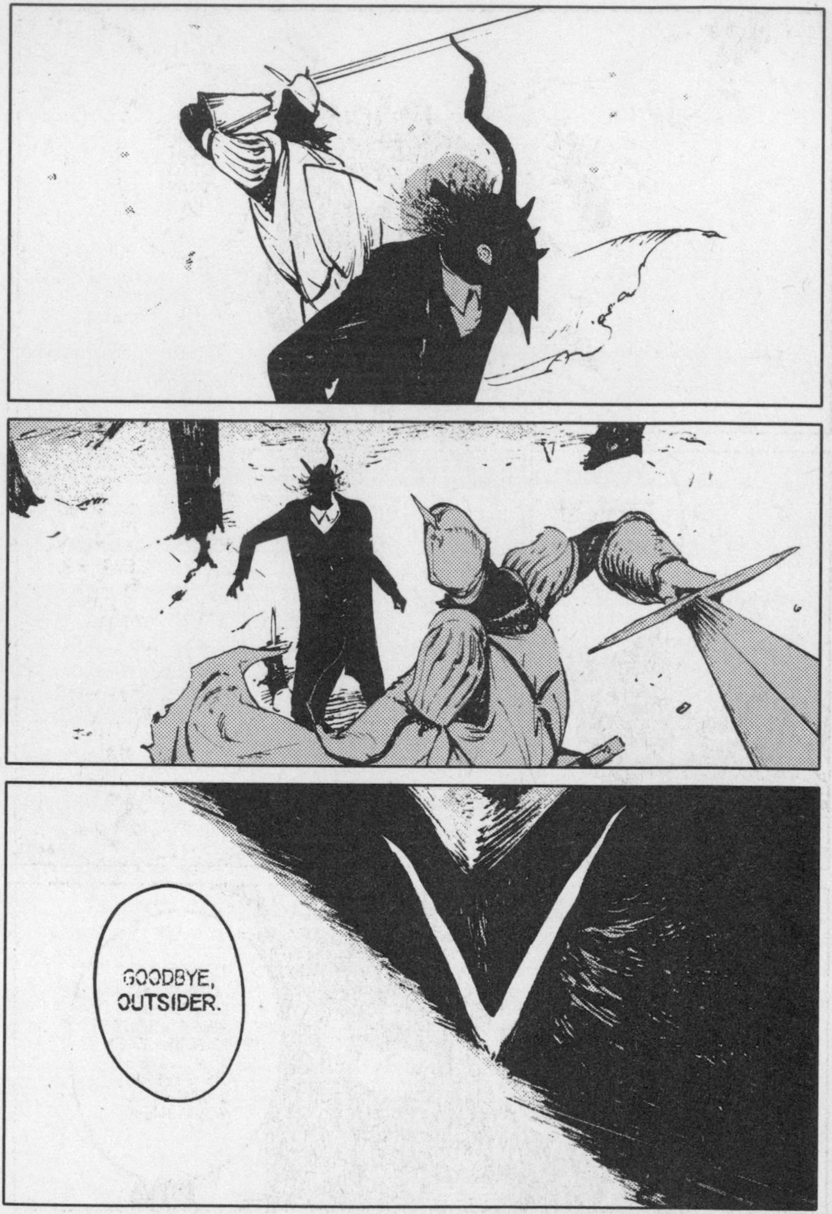
GOODBYE,
OUTSIDER.

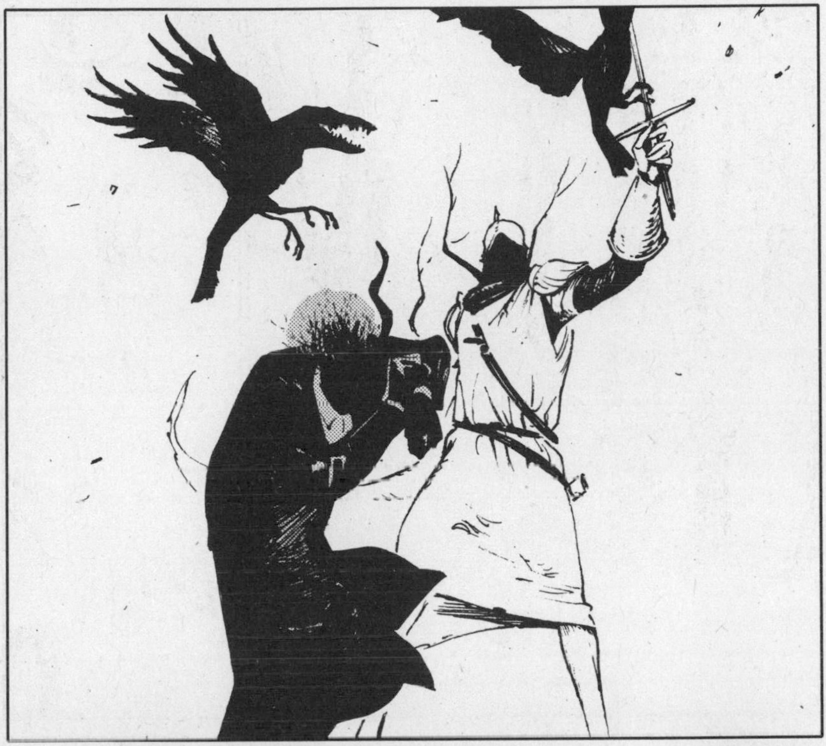

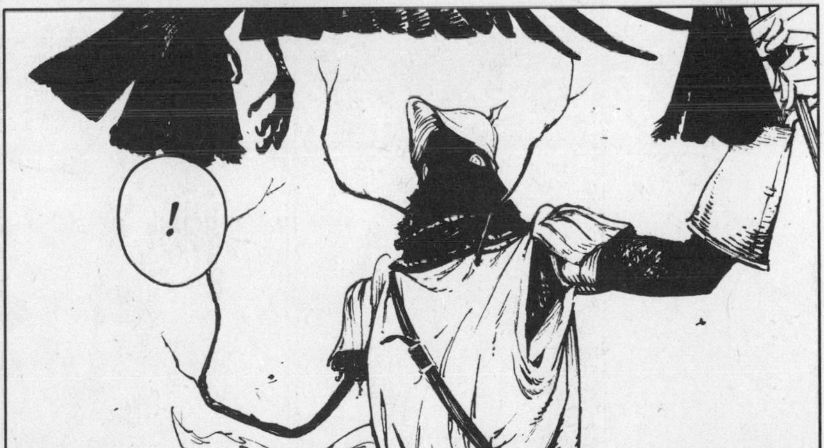
!

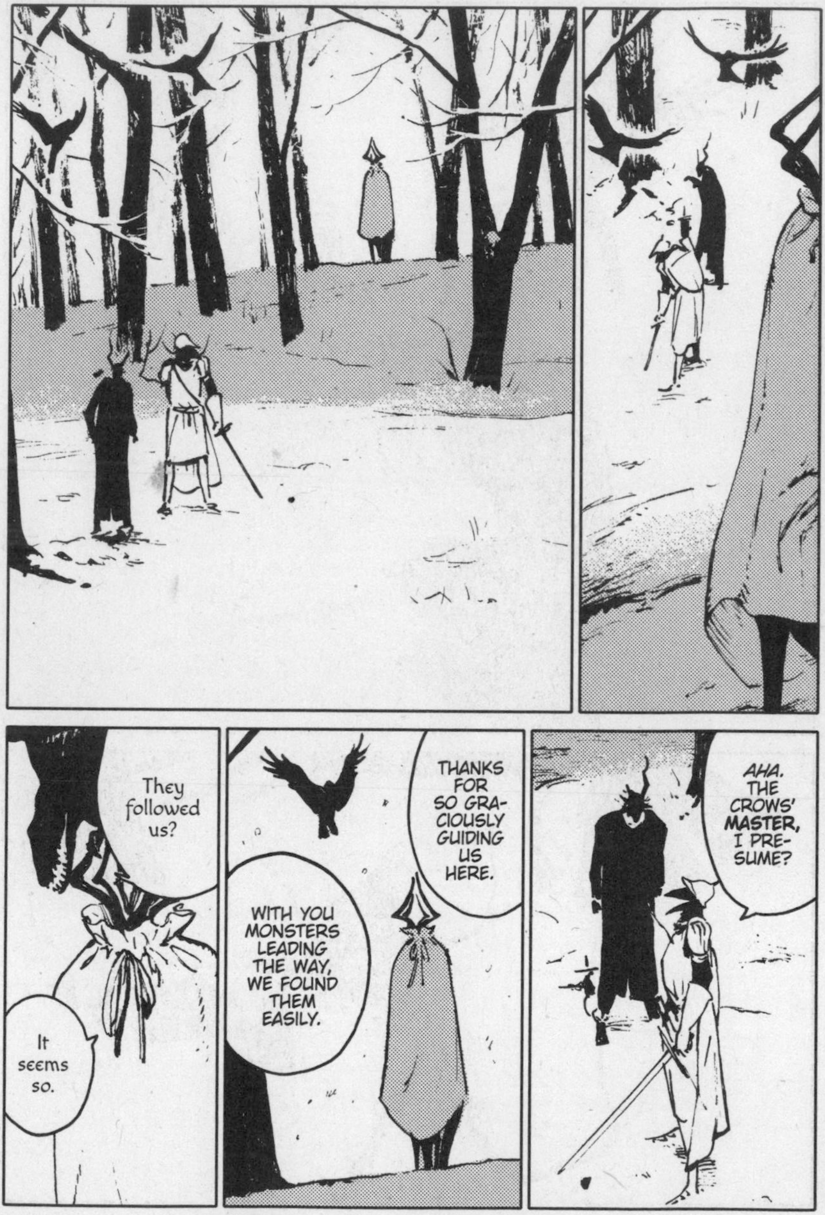
AHA. THE CROWS' MASTER, I PRESUME?
THANKS FOR SO GRACIOUSLY GUIDING US HERE.
WITH YOU MONSTERS LEADING THE WAY, WE FOUND THEM EASILY.
They followed us?
It seems so.

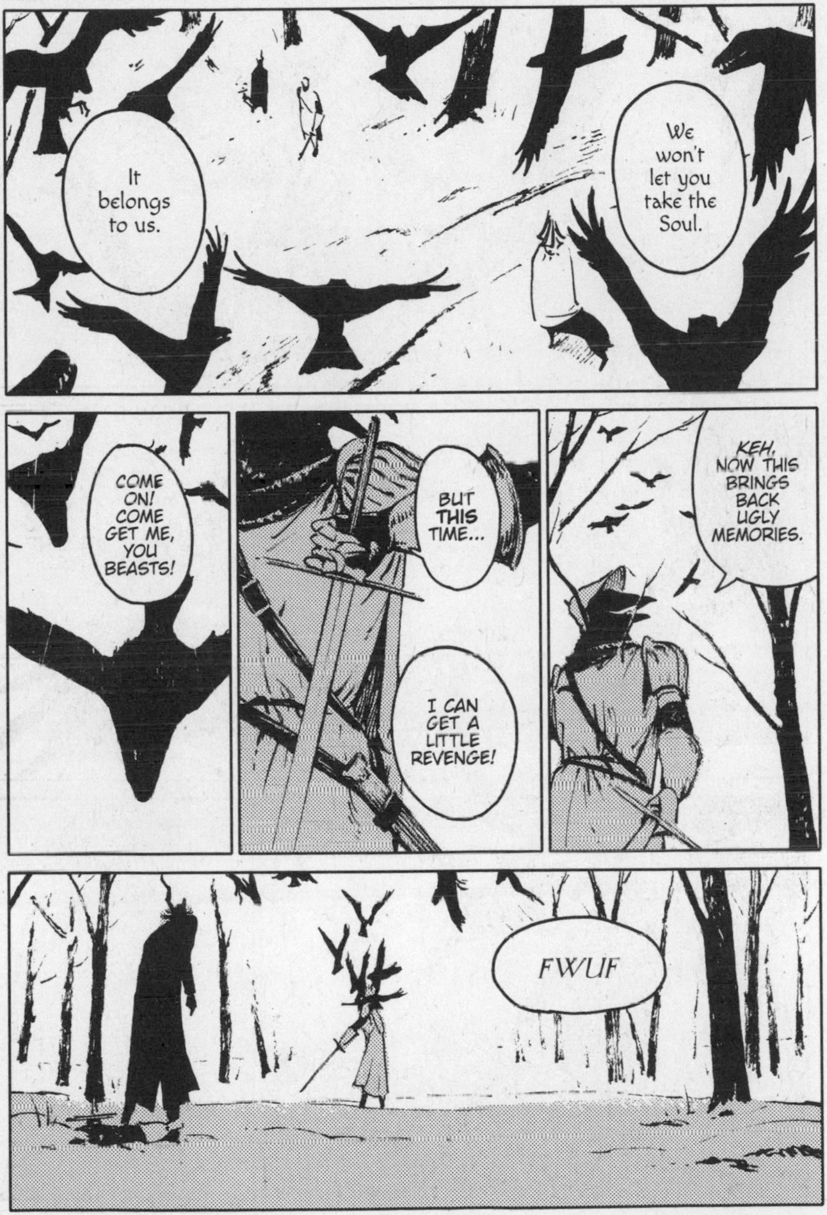
We won't let you take the Soul.
It belongs to us.
KEH, NOW THIS BRINGS BACK UGLY MEMORIES.
BUT THIS TIME...
I CAN GET A LITTLE REVENGE!
COME ON! COME GET ME, YOU BEASTS!
FWUF

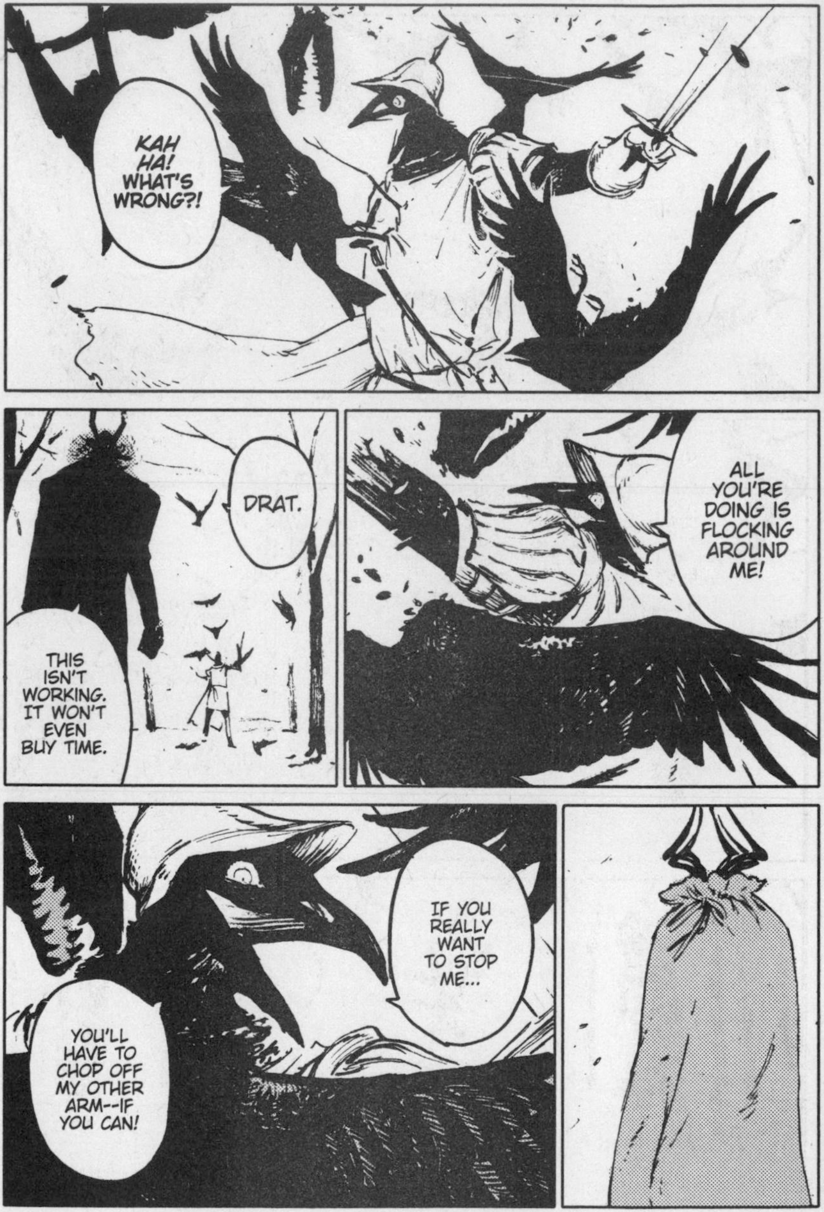
KAH HA! WHAT'S WRONG?!
ALL YOU'RE DOING IS FLOCKING AROUND ME!
DRAT.
THIS ISN'T WORKING. IT WON'T EVEN BUY TIME.
IF YOU REALLY WANT TO STOP ME...
YOU'LL HAVE TO CHOP OFF MY OTHER ARM--IF YOU CAN!

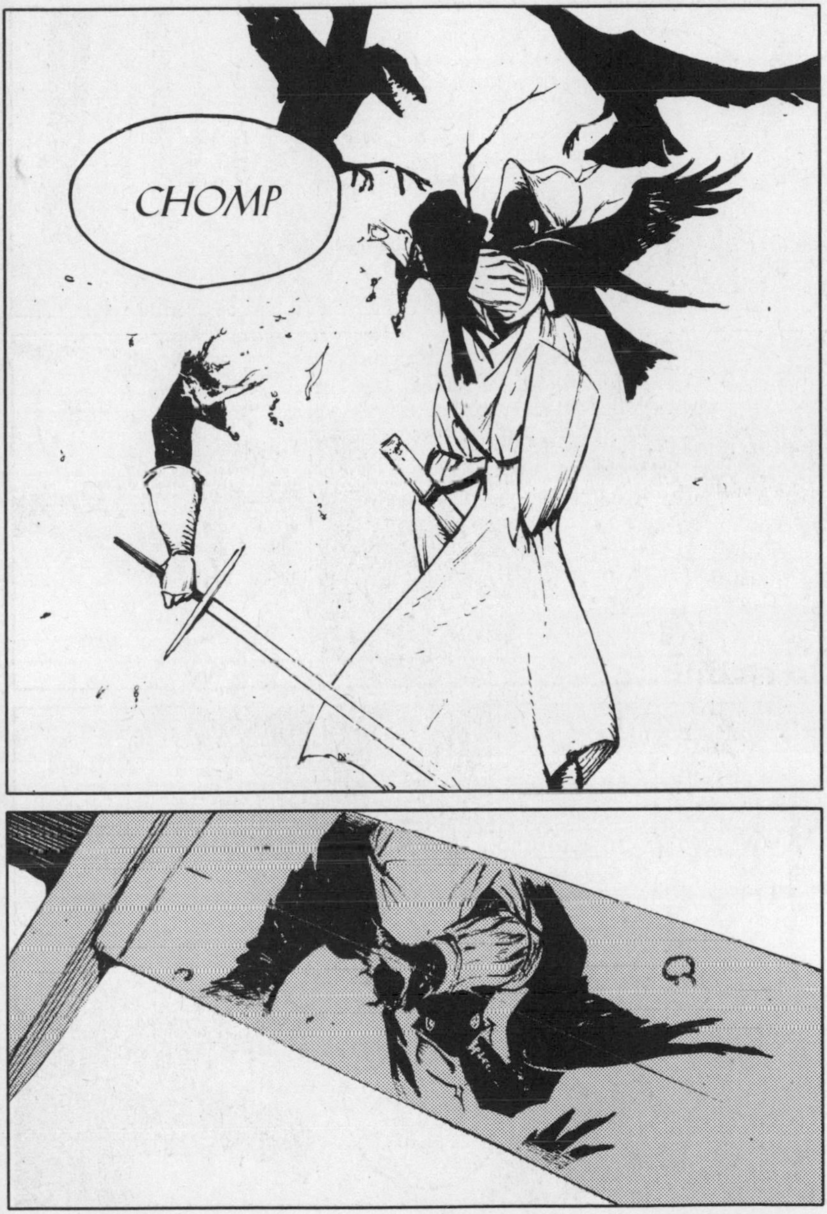
CHOMP

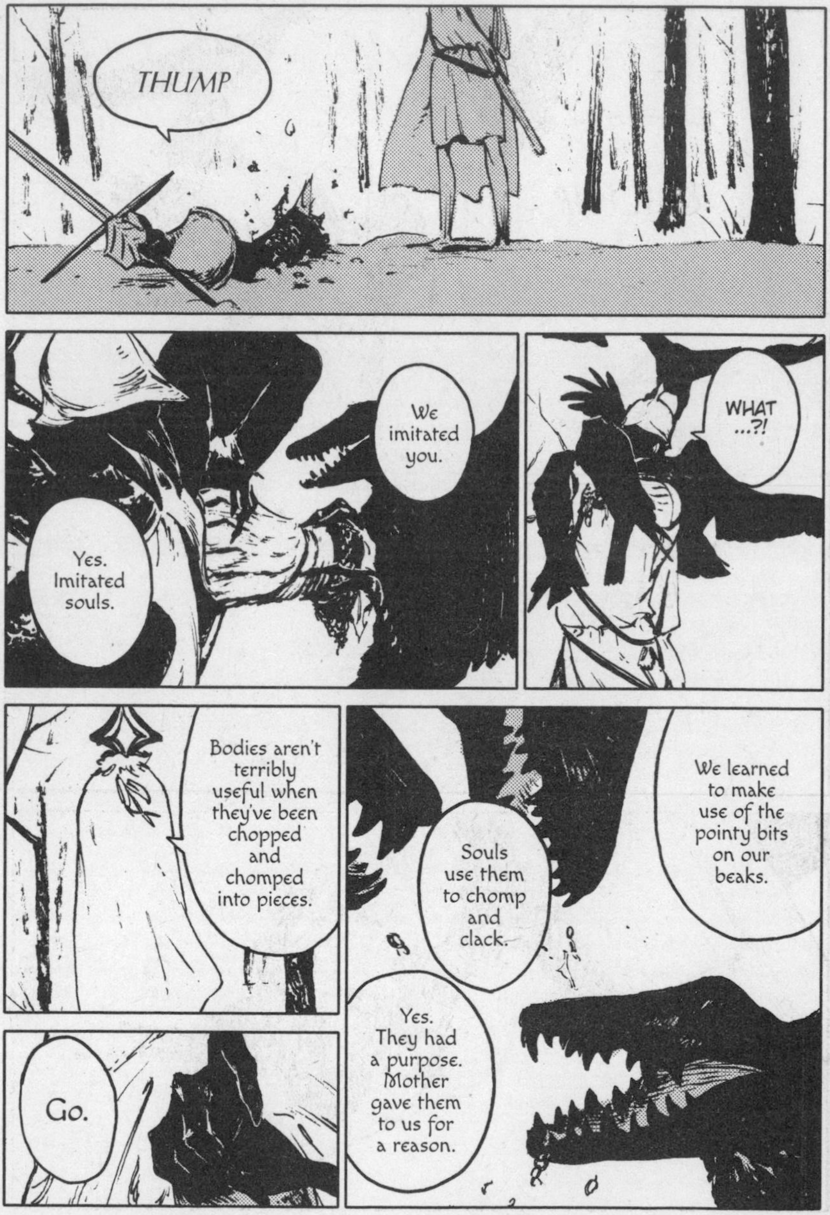
THUMP
WHAT ...?!
We imitated you.
Yes. Imitated souls.
We learned to make use of the pointy bits on our beaks.
Souls use them to chomp and clack.
Yes. They had a purpose. Mother gave them to us for a reason.
Bodies aren't terribly useful when they've been chopped and chomped into pieces.
Go.

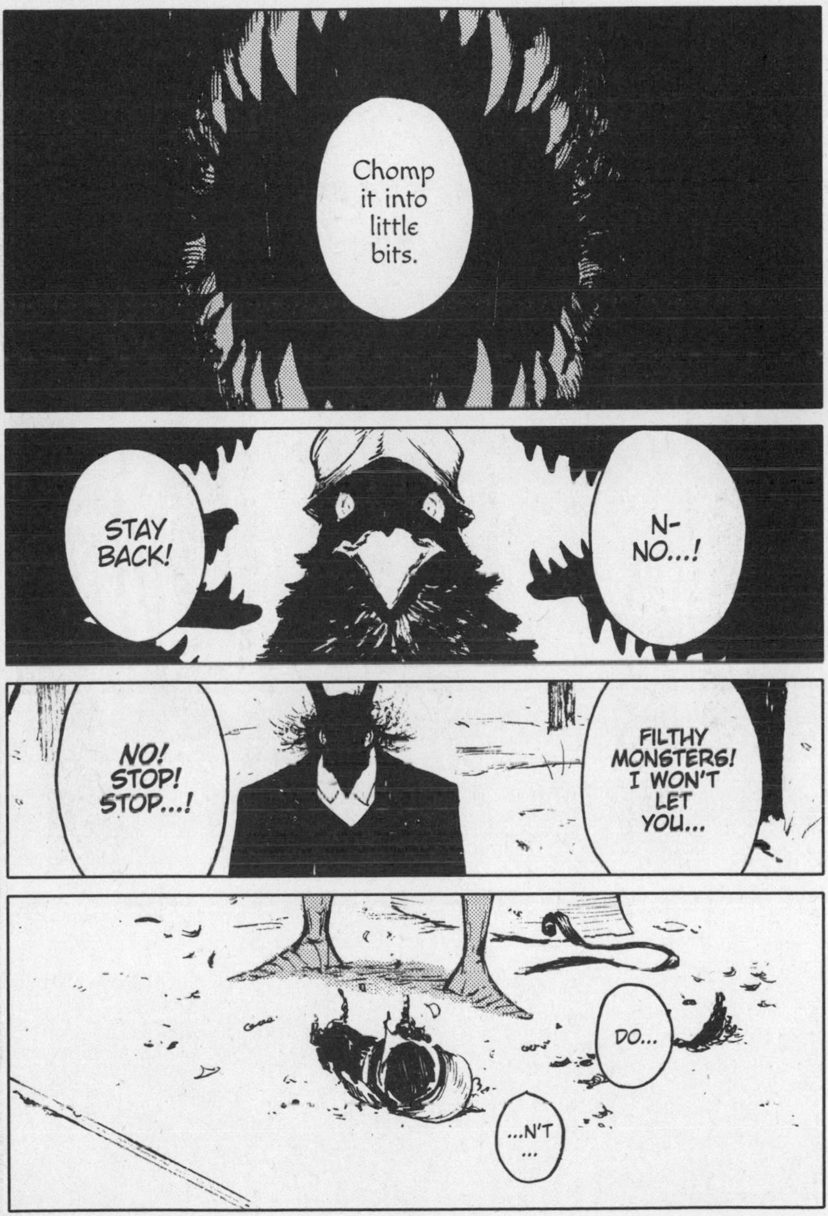
Chomp it into little bits.
N-NO...!
STAY BACK!
FILTHY MONSTERS! I WON'T LET YOU...
NO! STOP! STOP...!
DO...
...N'T ...

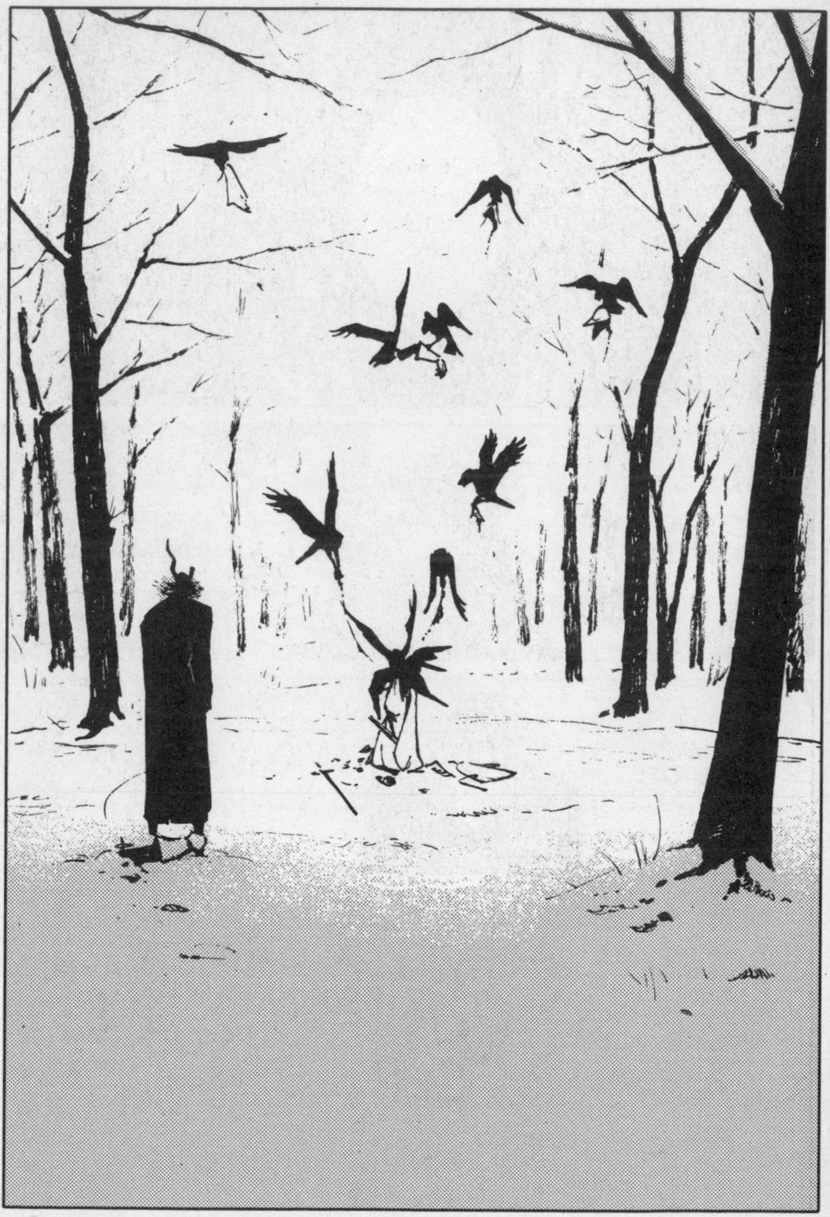

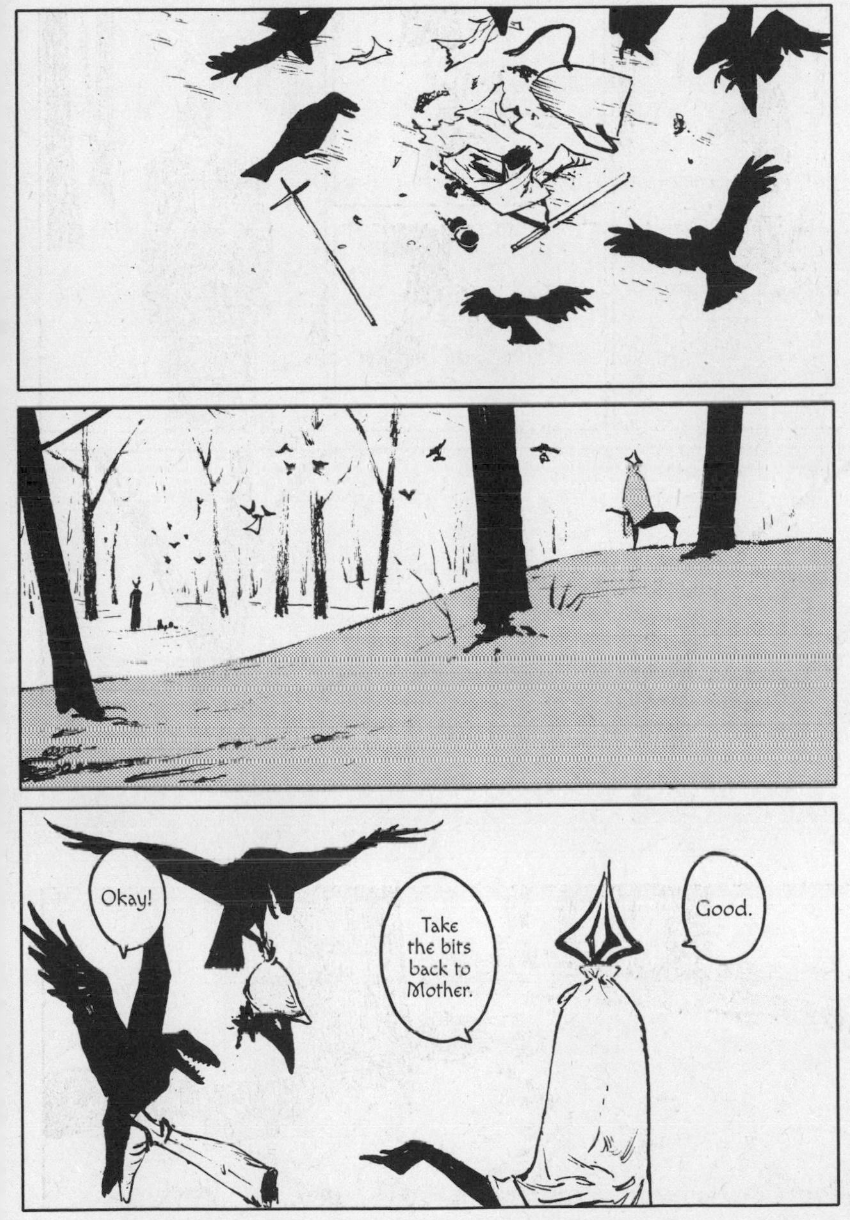
Good.
Take the bits back to Mother.
Okay!

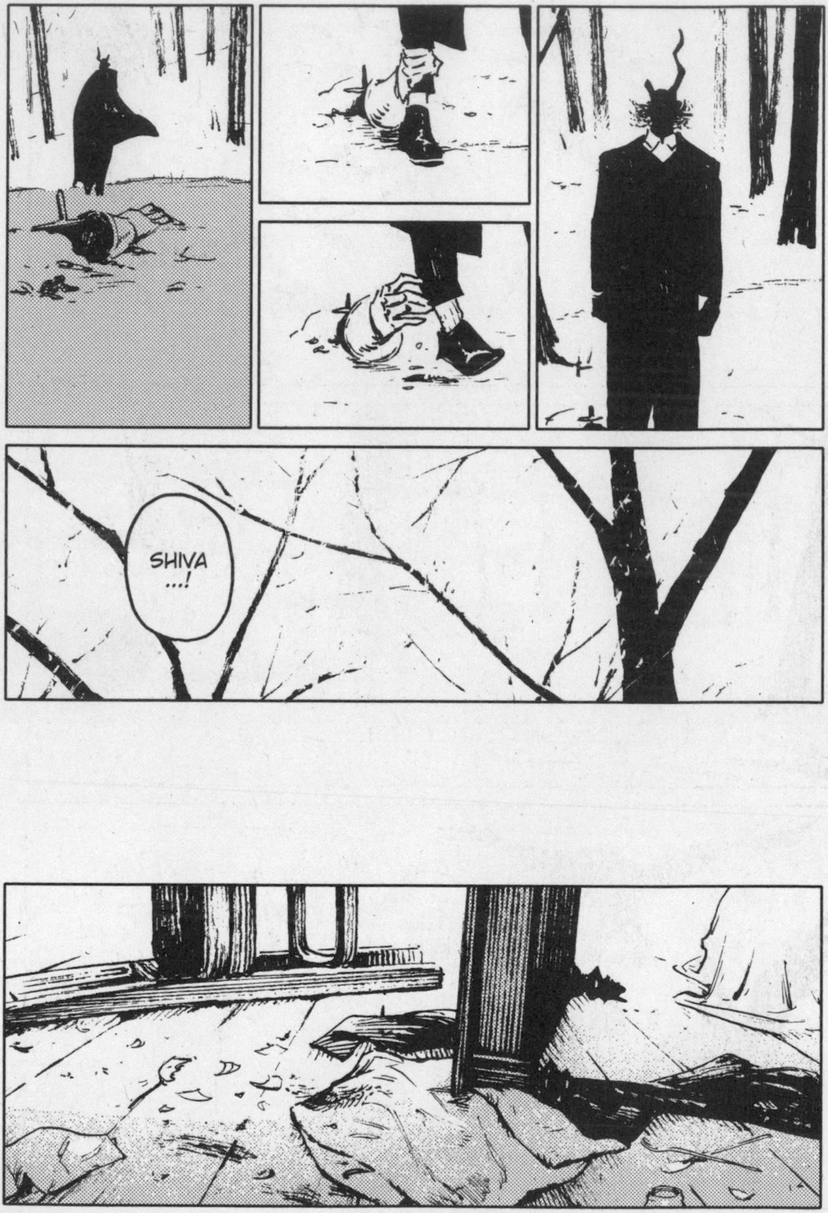
SHIVA ...!

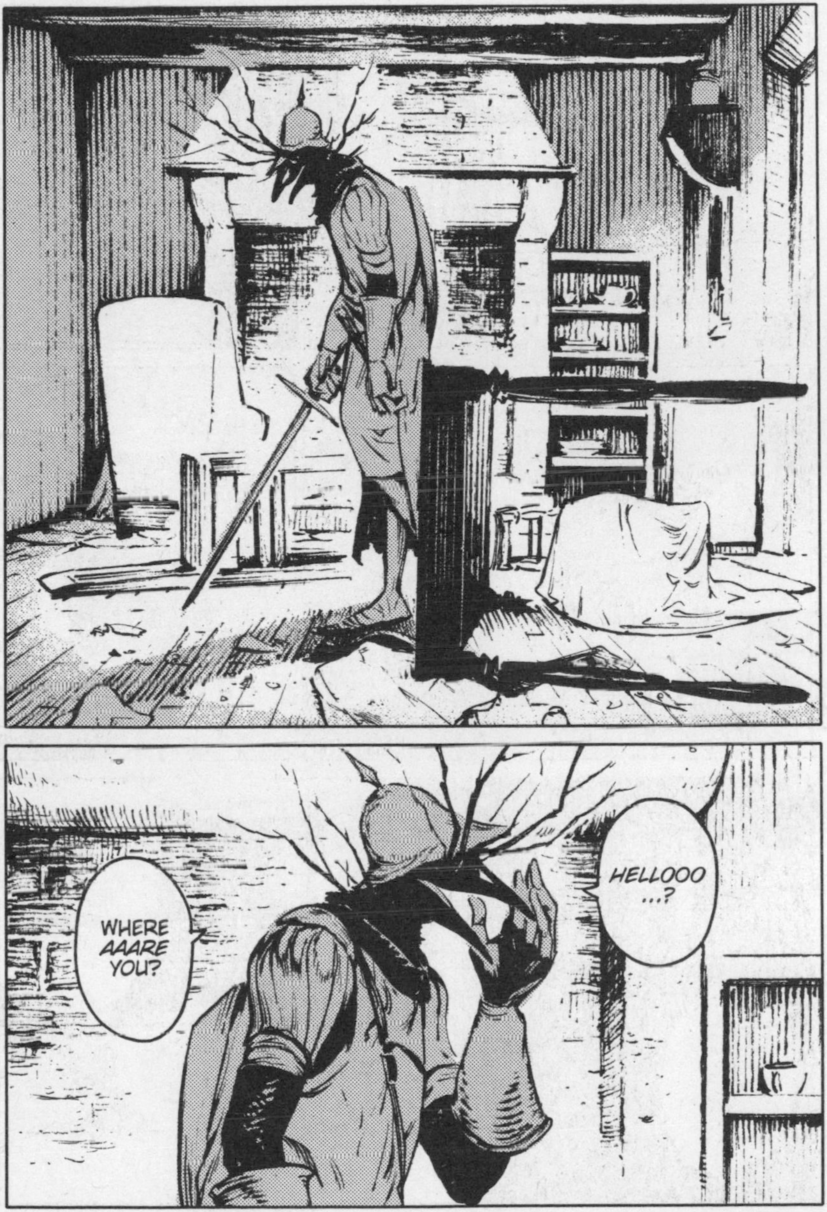
HELLOOO ...?
WHERE AAARE YOU?

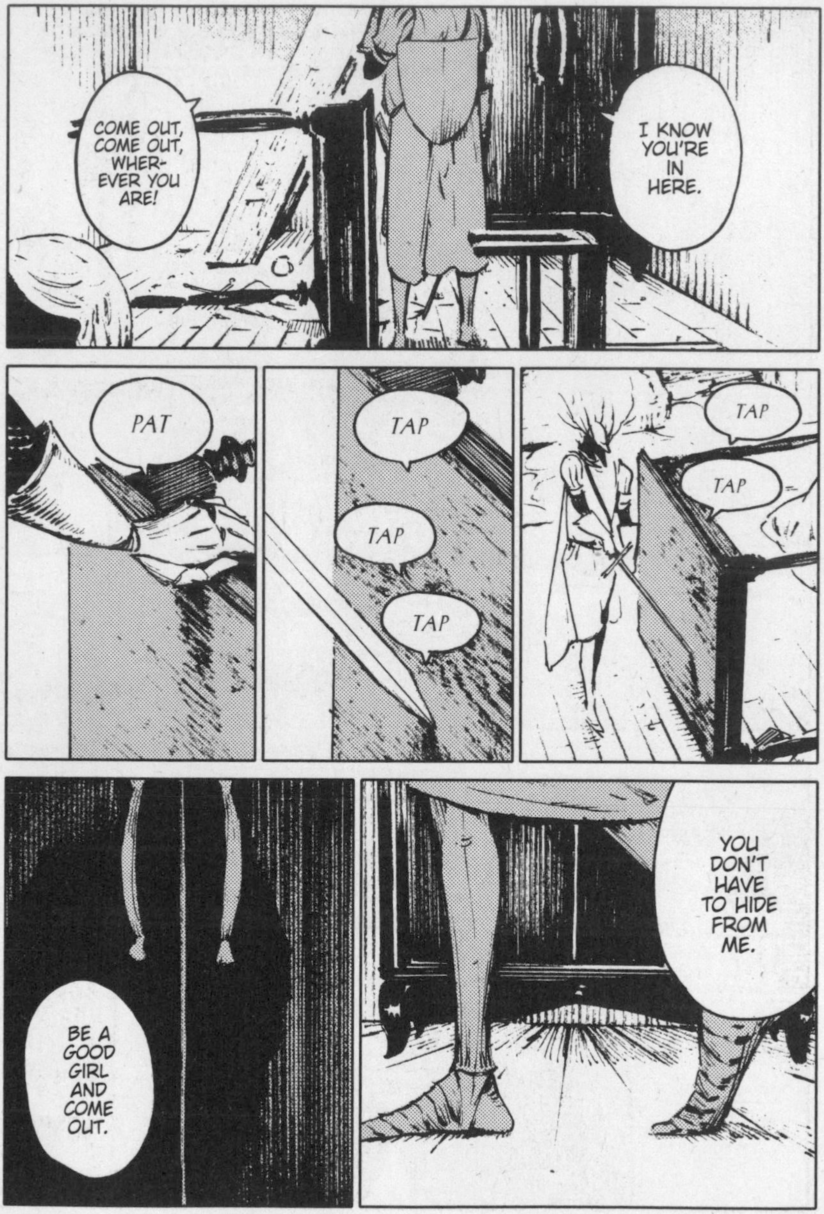
I KNOW YOU'RE IN HERE.
COME OUT, COME OUT, WHER-EVER YOU ARE!
TAP
TAP
TAP
TAP
TAP
PAT
YOU DON'T HAVE TO HIDE FROM ME.
BE A GOOD GIRL AND COME OUT.

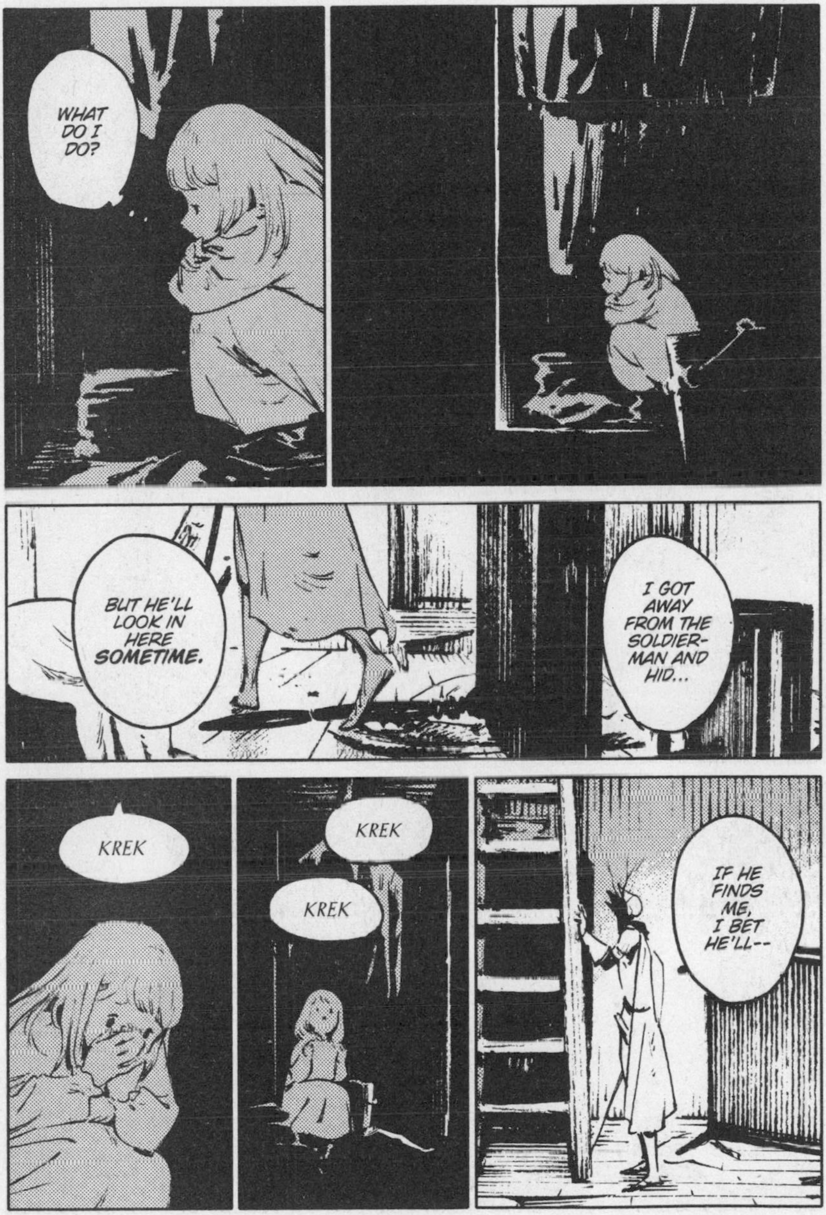
WHAT DO I DO?
I GOT AWAY FROM THE SOLDIER-MAN AND HID...
BUT HE'LL LOOK IN HERE SOMETIME.
IF HE FINDS ME, I BET HE'LL--
KREK
KREK
KREK

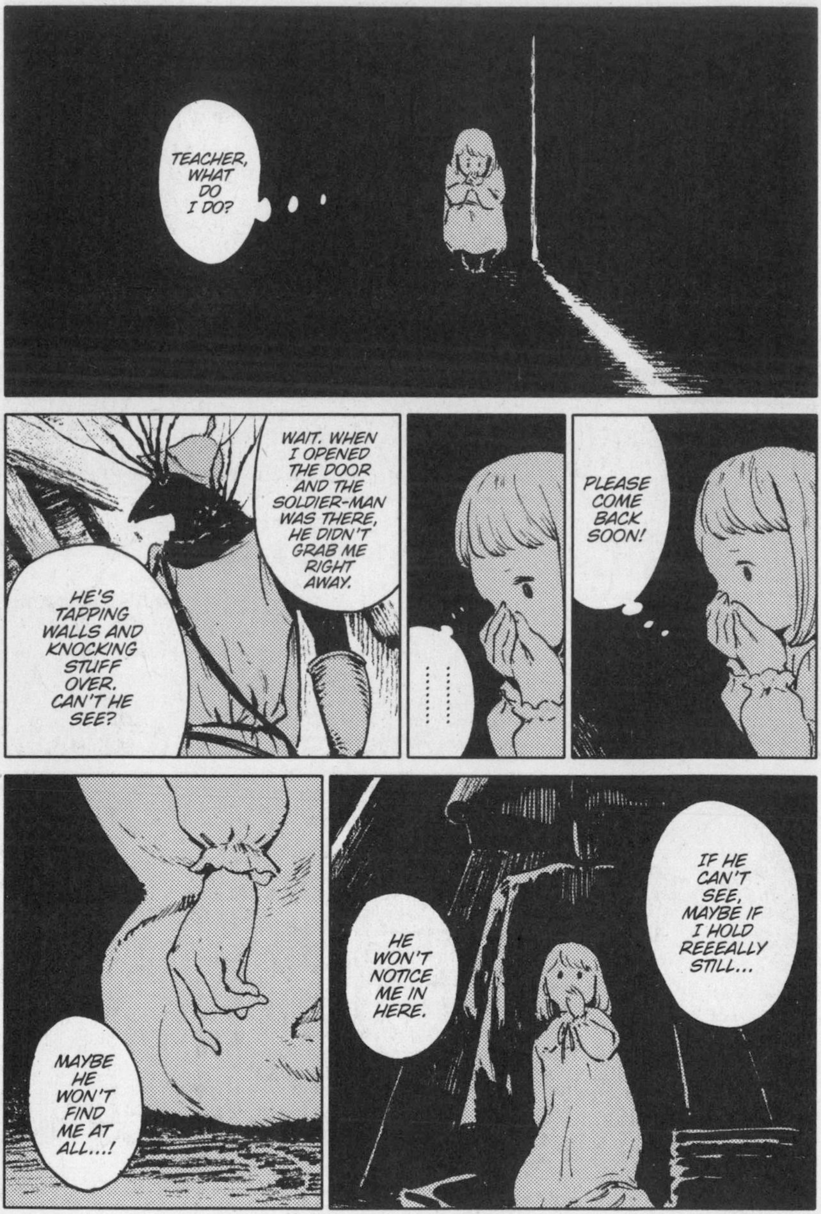
TEACHER, WHAT DO I DO?
PLEASE COME BACK SOON!
......
WAIT. WHEN I OPENED THE DOOR AND THE SOLDIER-MAN WAS THERE, HE DIDN'T GRAB ME RIGHT AWAY.
HE'S TAPPING WALLS AND KNOCKING STUFF OVER. CAN'T HE SEE?
IF HE CAN'T SEE, MAYBE IF I HOLD REEEALLY STILL...
HE WON'T NOTICE ME IN HERE.
MAYBE HE WON'T FIND ME AT ALL...!

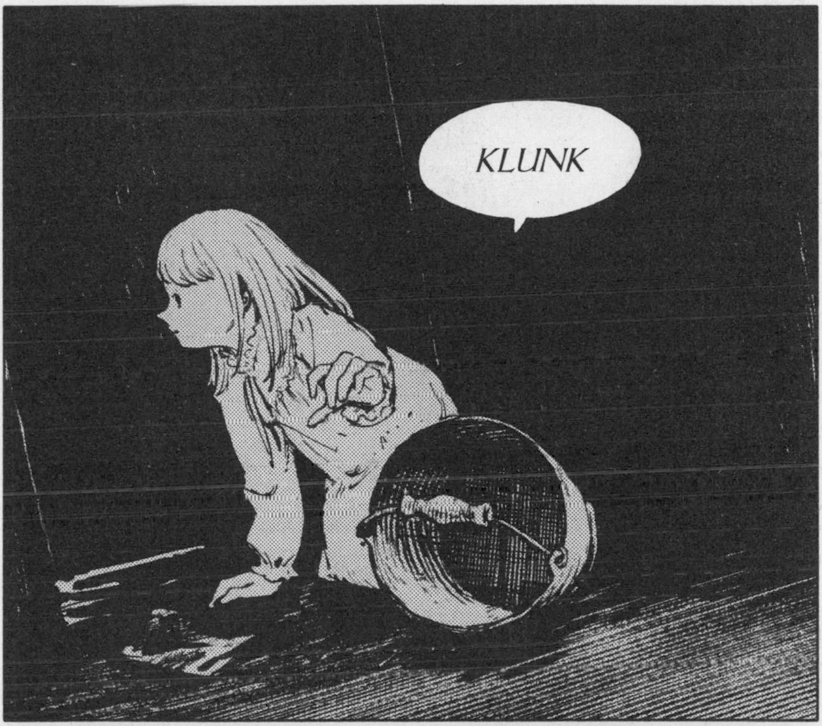
KLUNK
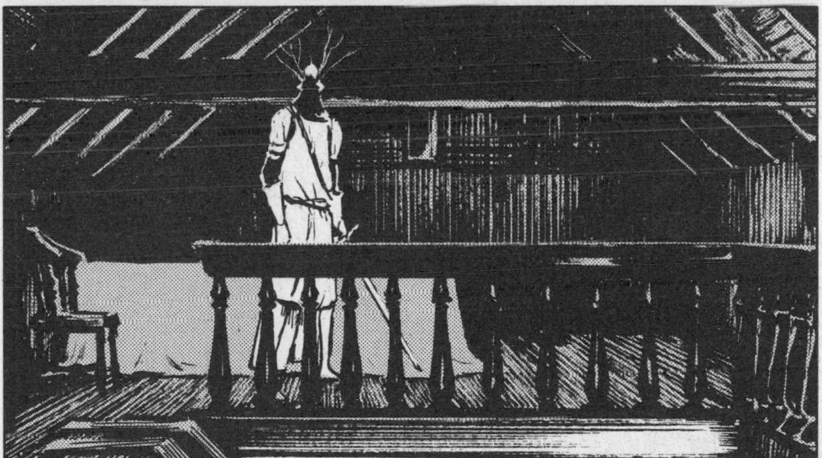

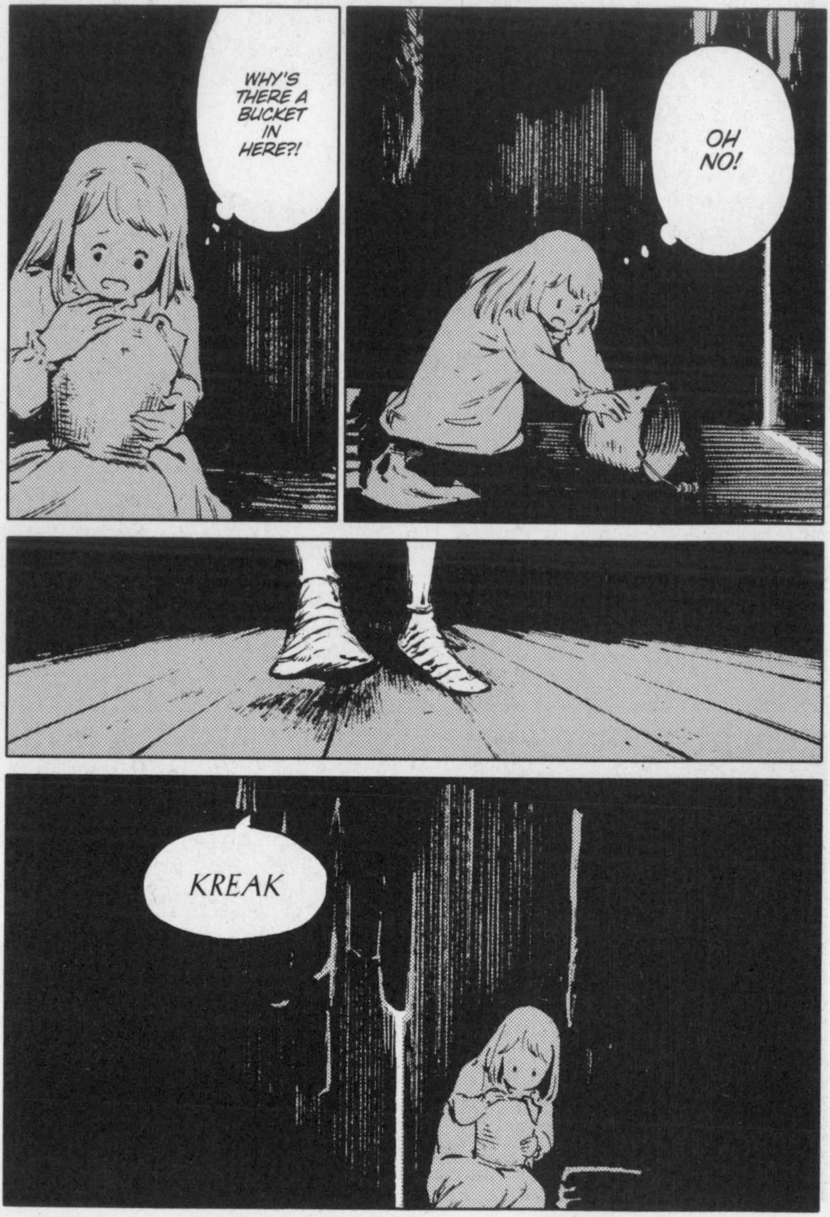
OH NO!
WHY'S THERE A BUCKET IN HERE?!
KREAK

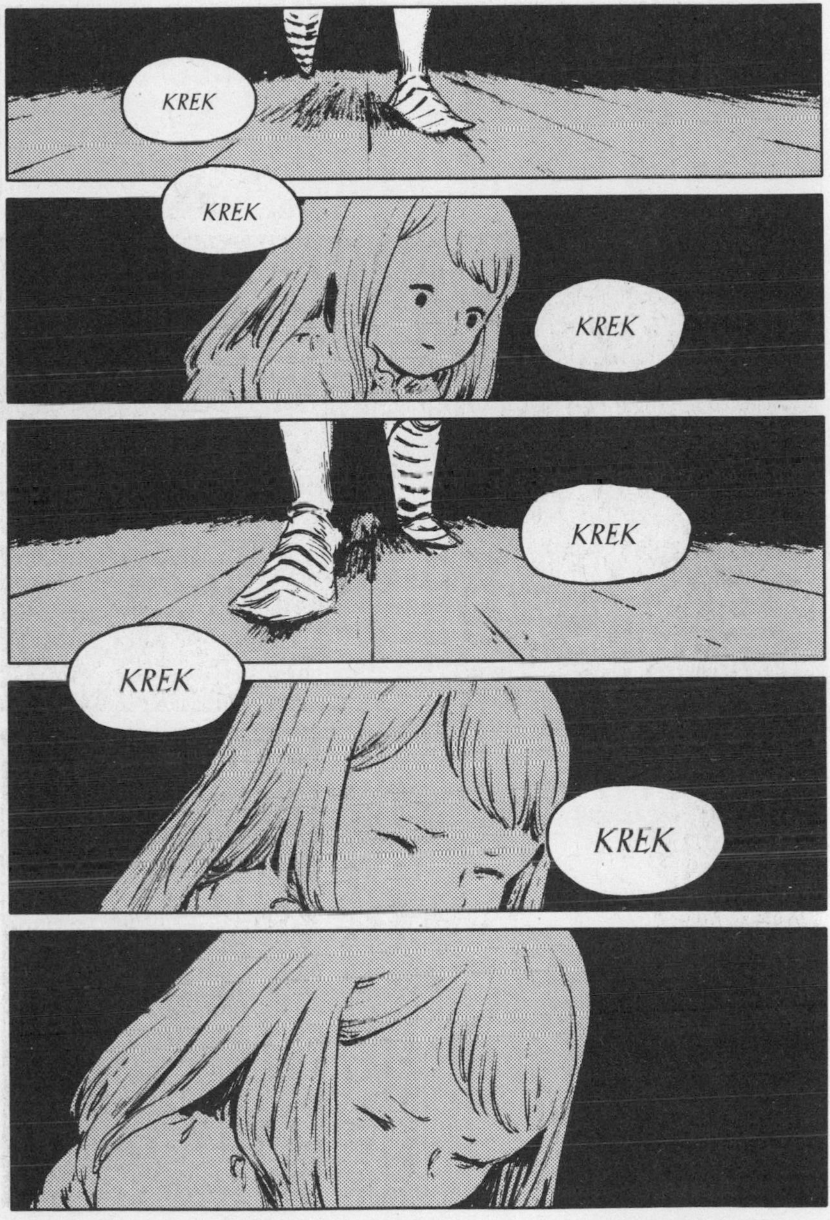
KREK
KREK
KREK
KREK
KREK
KREK

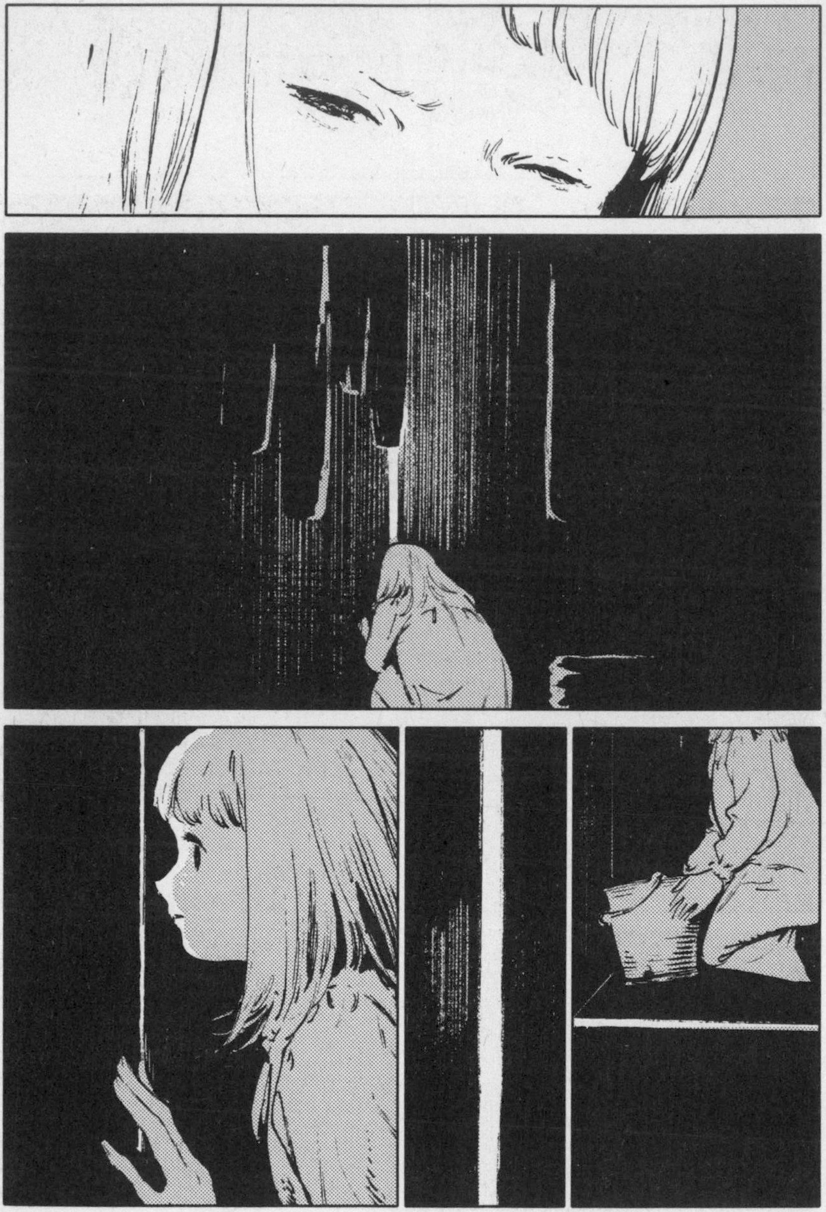

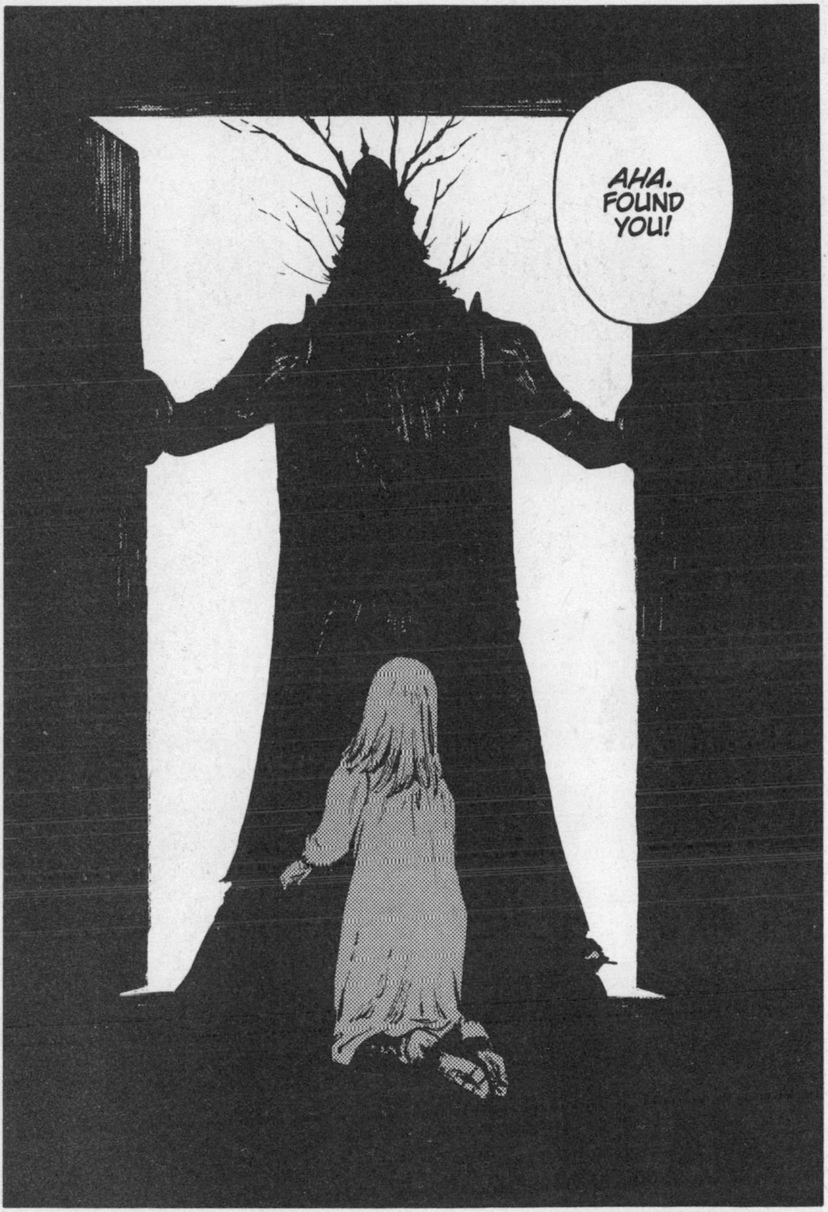
AHA. FOUND YOU!

Chapter 32

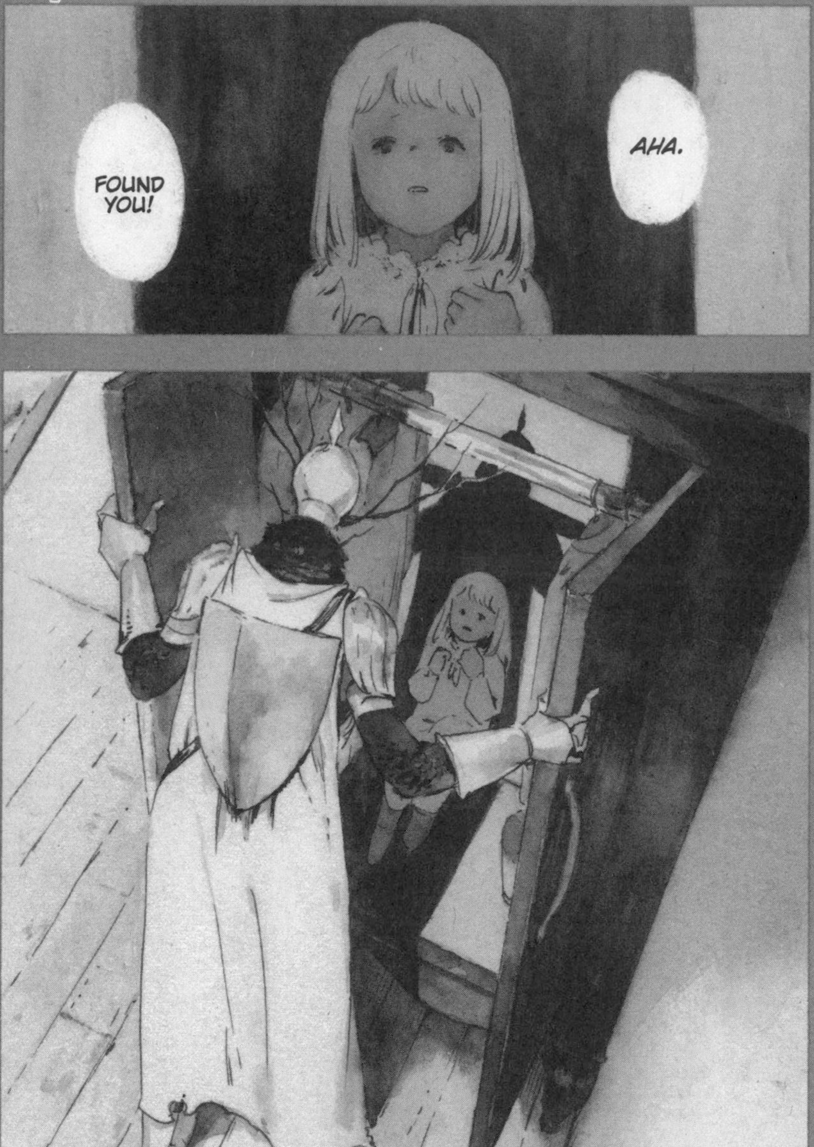
AHA.
FOUND YOU!

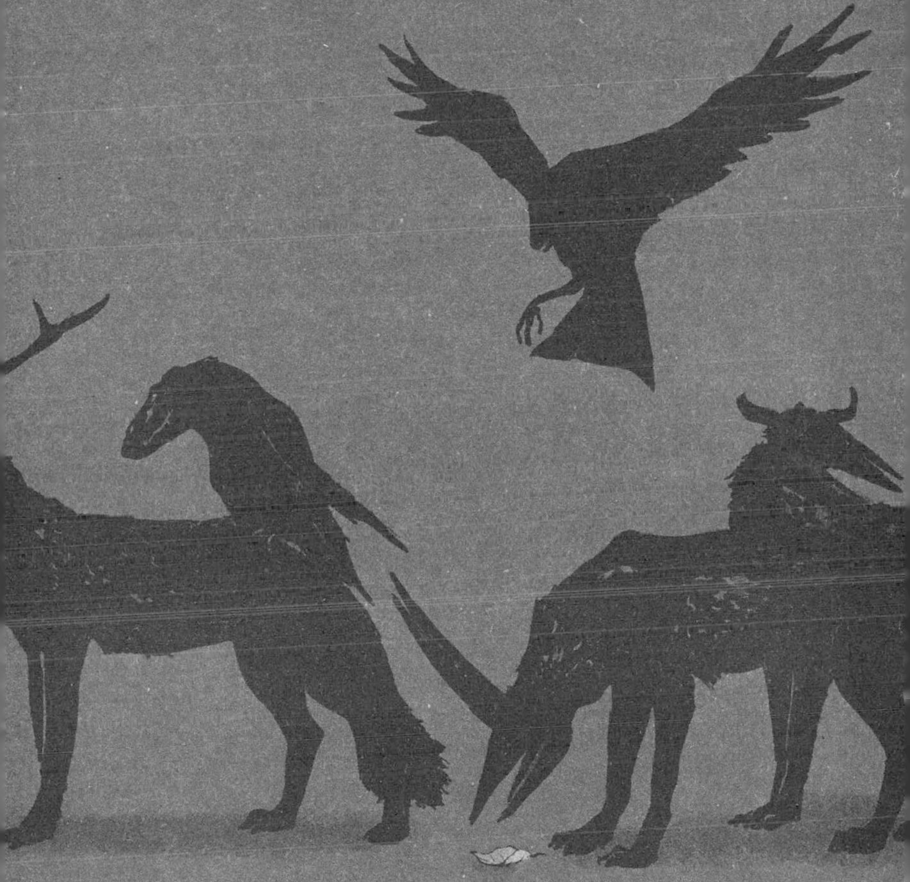

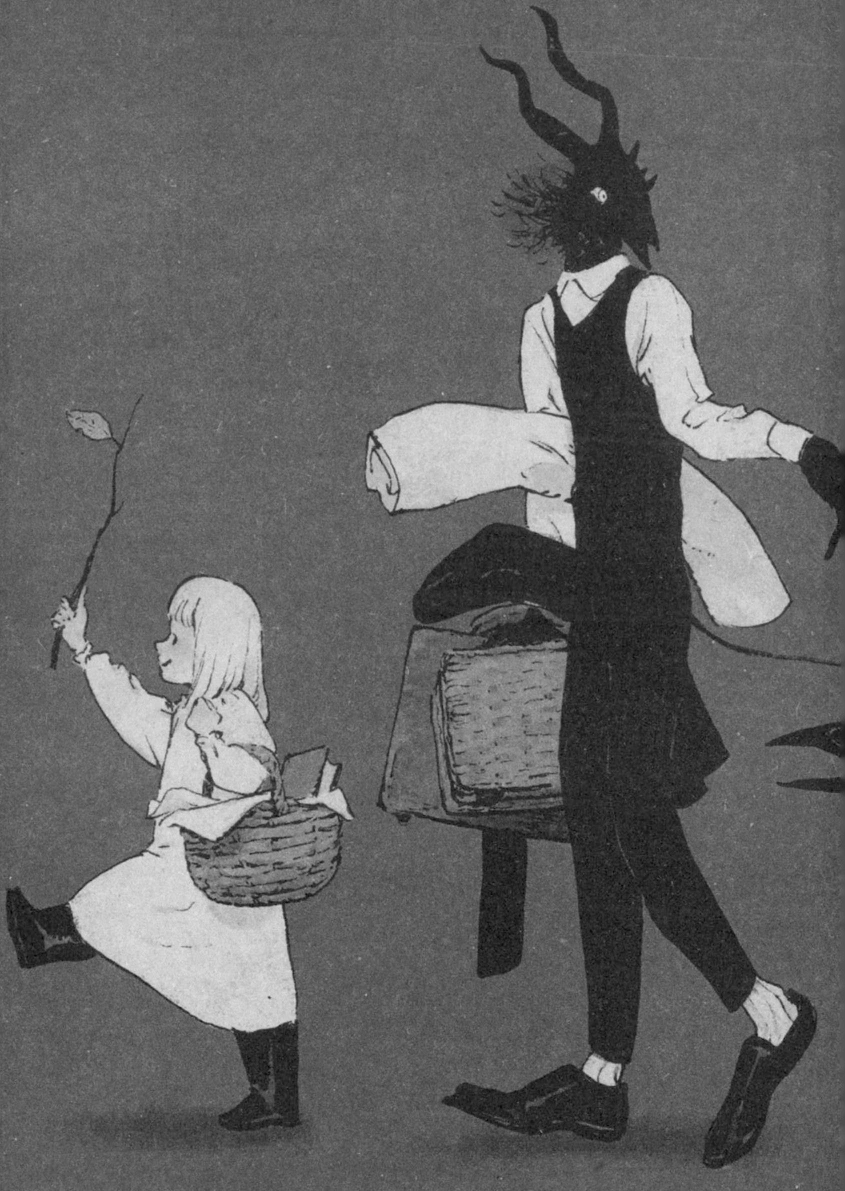

Chapter 32

Siúil, a Rún
The Girl from the Other Side

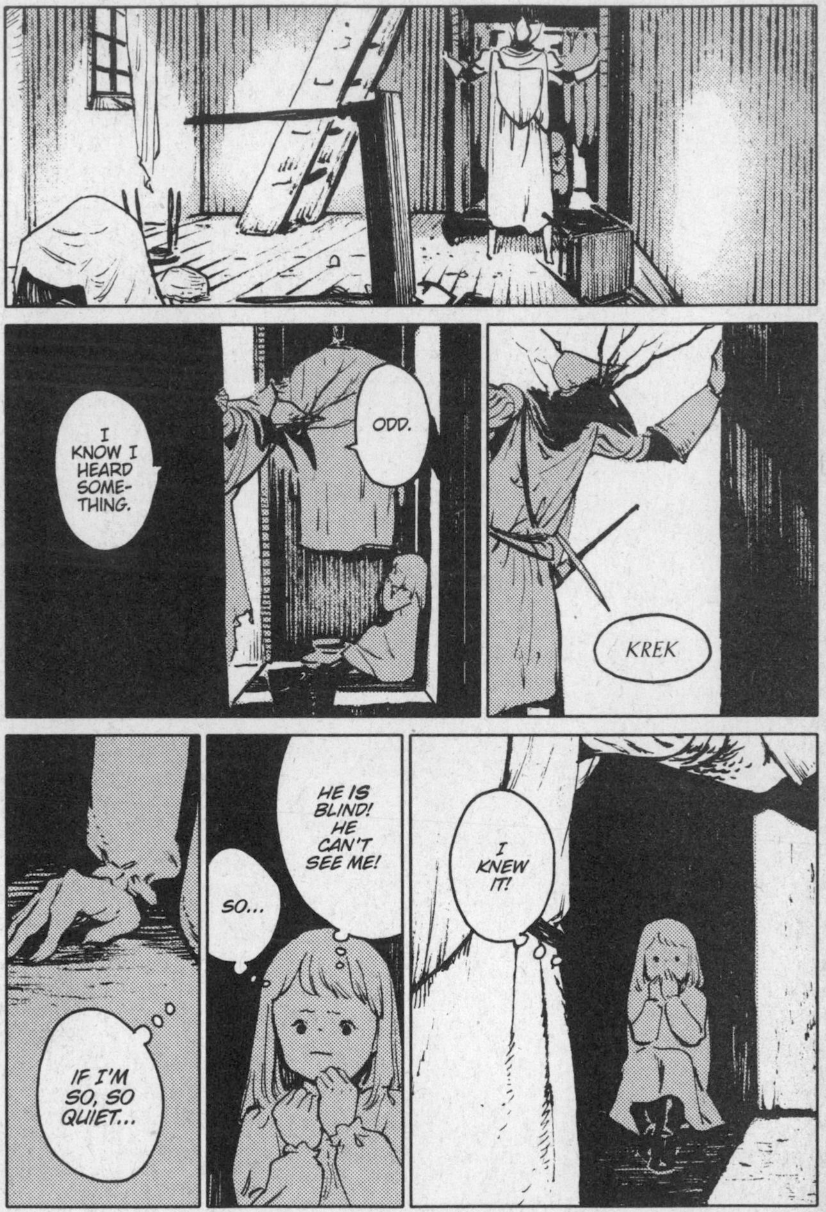
KREK
ODD.
I KNOW I HEARD SOMETHING.
I KNEW IT!
HE IS BLIND! HE CAN'T SEE ME!
SO...
IF I'M SO, SO QUIET...

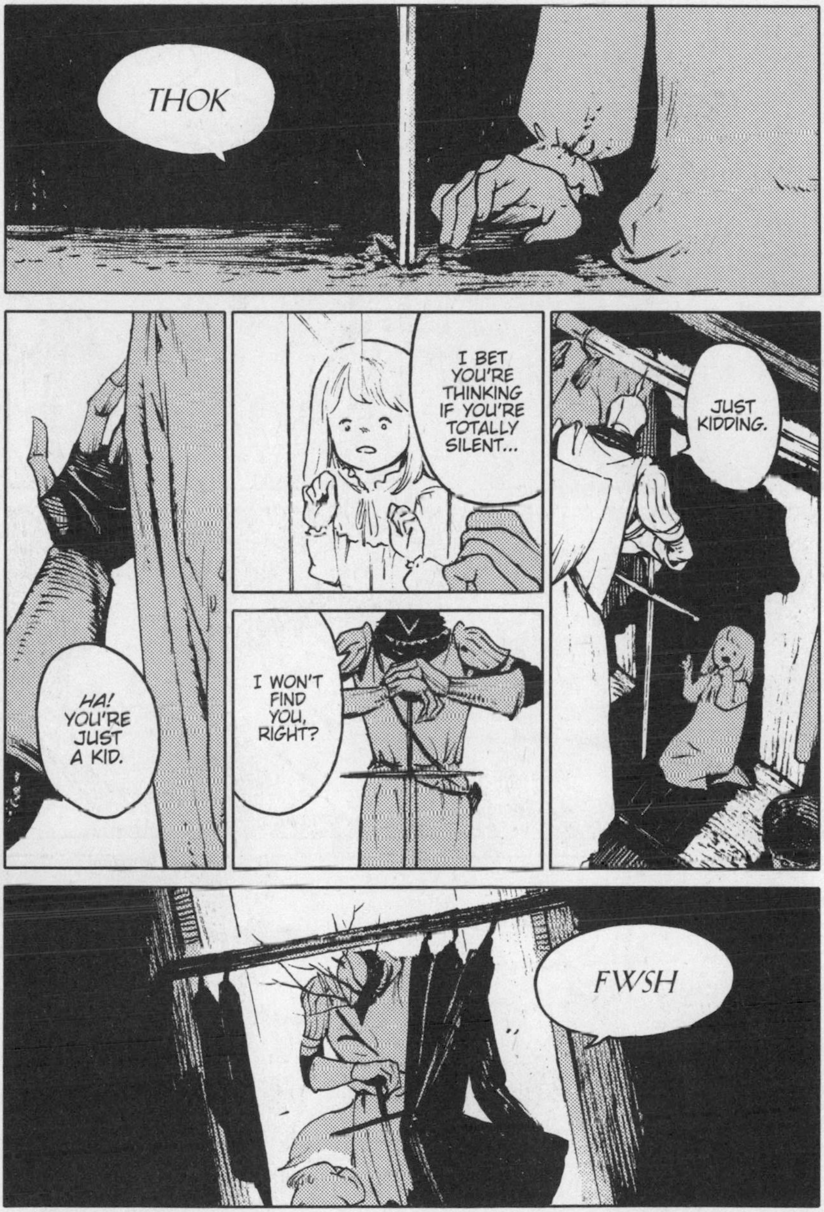
THOK
JUST KIDDING.
I BET YOU'RE THINKING IF YOU'RE TOTALLY SILENT...
I WON'T FIND YOU, RIGHT?
HA! YOU'RE JUST A KID.
FWSH

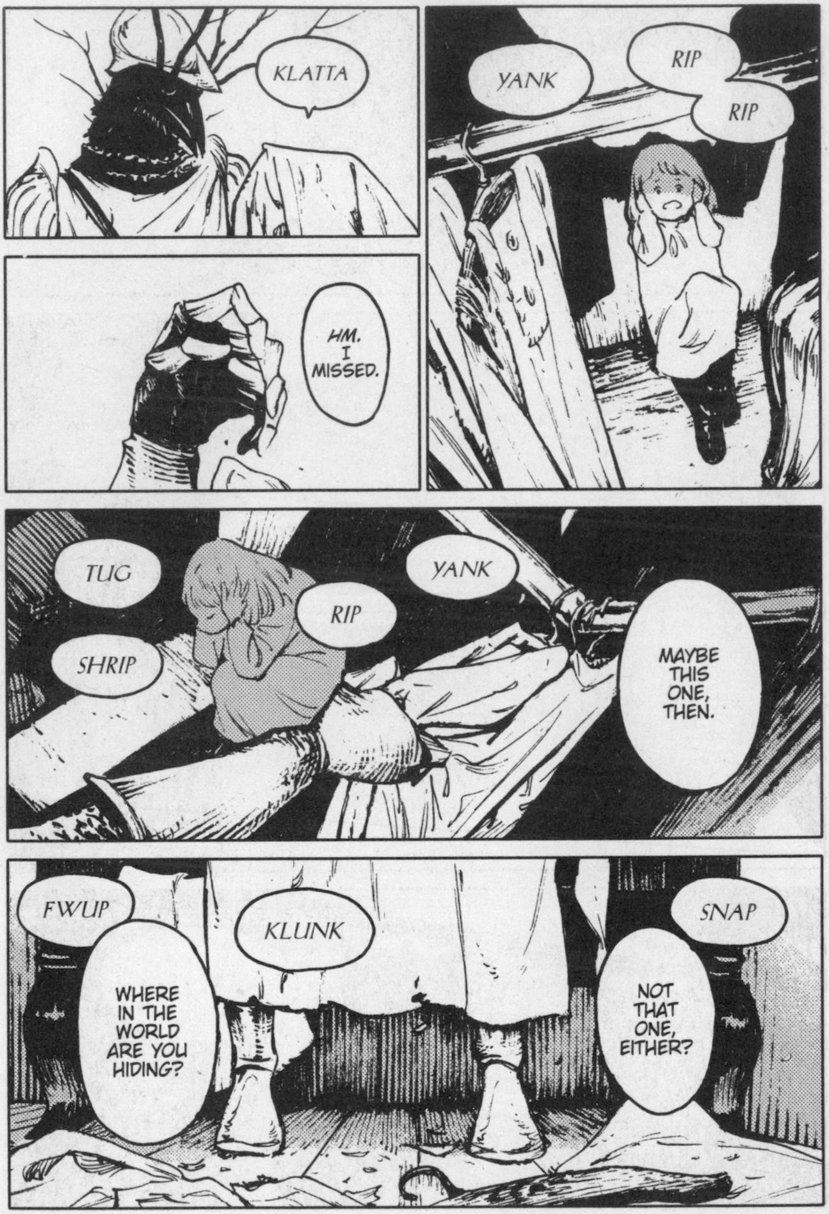
RIP
RIP
YANK
KLATTA
HM. I MISSED.
MAYBE THIS ONE, THEN.
YANK
RIP
TUG
SHRIP
SNAP
NOT THAT ONE, EITHER?
KLUNK
FWUP
WHERE IN THE WORLD ARE YOU HIDING?

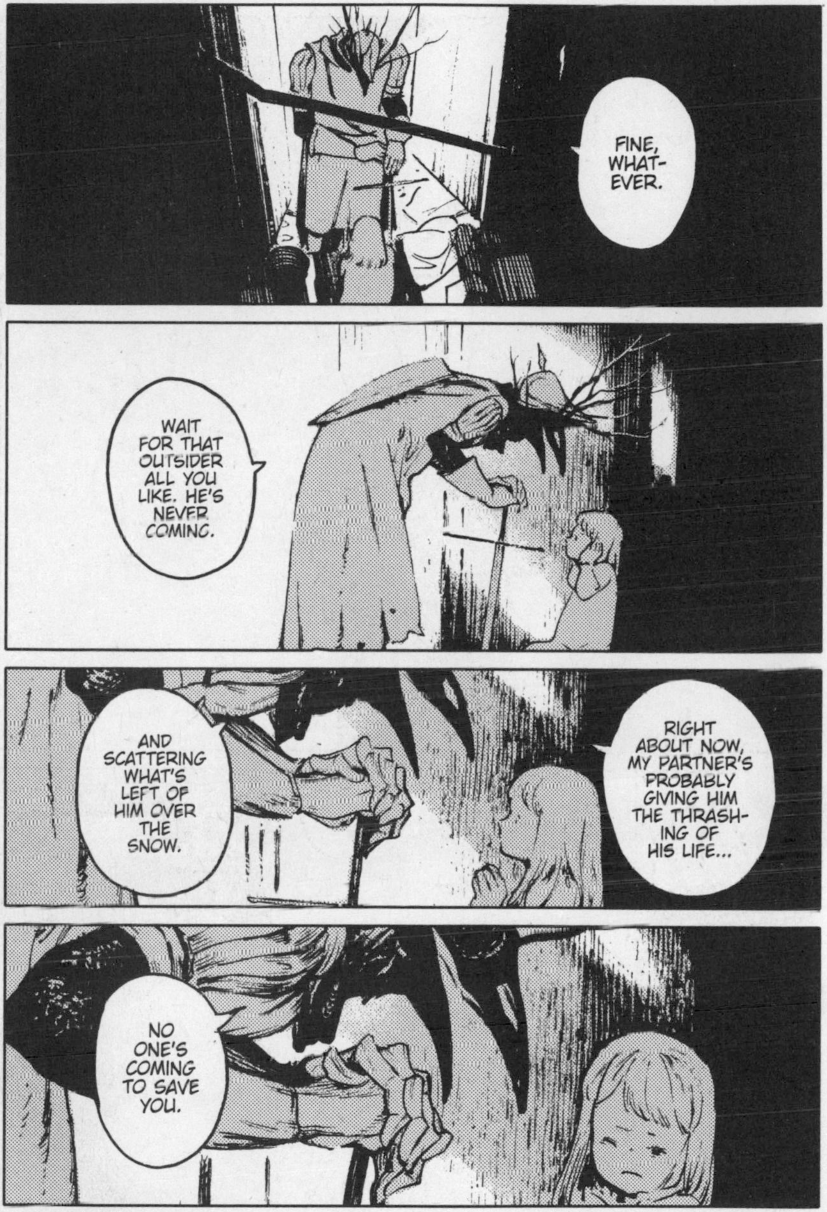
FINE, WHATEVER.
WAIT FOR THAT OUTSIDER ALL YOU LIKE. HE'S NEVER COMING.
RIGHT ABOUT NOW, MY PARTNER'S PROBABLY GIVING HIM THE THRASHING OF HIS LIFE...
AND SCATTERING WHAT'S LEFT OF HIM OVER THE SNOW.
NO ONE'S COMING TO SAVE YOU.

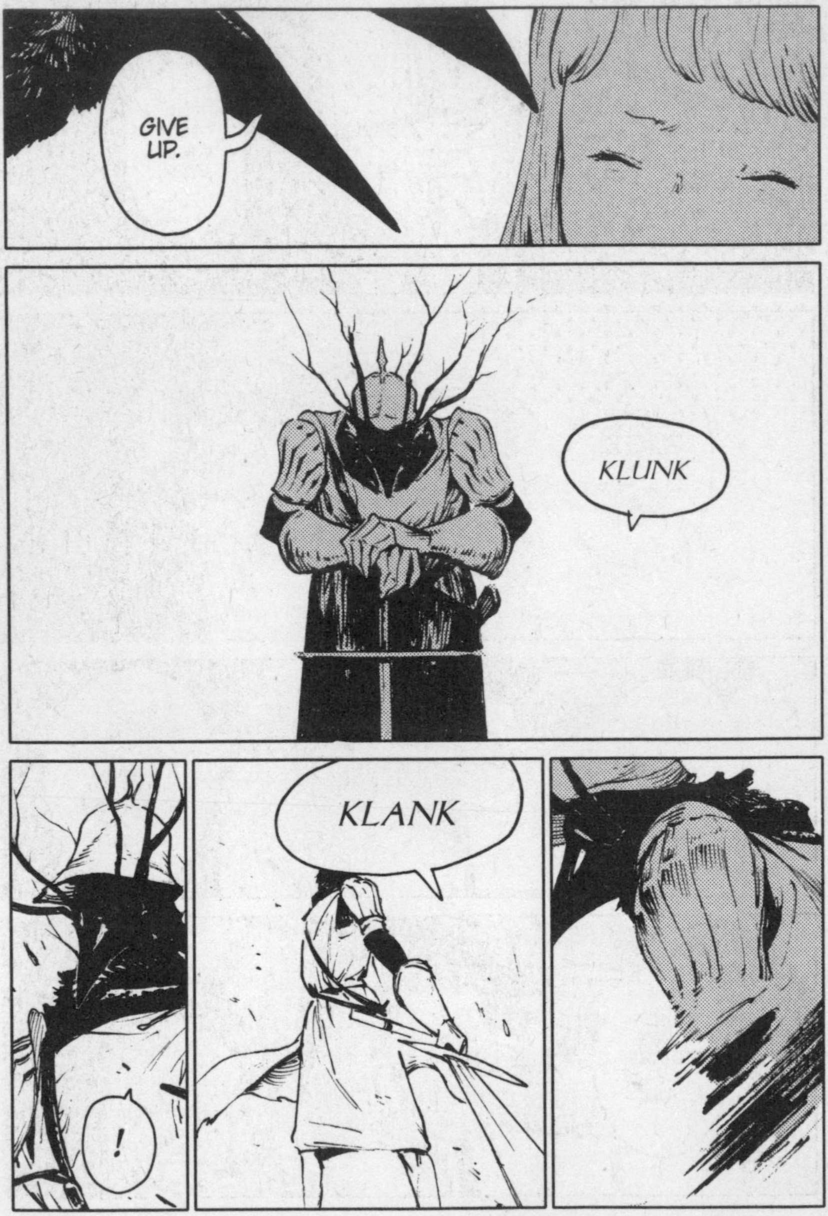
GIVE UP.
KLUNK
KLANK
!

THAT'S NOT THE GIRL.

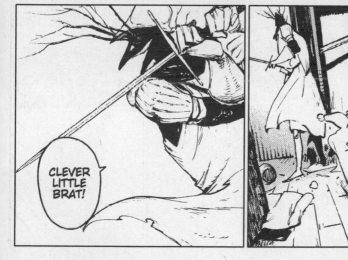

CLEVER LITTLE BRAT!

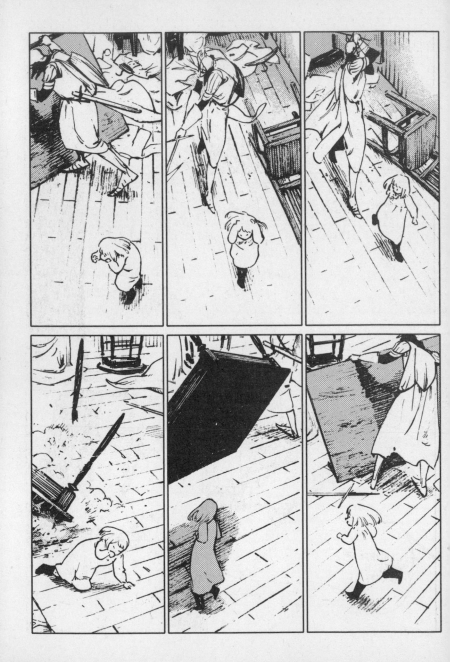

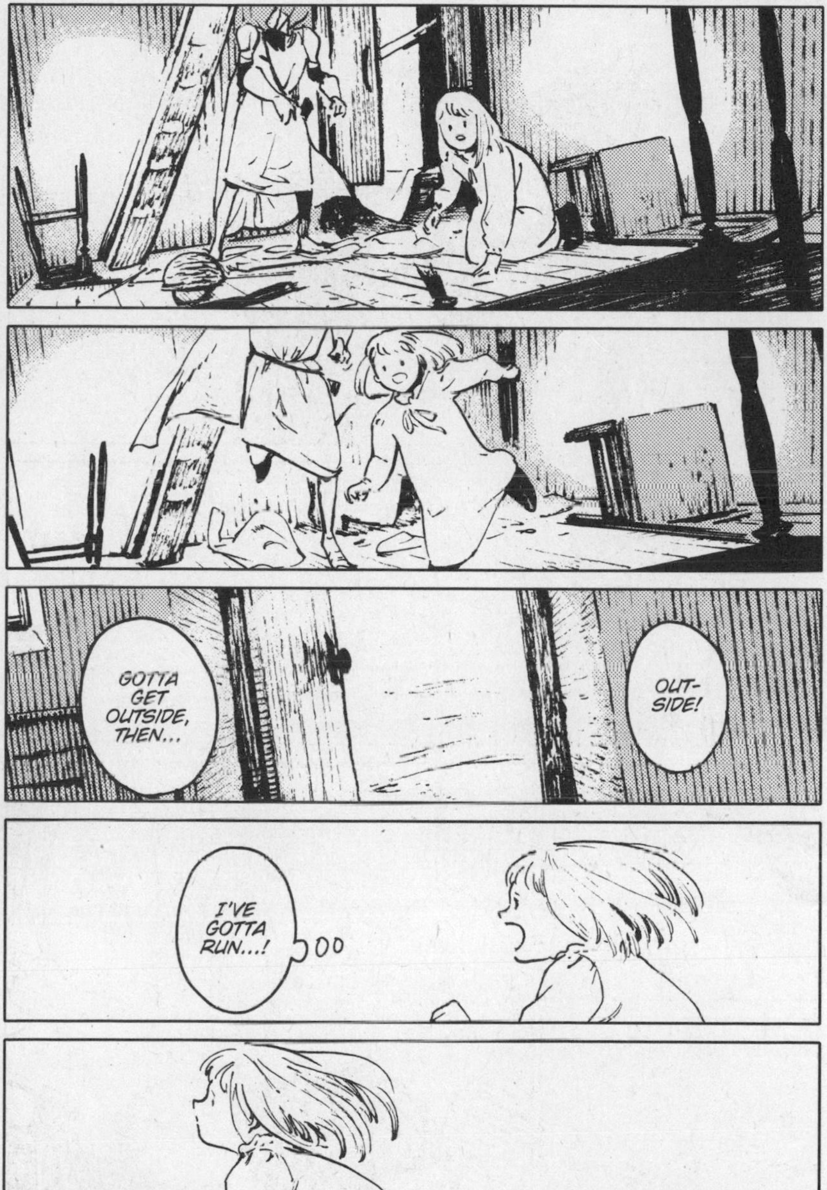
OUT-SIDE!
GOTTA GET OUTSIDE, THEN...
I'VE GOTTA RUN...!

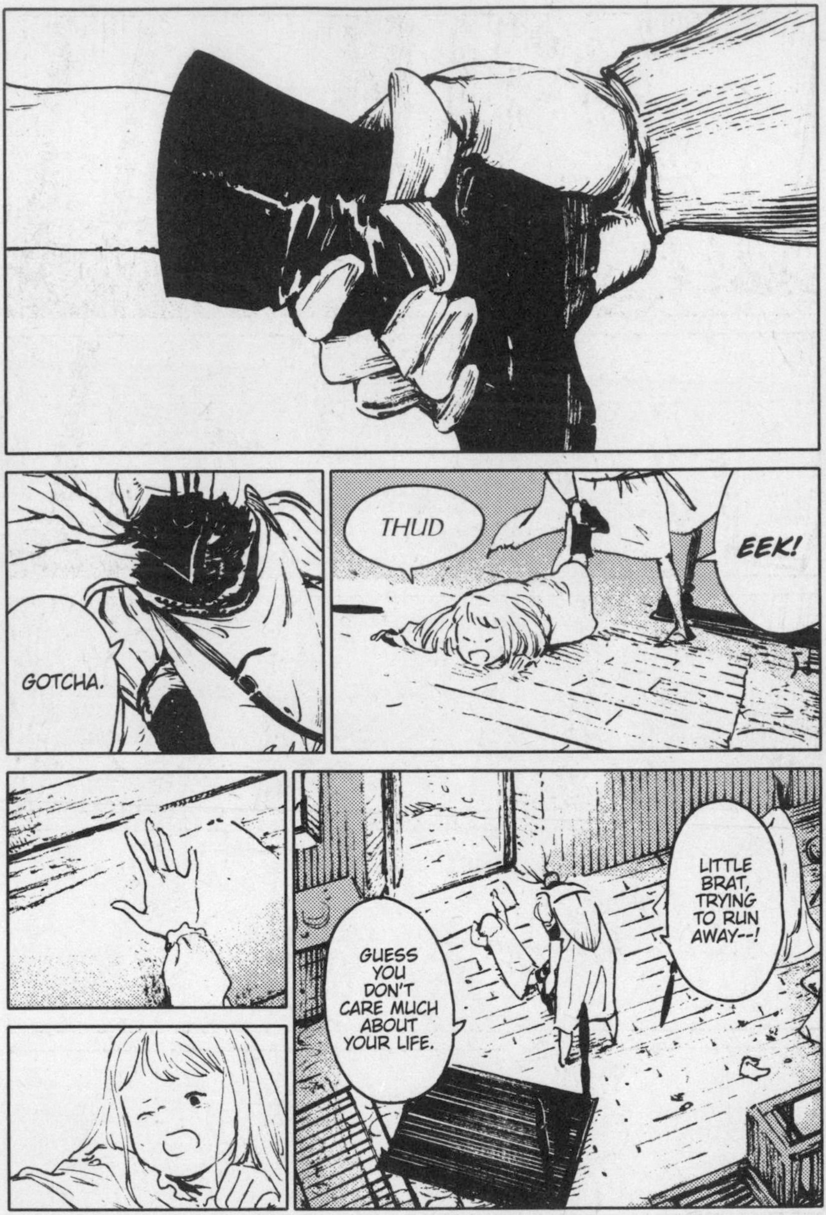
EEK!
THUD
GOTCHA.
LITTLE BRAT, TRYING TO RUN AWAY--!
GUESS YOU DON'T CARE MUCH ABOUT YOUR LIFE.

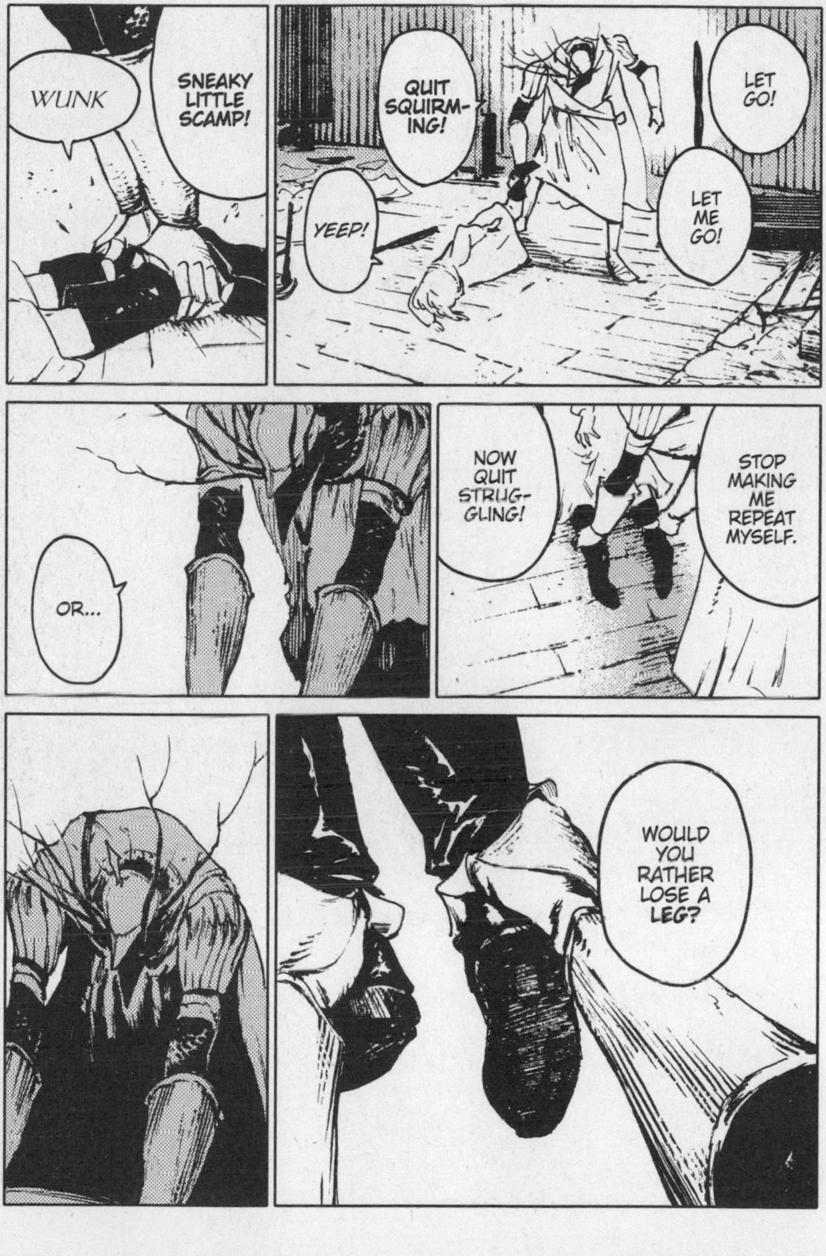
LET GO!
QUIT SQUIRMING!
LET ME GO!
YEEP!
SNEAKY LITTLE SCAMP!
WUNK
STOP MAKING ME REPEAT MYSELF.
NOW QUIT STRUGGLING!
OR...
WOULD YOU RATHER LOSE A LEG?

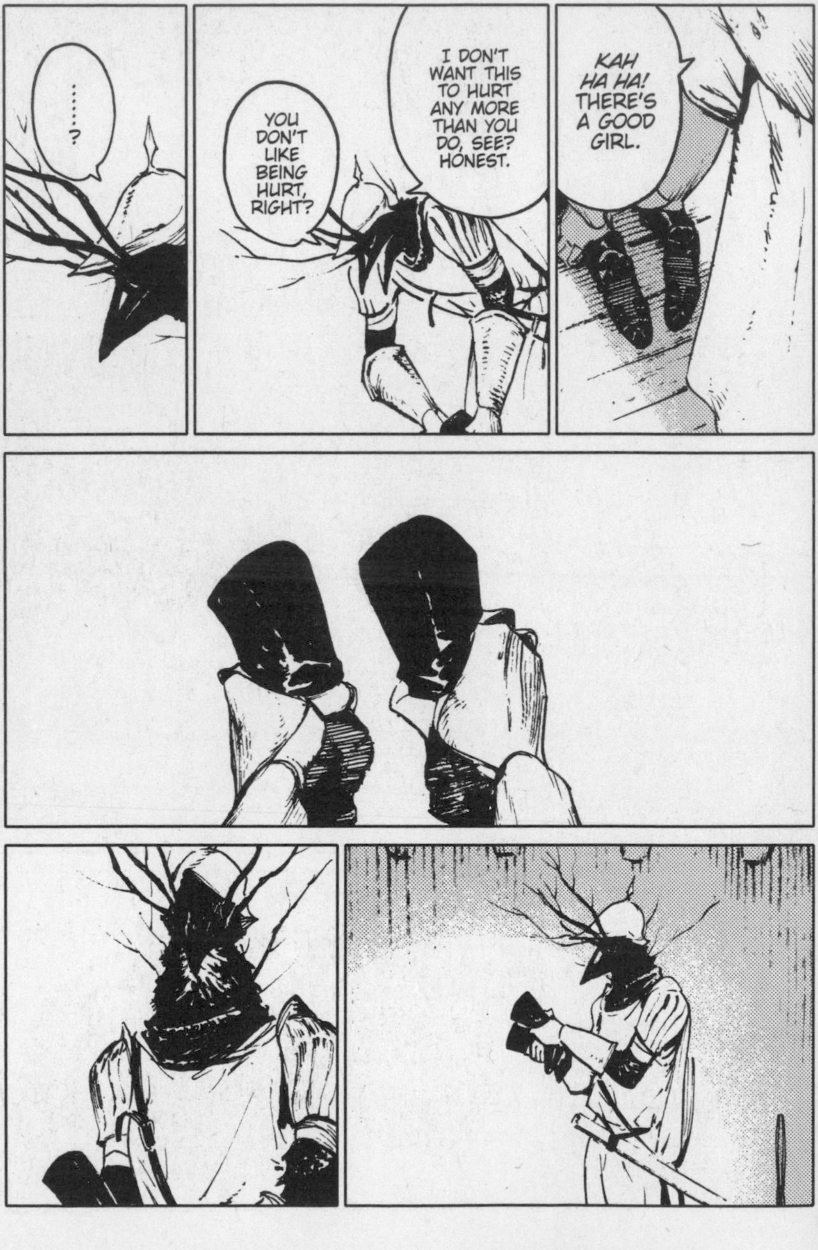
KAH HA HA! THERE'S A GOOD GIRL.
I DON'T WANT THIS TO HURT ANY MORE THAN YOU DO, SEE? HONEST.
YOU DON'T LIKE BEING HURT, RIGHT?
......?

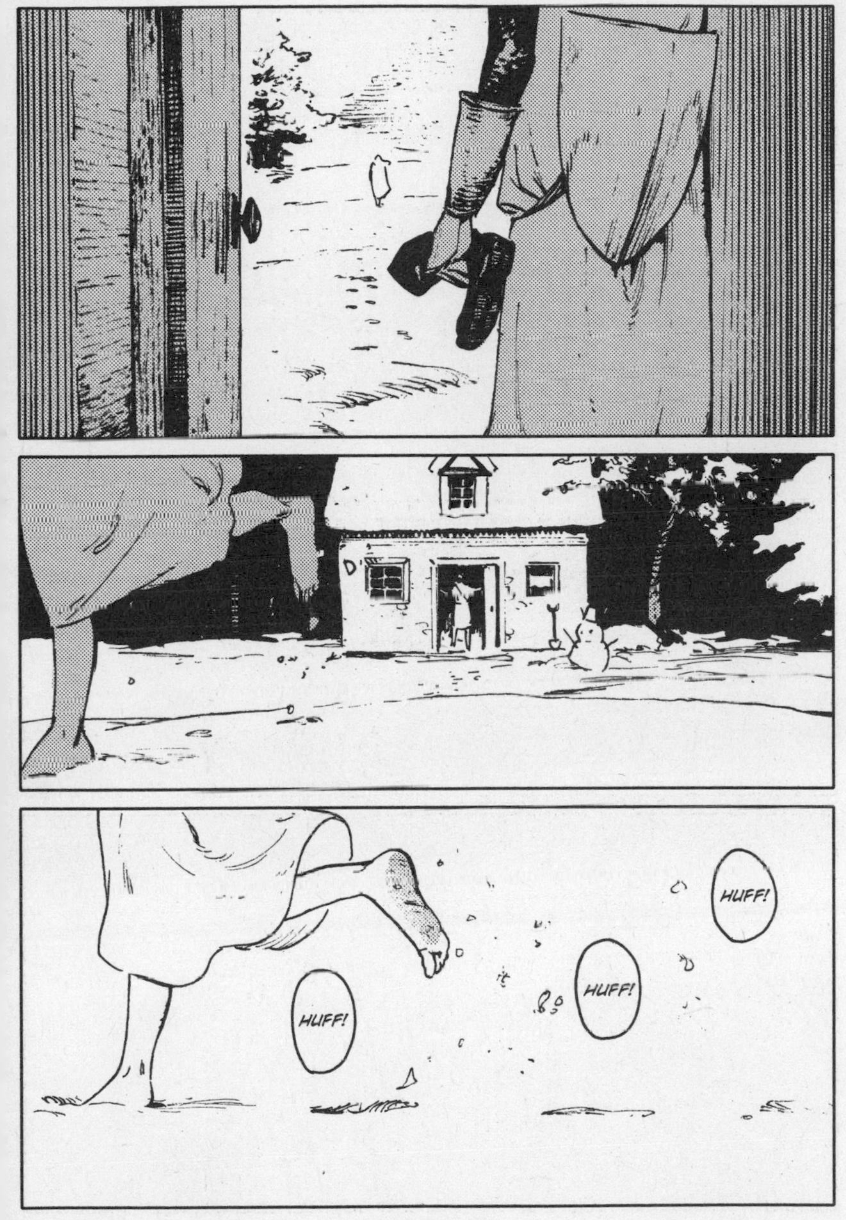
HUFF!
HUFF!
HUFF!

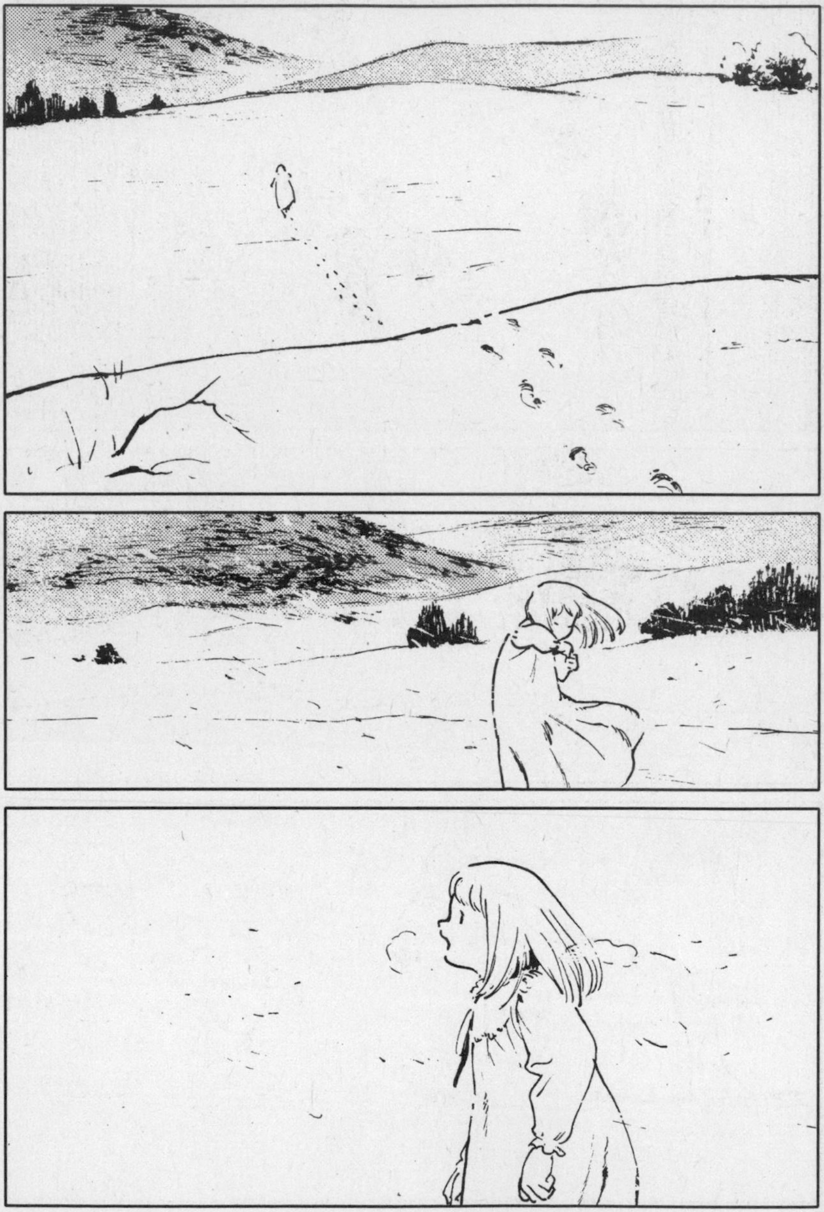

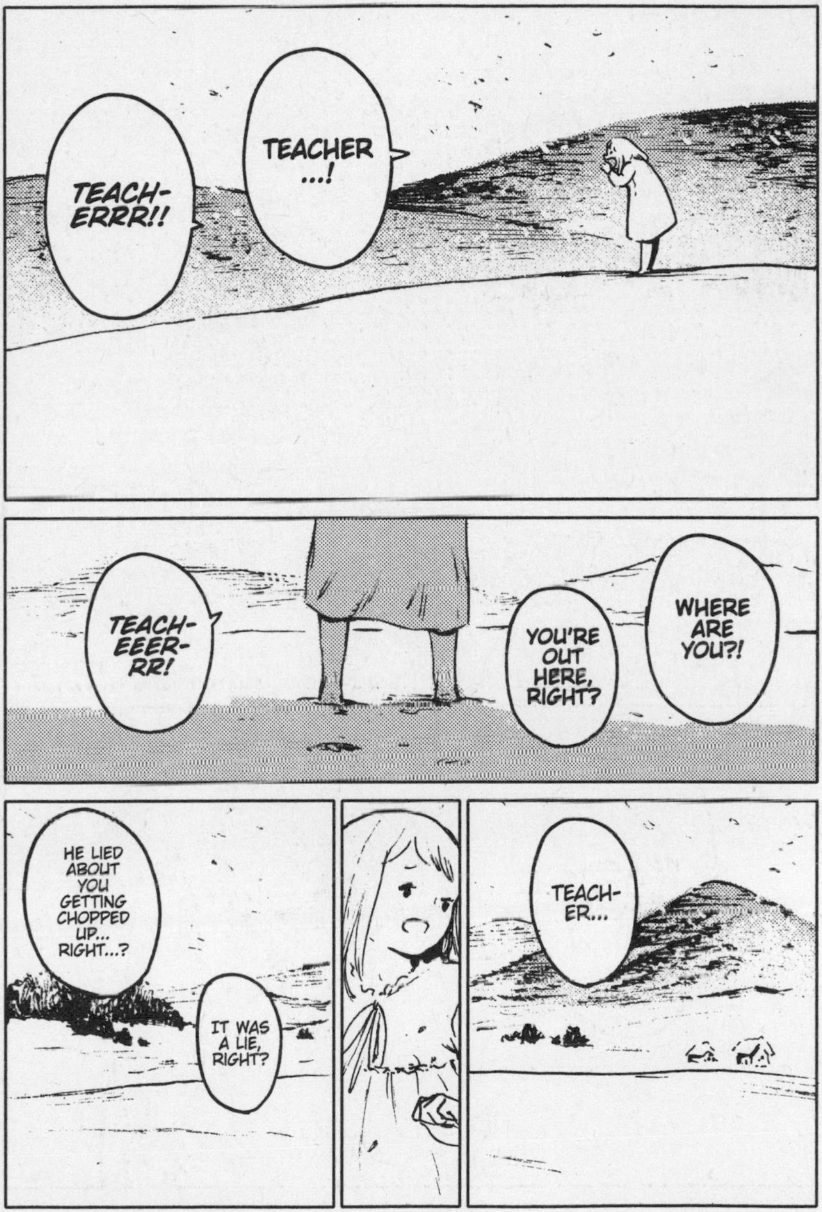
TEACHER ...!
TEACH-ERRR!!
WHERE ARE YOU?!
YOU'RE OUT HERE, RIGHT?
TEACH-EEER-RR!
TEACH-ER...
HE LIED ABOUT YOU GETTING CHOPPED UP... RIGHT...?
IT WAS A LIE, RIGHT?

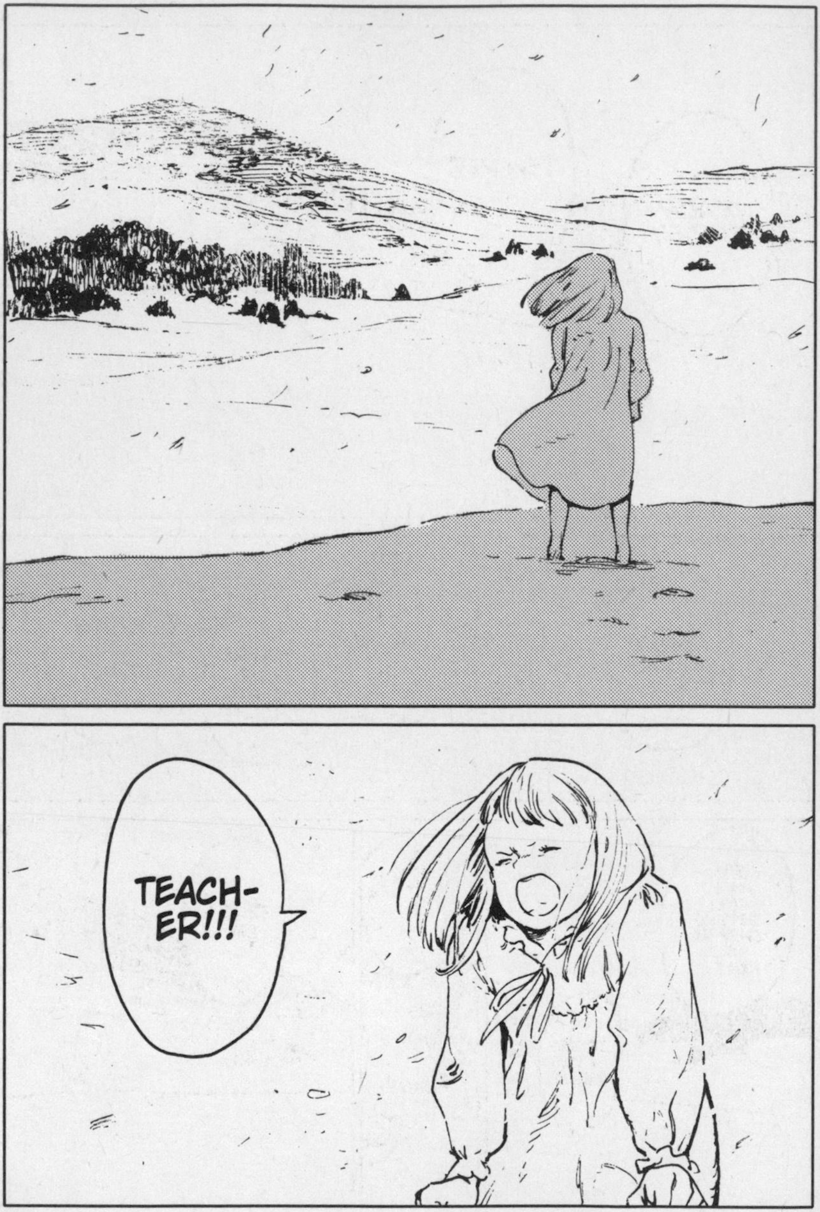
TEACH-
ER!!!

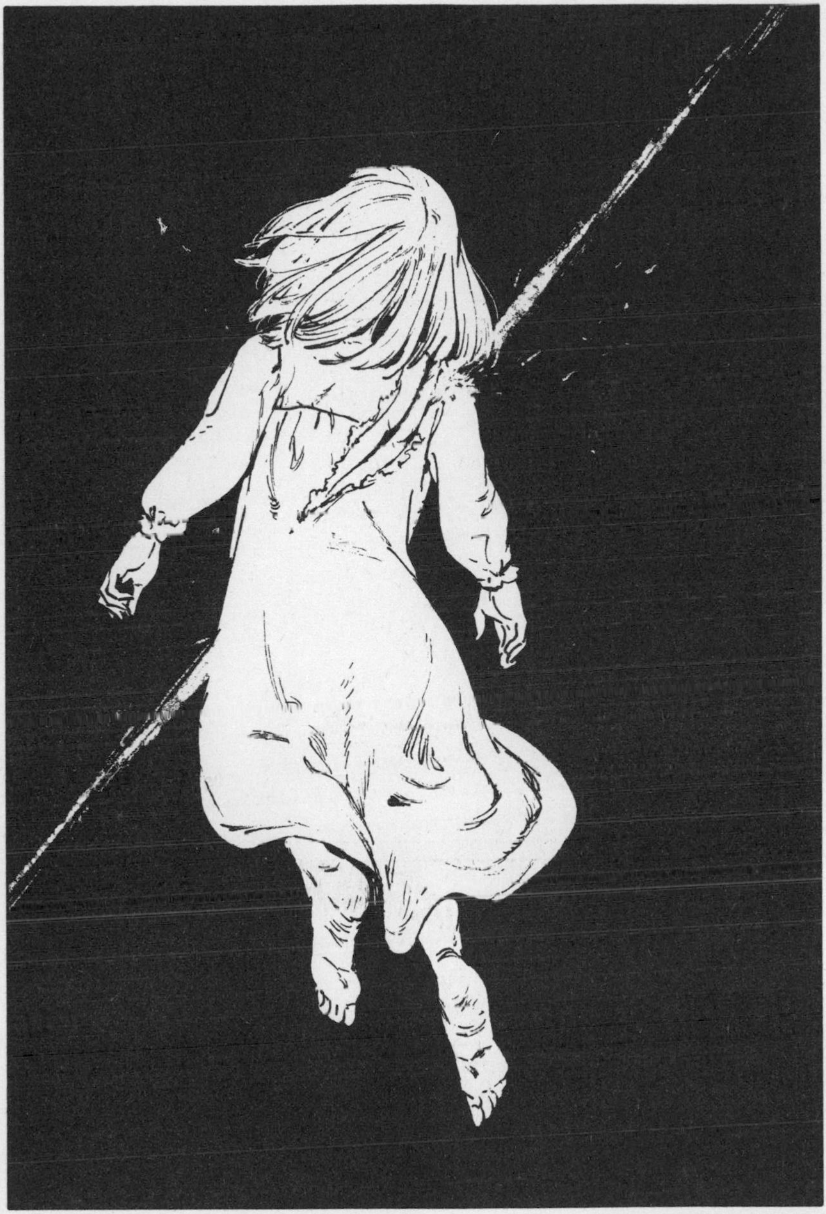

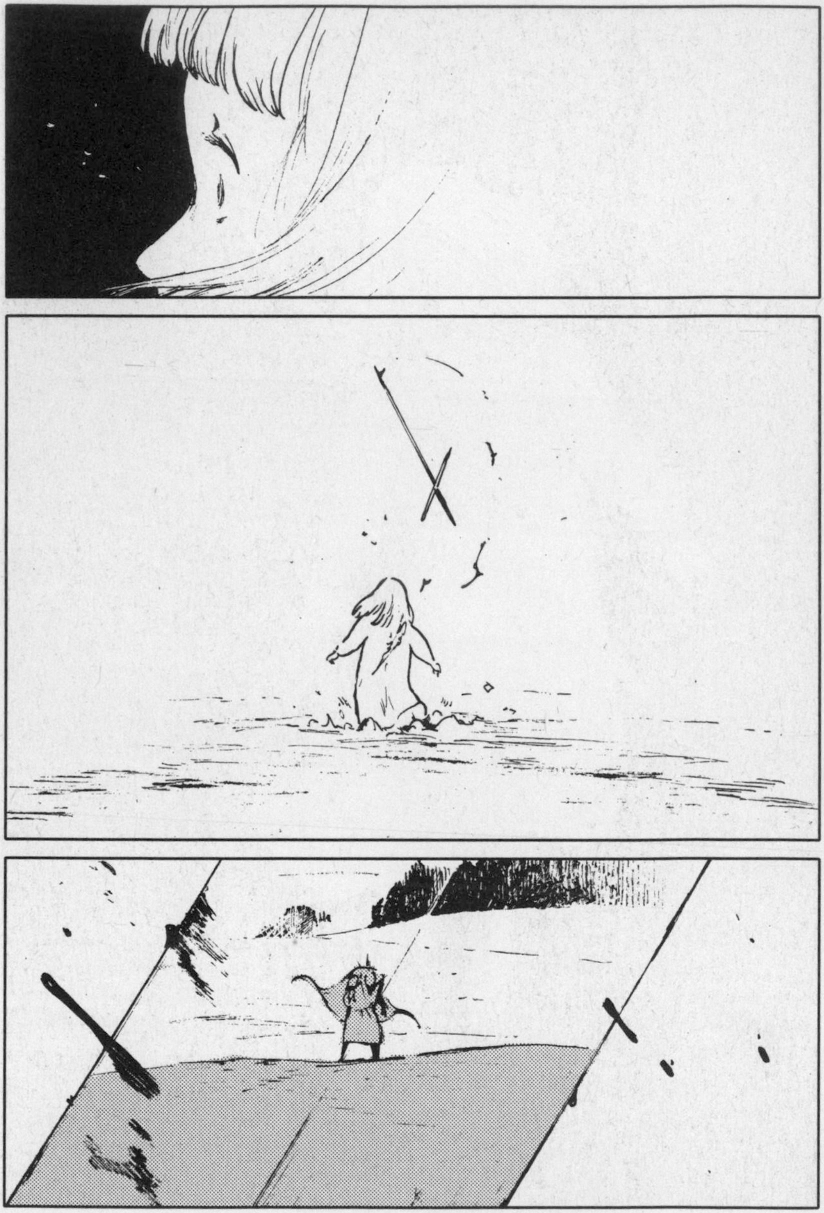

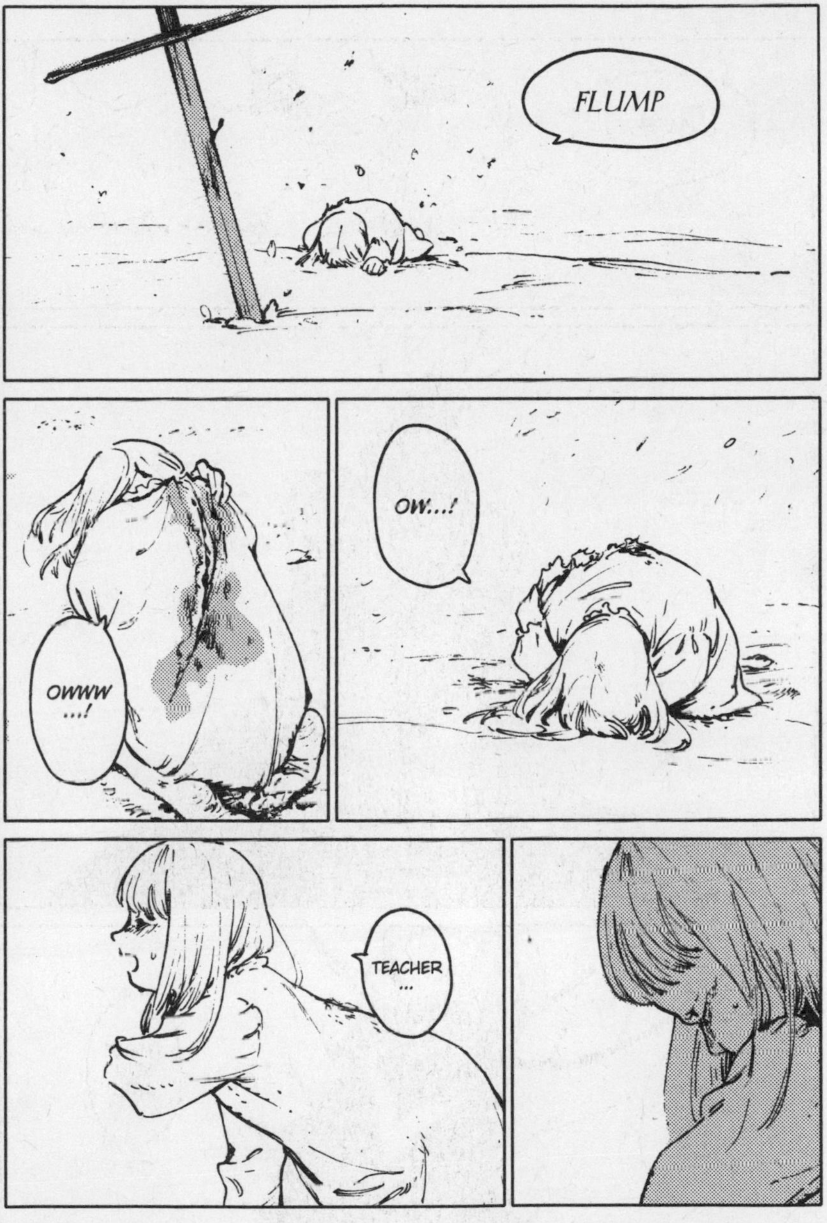
FLUMP
OW...!
OWWW ...!
TEACHER ...

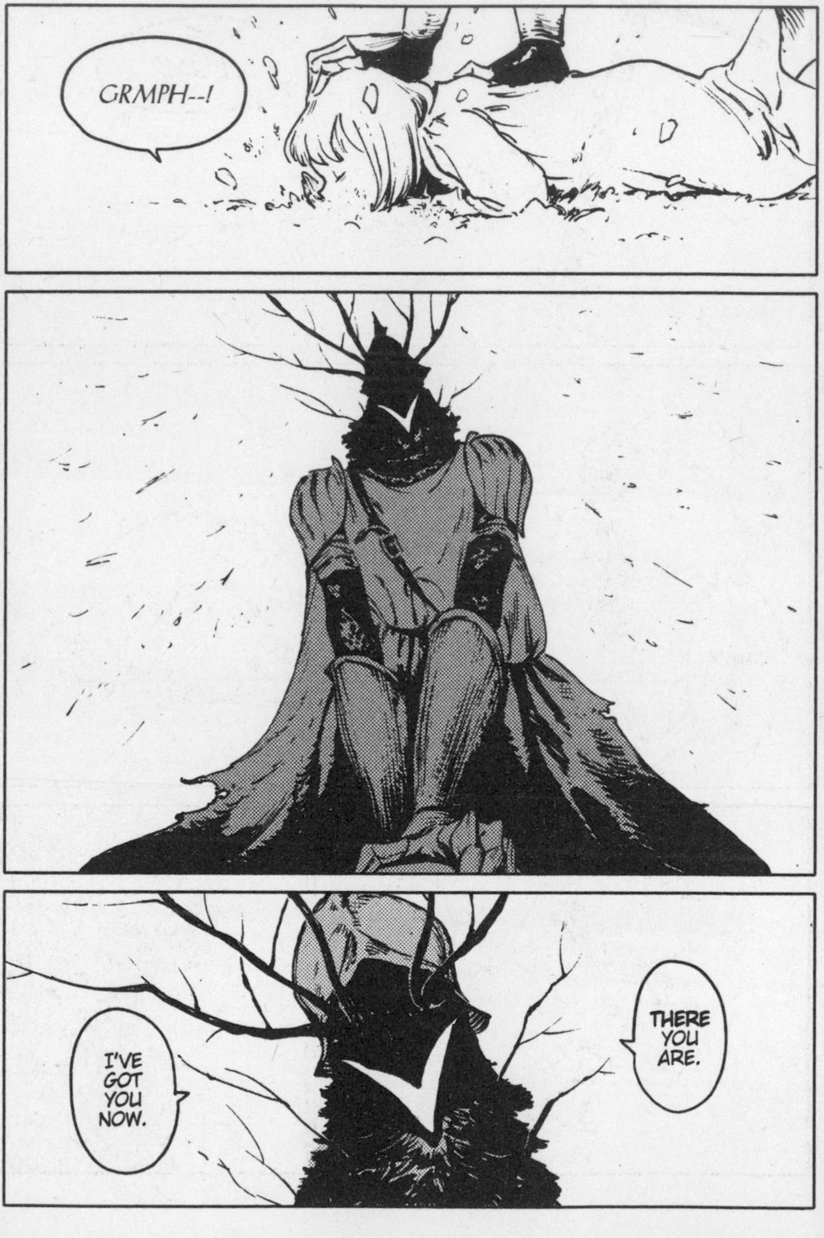
GRMPH--!
THERE YOU ARE.
I'VE GOT YOU NOW.

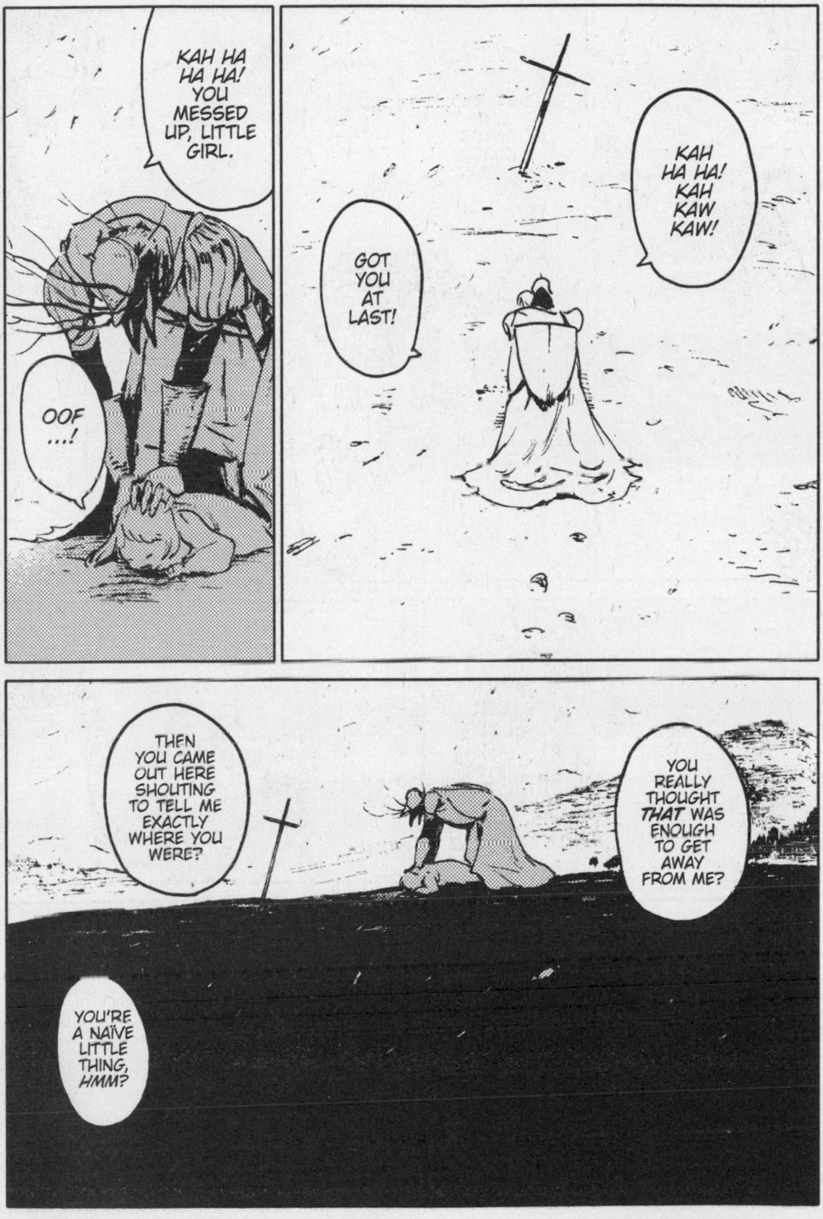
KAH HA HA! KAH KAW KAW!
GOT YOU AT LAST!
KAH HA HA HA! YOU MESSED UP, LITTLE GIRL.
OOF ...!
YOU REALLY THOUGHT *THAT* WAS ENOUGH TO GET AWAY FROM ME?
THEN YOU CAME OUT HERE SHOUTING TO TELL ME EXACTLY WHERE YOU WERE?
YOU'RE A NAÏVE LITTLE THING, *HMM?*

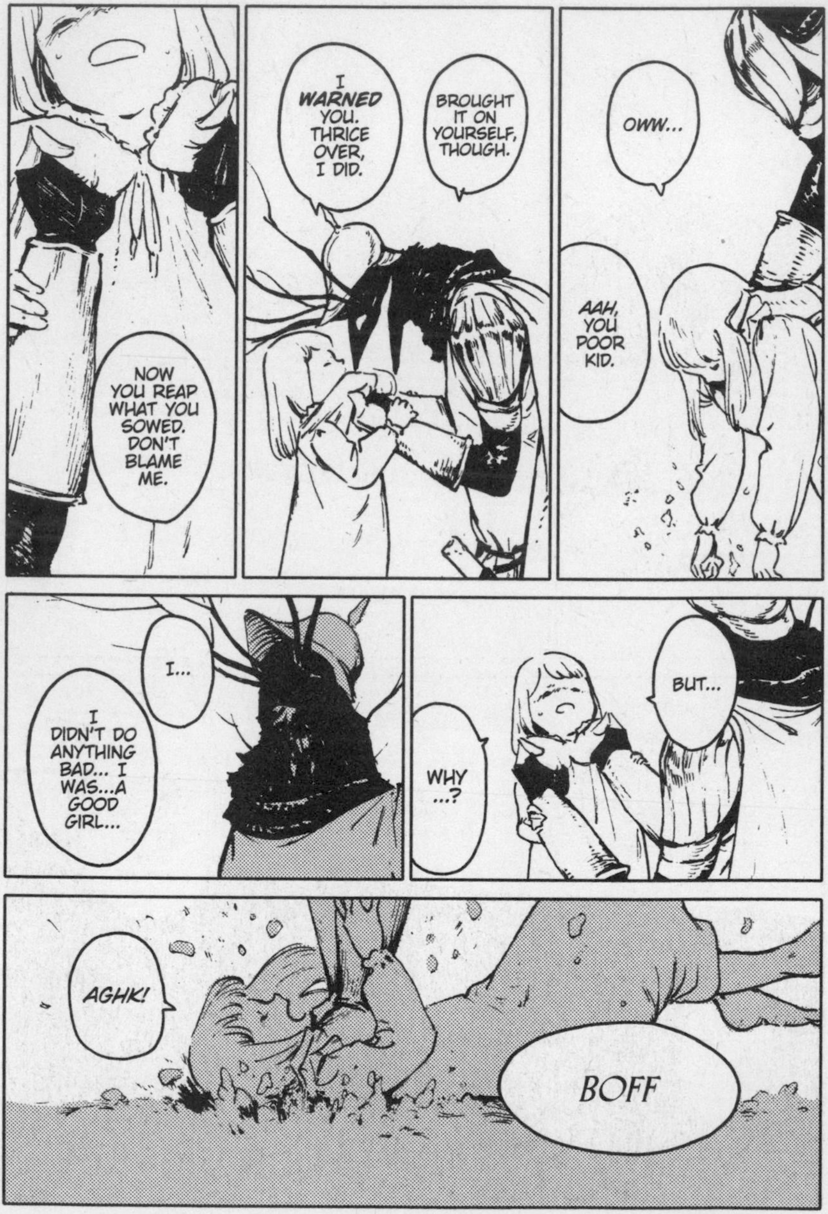
OWW...
AAH, YOU POOR KID.
BROUGHT IT ON YOURSELF, THOUGH.
I WARNED YOU. THRICE OVER, I DID.
NOW YOU REAP WHAT YOU SOWED. DON'T BLAME ME.
BUT...
WHY ...?
I...
I DIDN'T DO ANYTHING BAD... I WAS...A GOOD GIRL...
BOFF
AGHK!

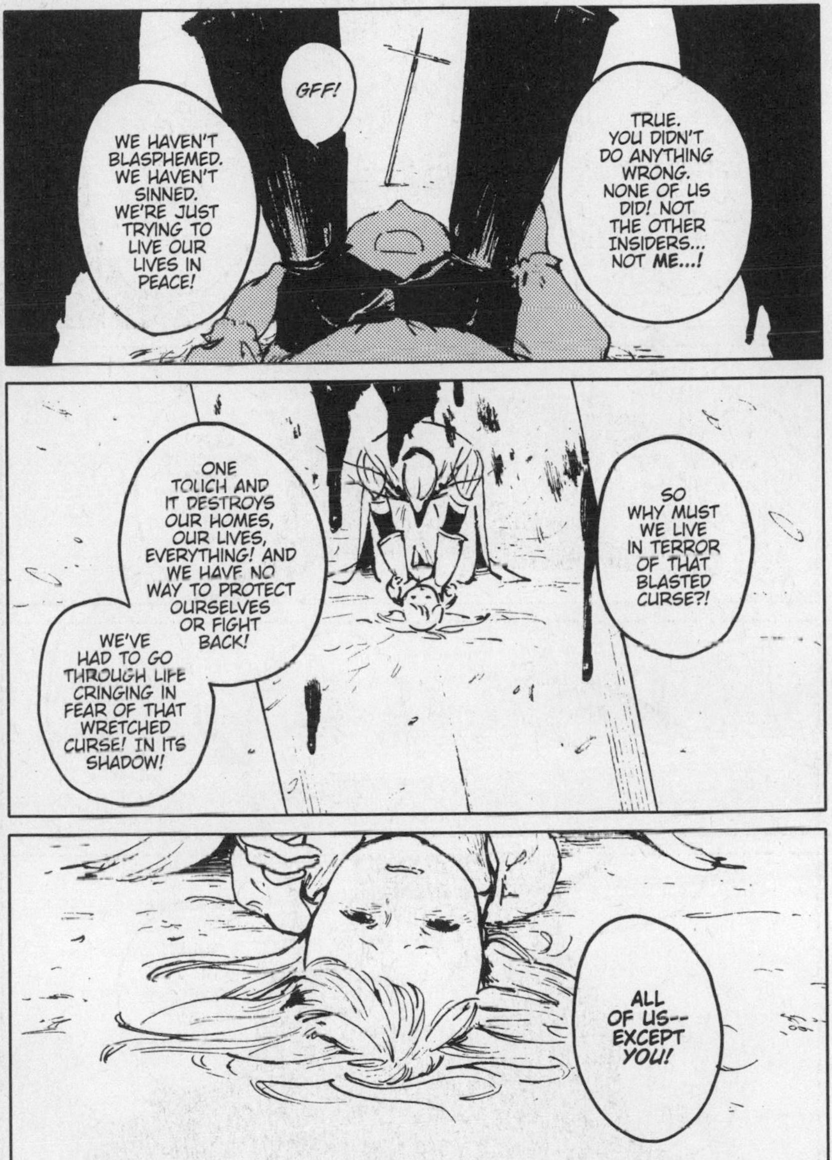
TRUE. YOU DIDN'T DO ANYTHING WRONG. NONE OF US DID! NOT THE OTHER INSIDERS... NOT ME...!
GFF!
WE HAVEN'T BLASPHEMED. WE HAVEN'T SINNED. WE'RE JUST TRYING TO LIVE OUR LIVES IN PEACE!
SO WHY MUST WE LIVE IN TERROR OF THAT BLASTED CURSE?!
ONE TOUCH AND IT DESTROYS OUR HOMES, OUR LIVES, EVERYTHING! AND WE HAVE NO WAY TO PROTECT OURSELVES OR FIGHT BACK!
WE'VE HAD TO GO THROUGH LIFE CRINGING IN FEAR OF THAT WRETCHED CURSE! IN ITS SHADOW!
ALL OF US--EXCEPT YOU!

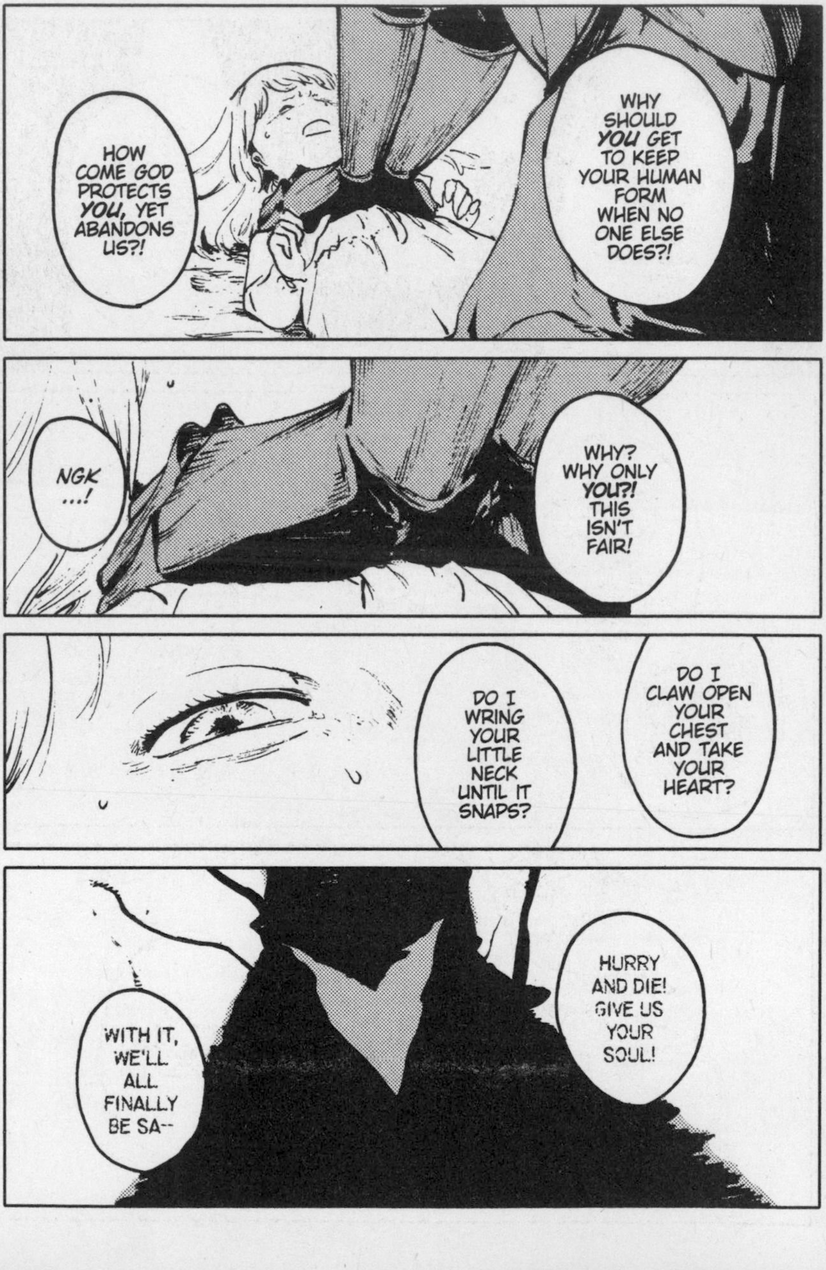
WHY SHOULD *YOU* GET TO KEEP YOUR HUMAN FORM WHEN NO ONE ELSE DOES?!
HOW COME GOD PROTECTS *YOU*, YET ABANDONS US?!
WHY? WHY ONLY *YOU*?! THIS ISN'T FAIR!
NGK ...!
DO I CLAW OPEN YOUR CHEST AND TAKE YOUR HEART?
DO I WRING YOUR LITTLE NECK UNTIL IT SNAPS?
HURRY AND DIE! GIVE US YOUR SOUL!
WITH IT, WE'LL ALL FINALLY BE SA--

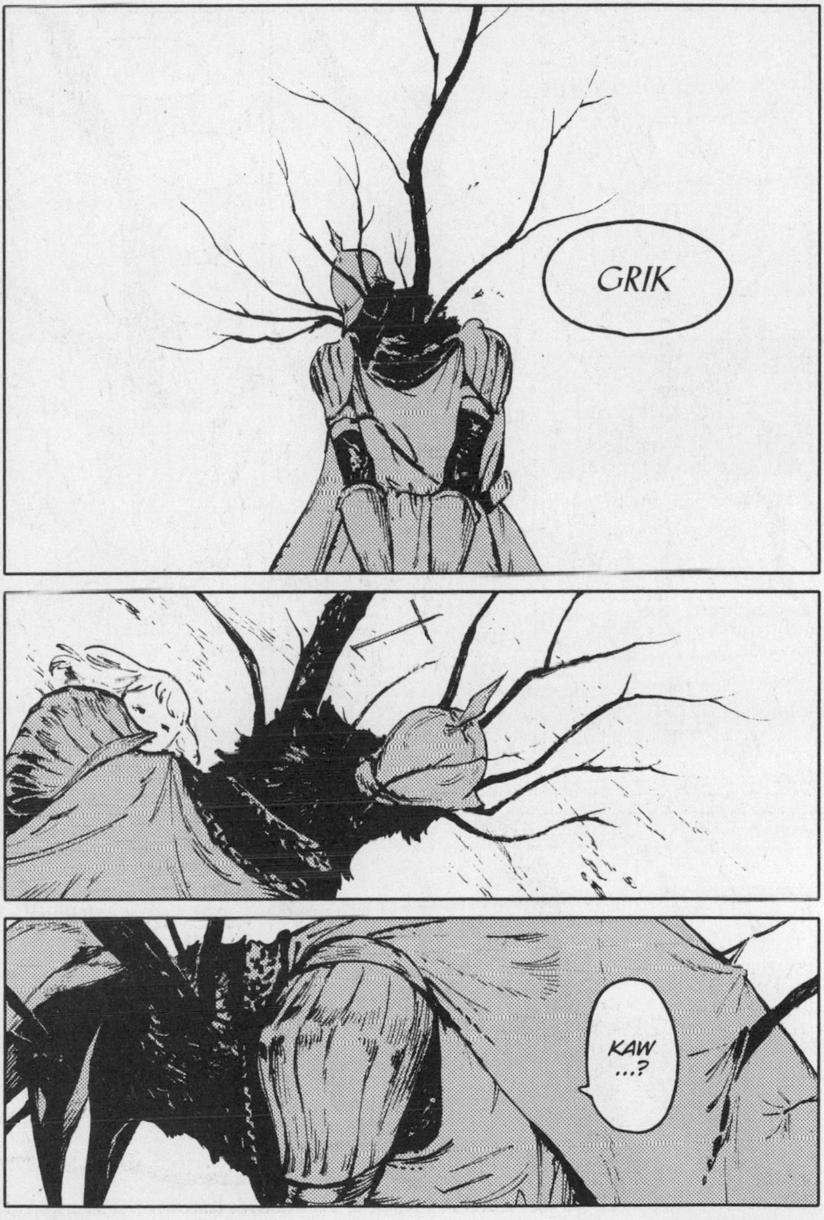
GRIK
KAW ...?

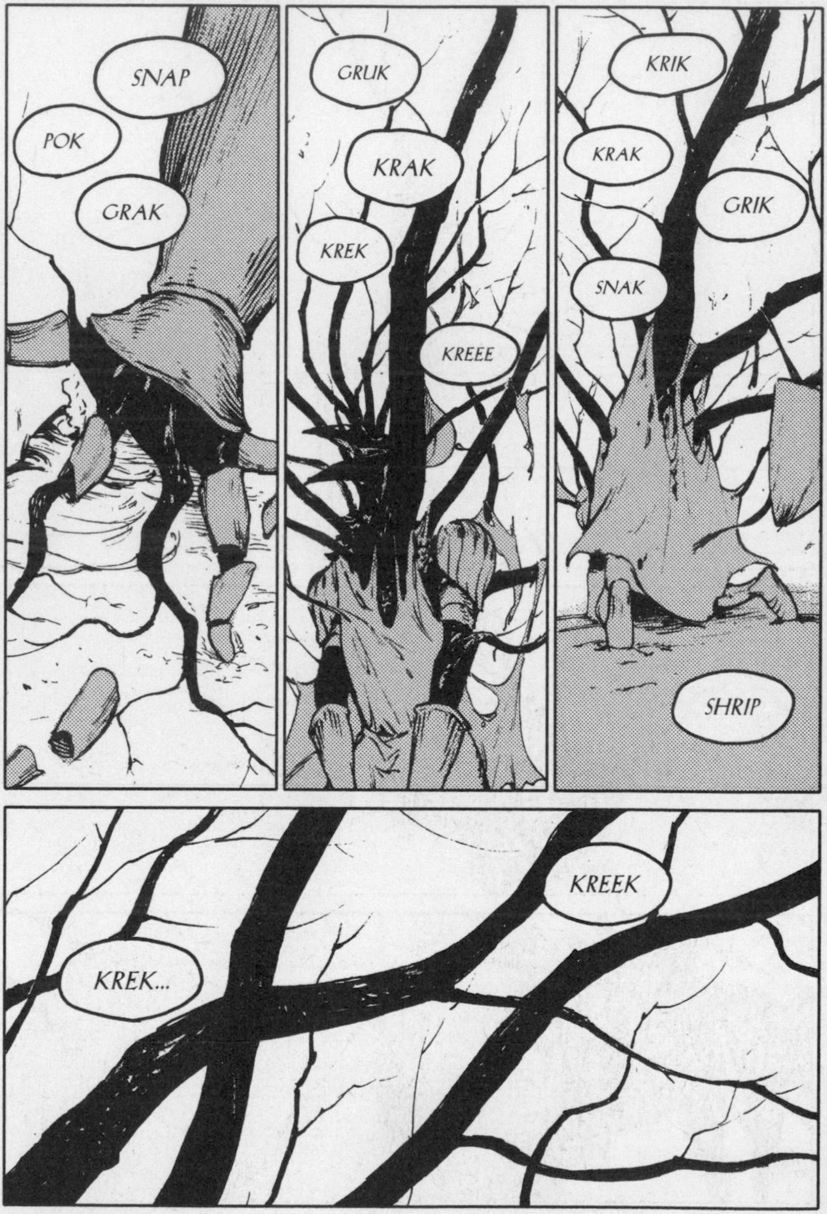
KRIK
KRAK
GRIK
SNAK
SHRIP
GRUK
KRAK
KREK
KREEE
SNAP
POK
GRAK
KREEK
KREK...

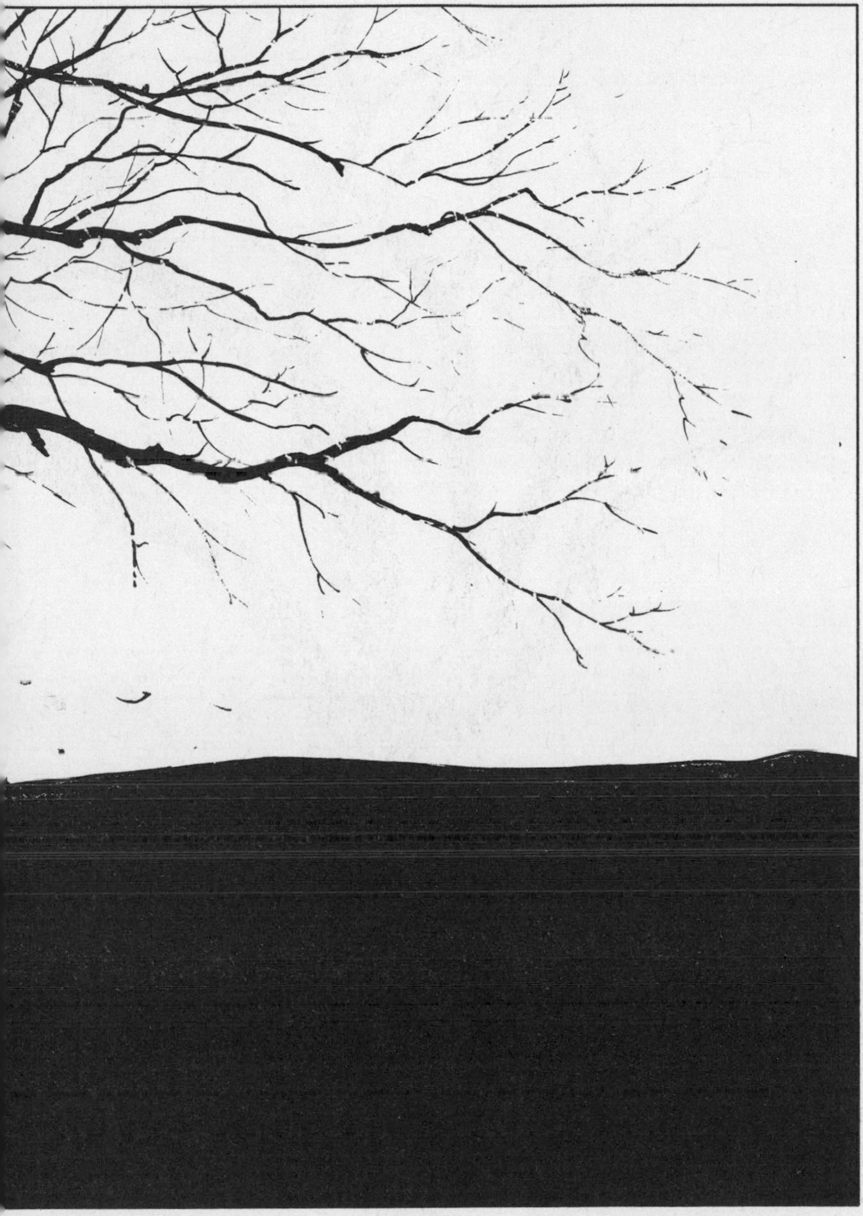

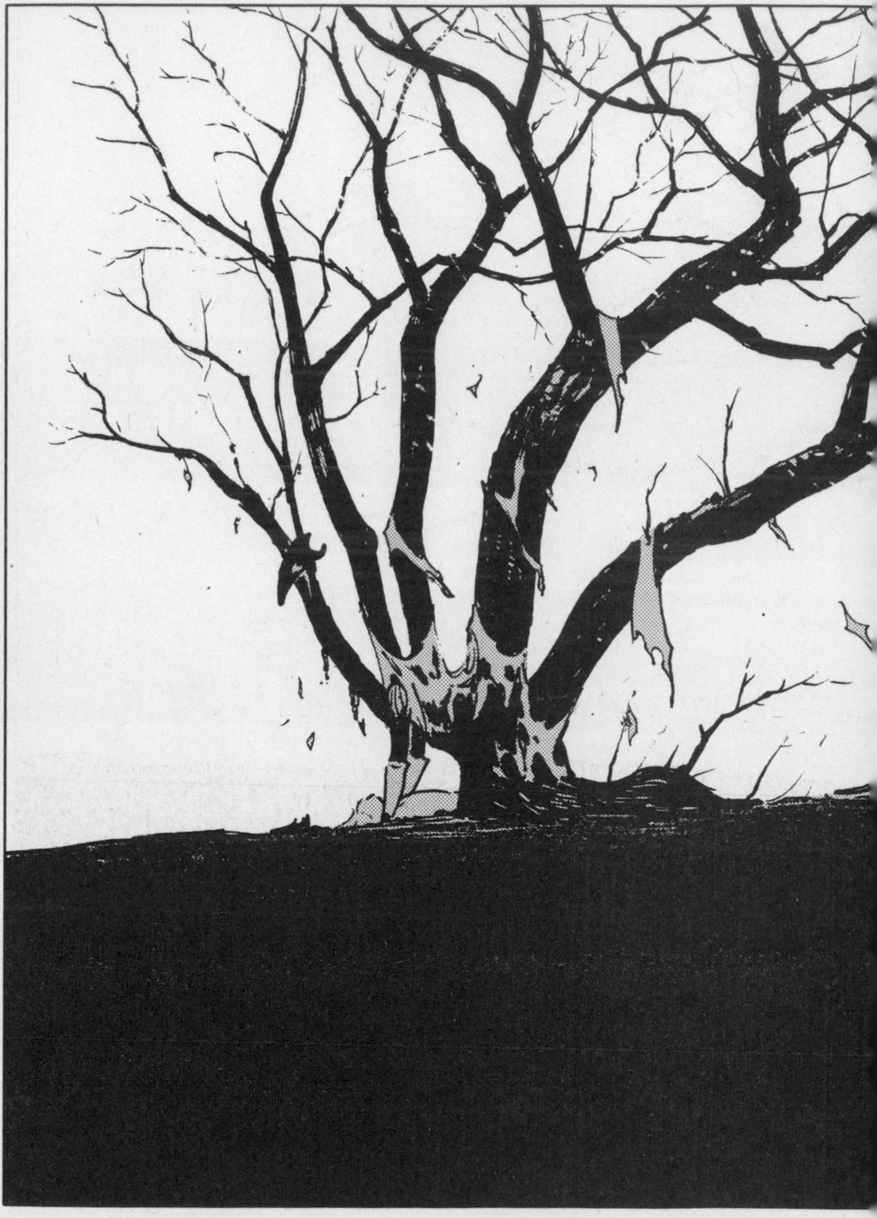

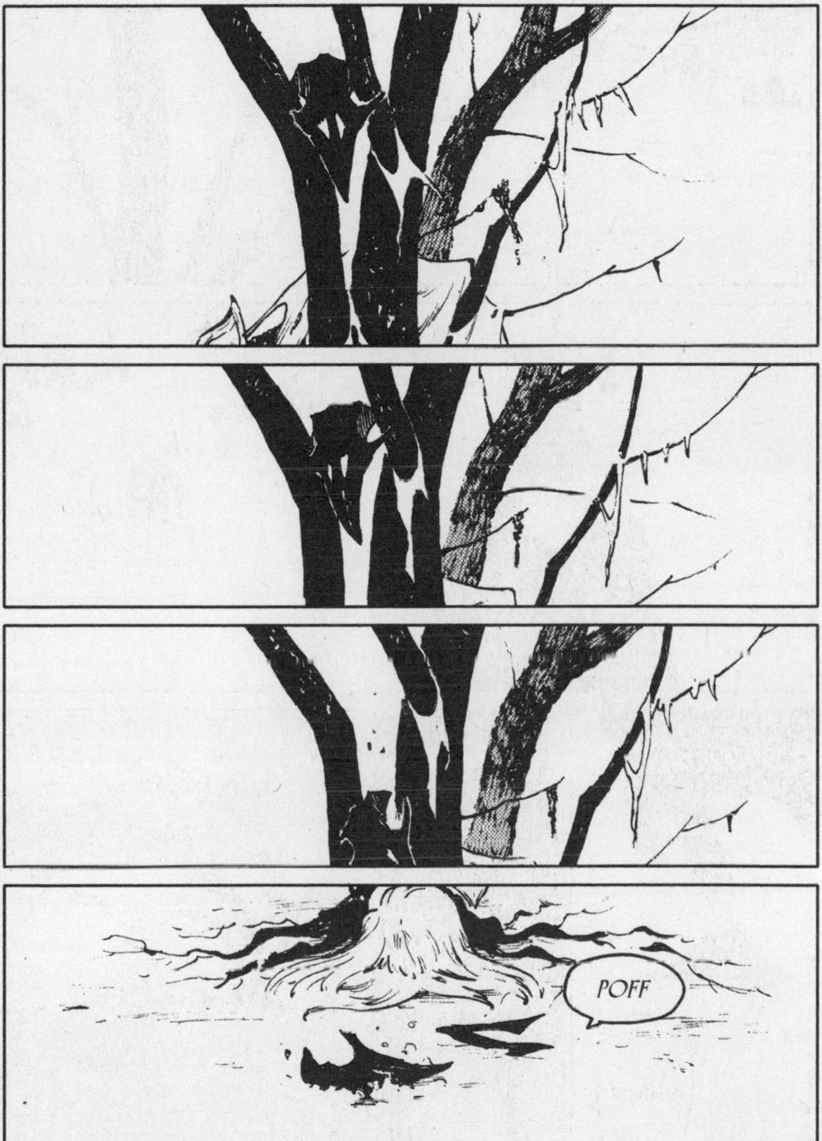
POFF

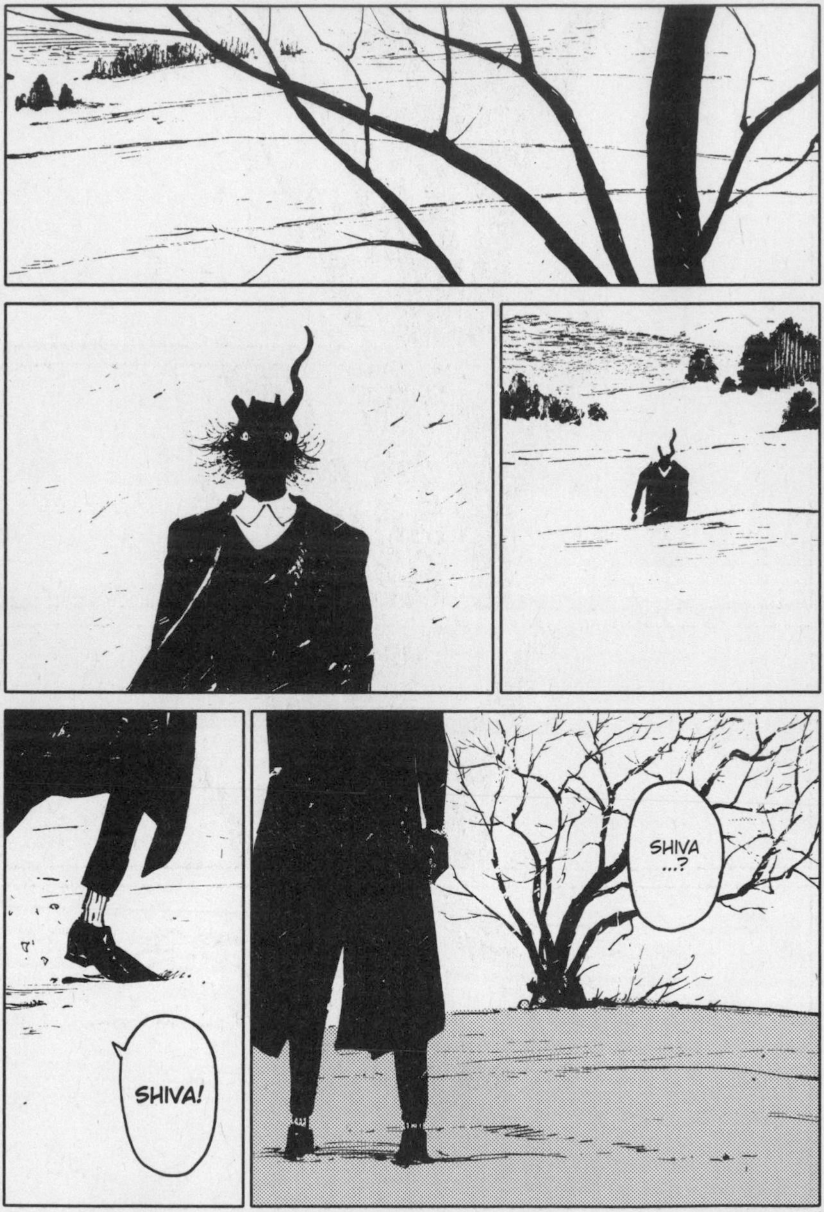
SHIVA ...?
SHIVA!

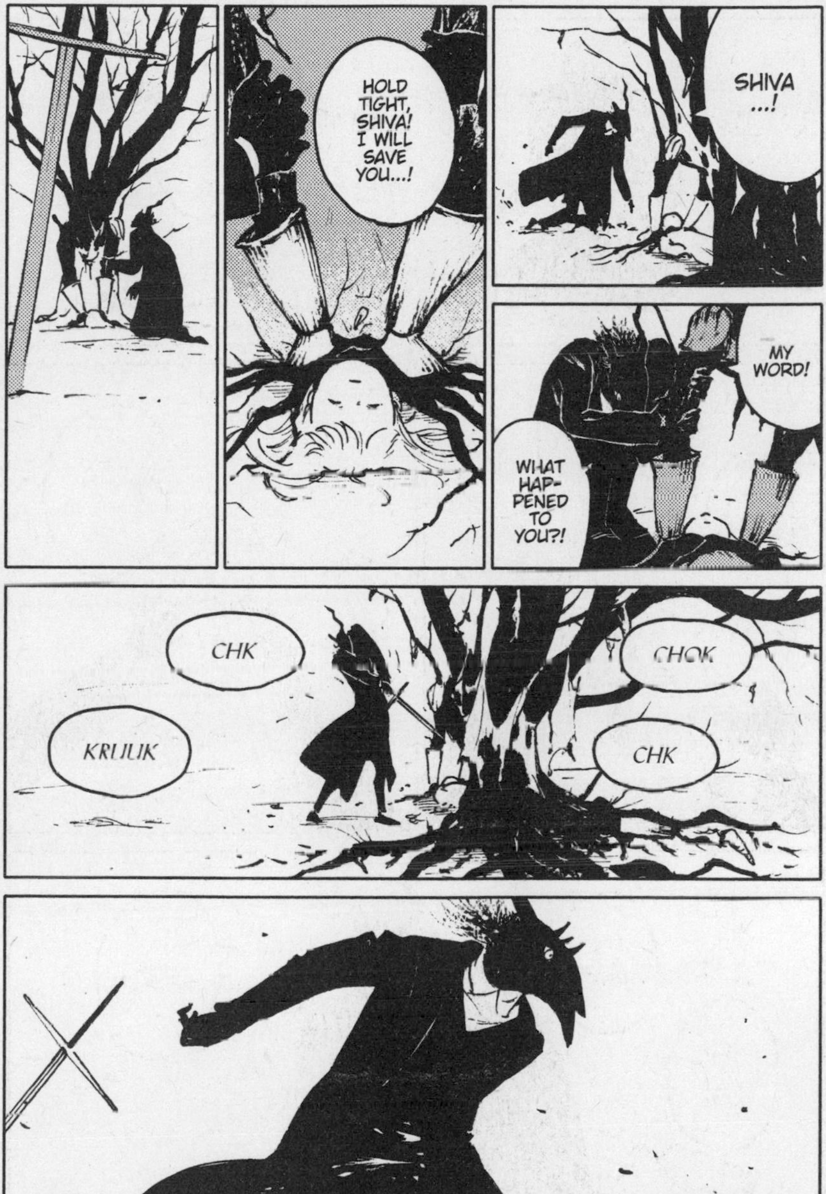
SHIVA ...!
MY WORD!
WHAT HAP-PENED TO YOU?!
HOLD TIGHT, SHIVA! I WILL SAVE YOU...!
CHOK
CHK
CHK
KRUUK

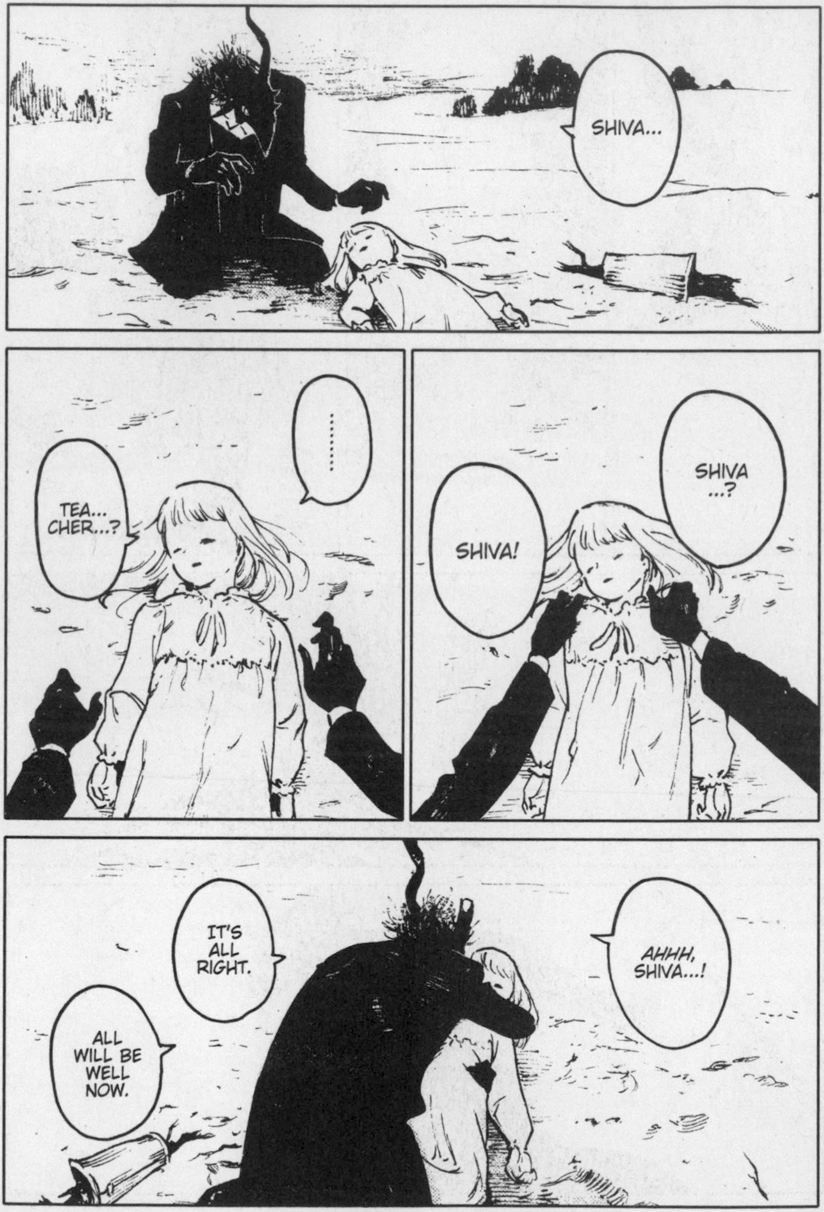
SHIVA...
SHIVA ...?
SHIVA!
......
TEA... CHER...?
AHHH, SHIVA...!
IT'S ALL RIGHT.
ALL WILL BE WELL NOW.

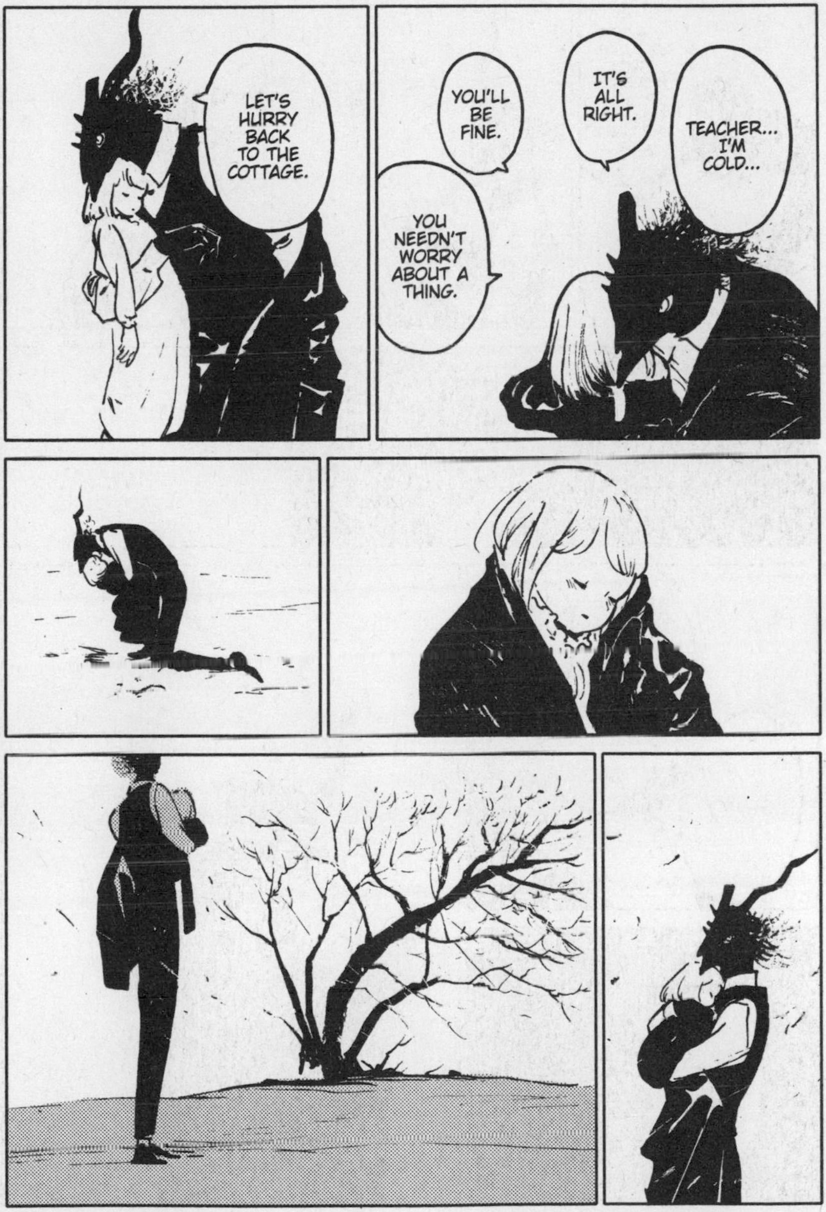
TEACHER... I'M COLD...
IT'S ALL RIGHT.
YOU'LL BE FINE.
YOU NEEDN'T WORRY ABOUT A THING.
LET'S HURRY BACK TO THE COTTAGE.

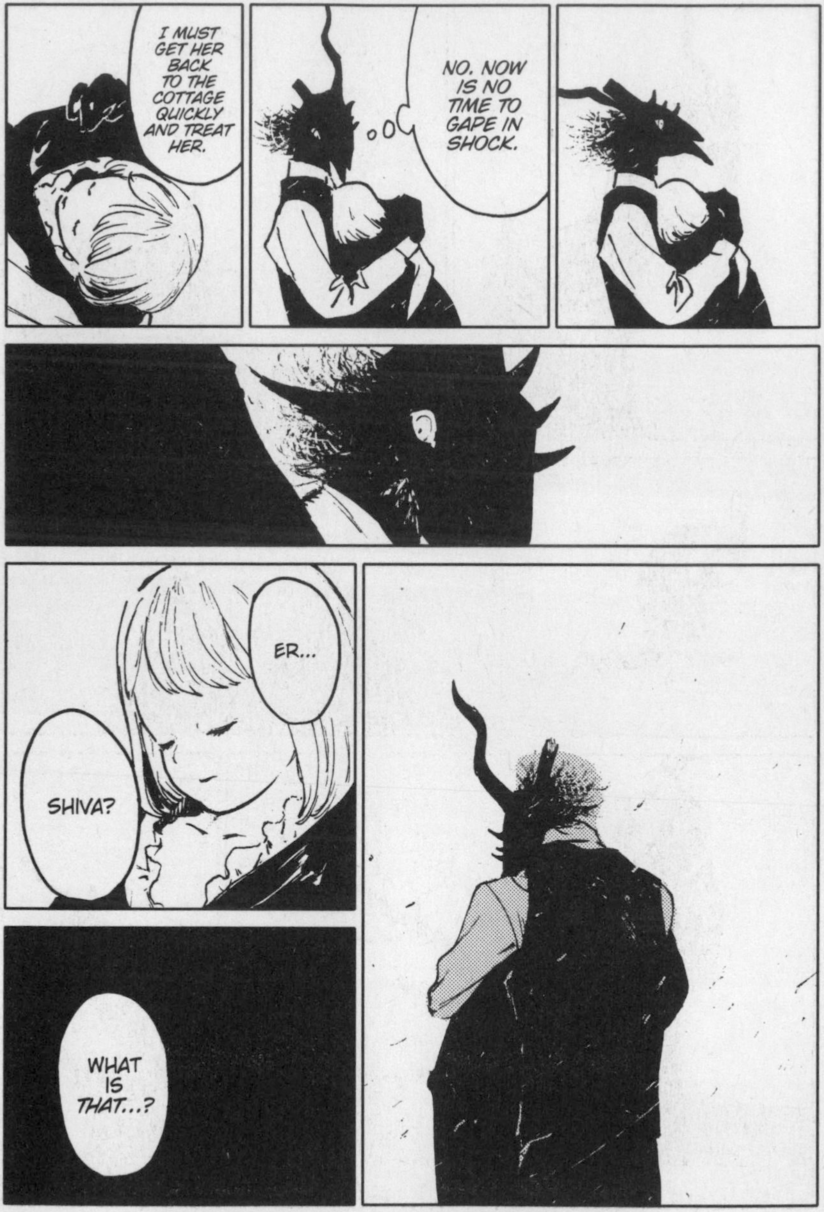
NO. NOW IS NO TIME TO GAPE IN SHOCK.
I MUST GET HER BACK TO THE COTTAGE QUICKLY AND TREAT HER.
ER...
SHIVA?
WHAT IS THAT...?

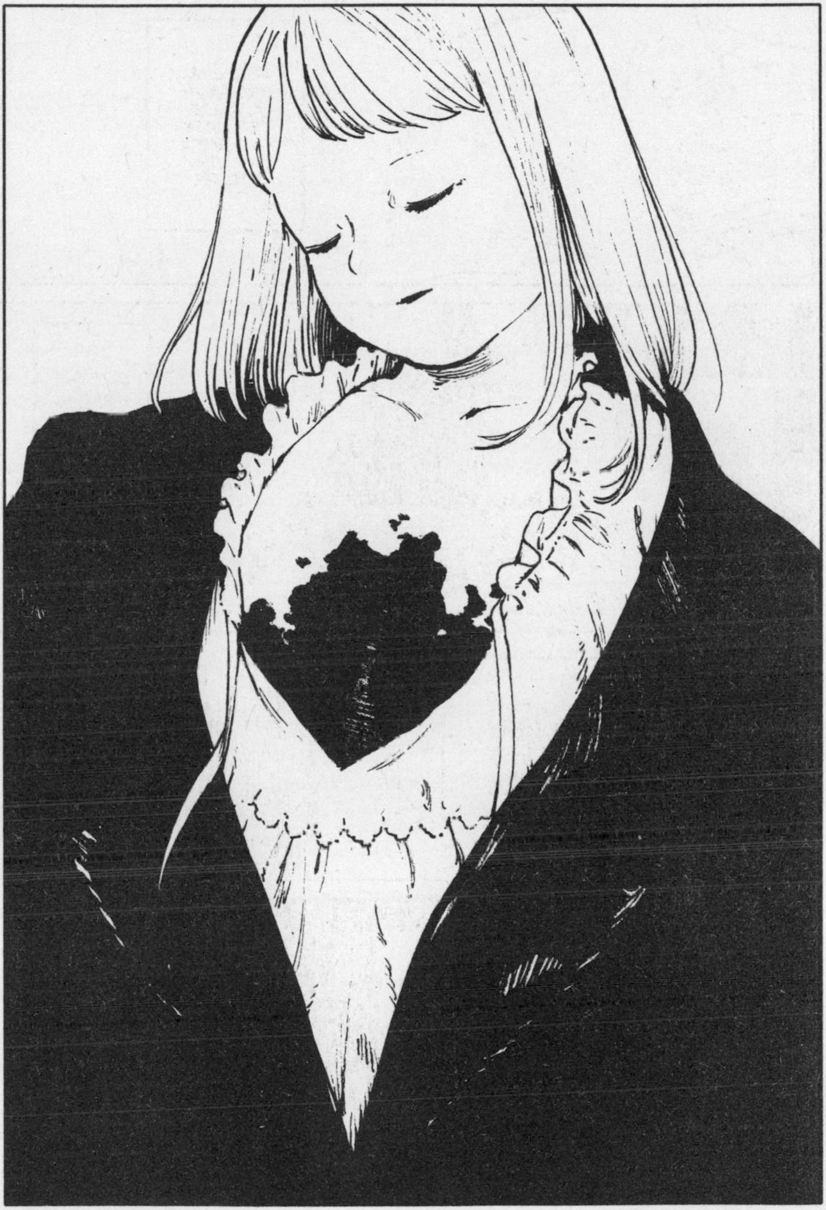

Chapter 33

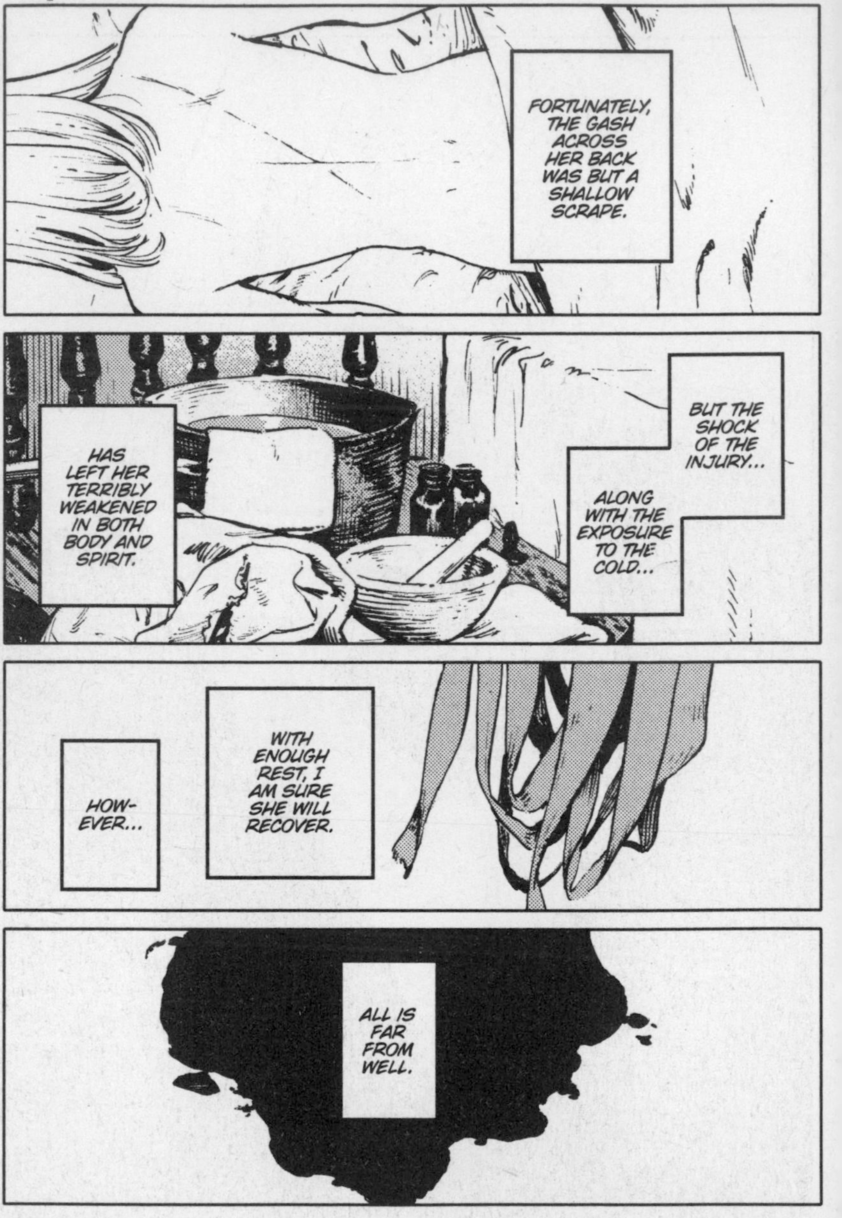
FORTUNATELY, THE GASH ACROSS HER BACK WAS BUT A SHALLOW SCRAPE.
BUT THE SHOCK OF THE INJURY...
ALONG WITH THE EXPOSURE TO THE COLD...
HAS LEFT HER TERRIBLY WEAKENED IN BOTH BODY AND SPIRIT.
WITH ENOUGH REST, I AM SURE SHE WILL RECOVER.
HOW-EVER...
ALL IS FAR FROM WELL.

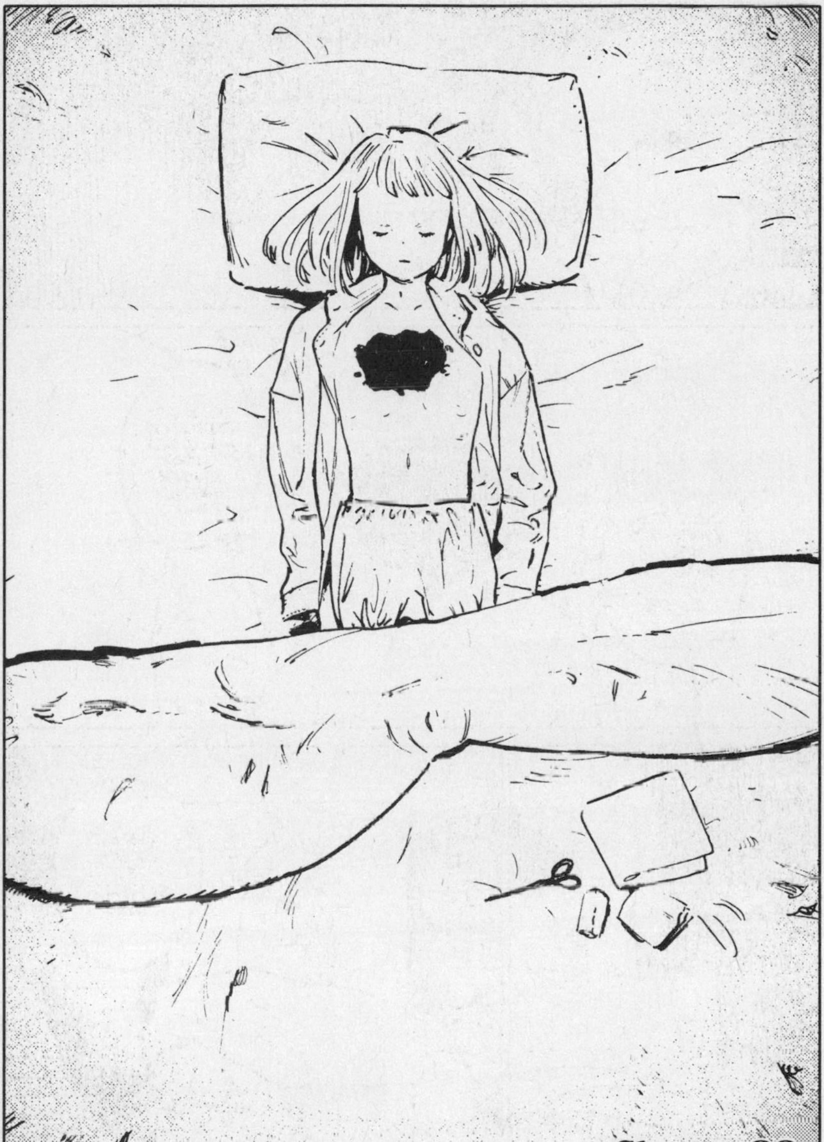
Chapter 33

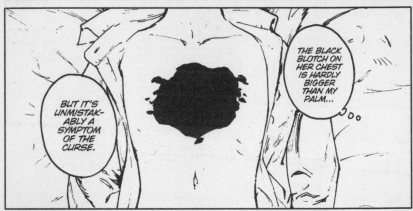

THE BLACK BLOTCH ON HER CHEST IS HARDLY BIGGER THAN MY PALM...

BUT IT'S UNMISTAKABLY A SYMPTOM OF THE CURSE.

AND BIT BY BIT, IT'S SPREADING.

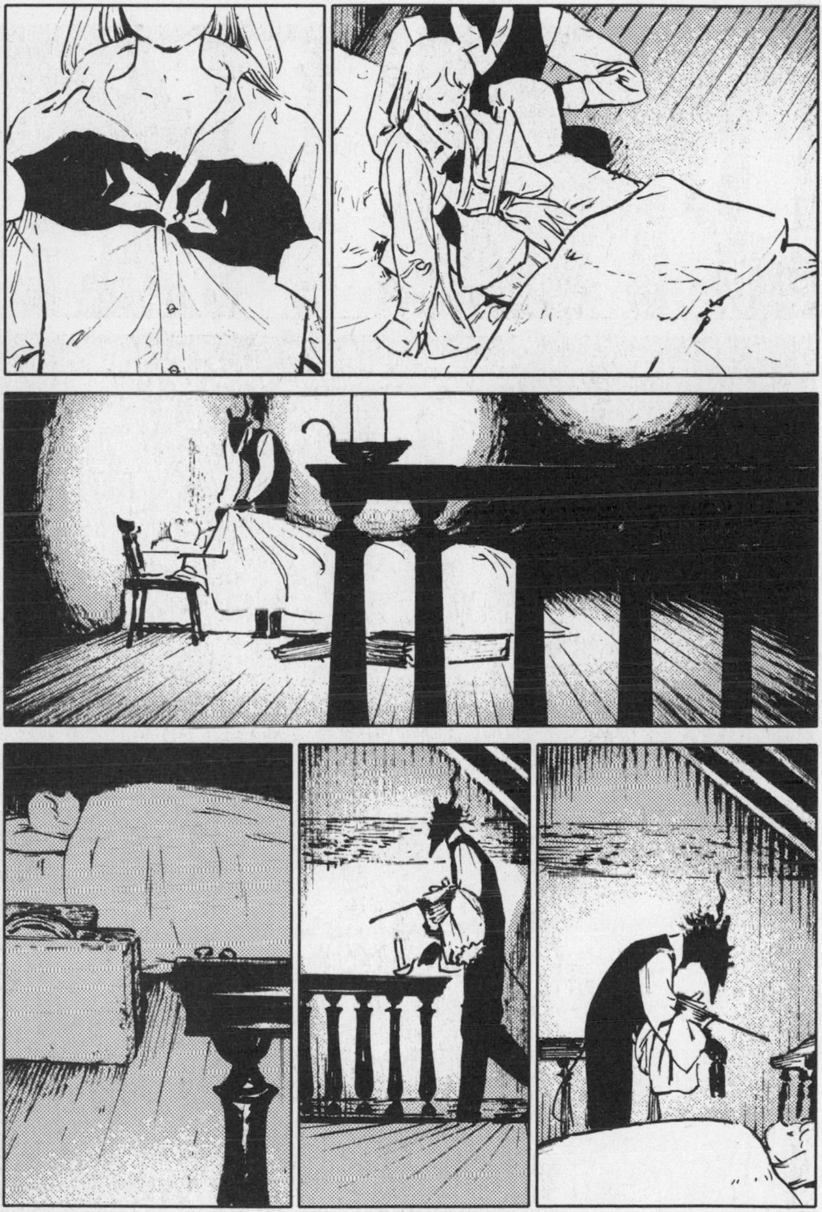

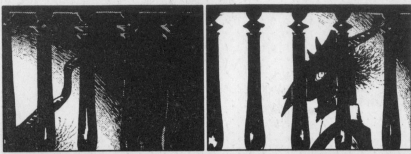

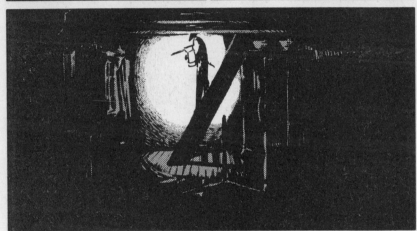

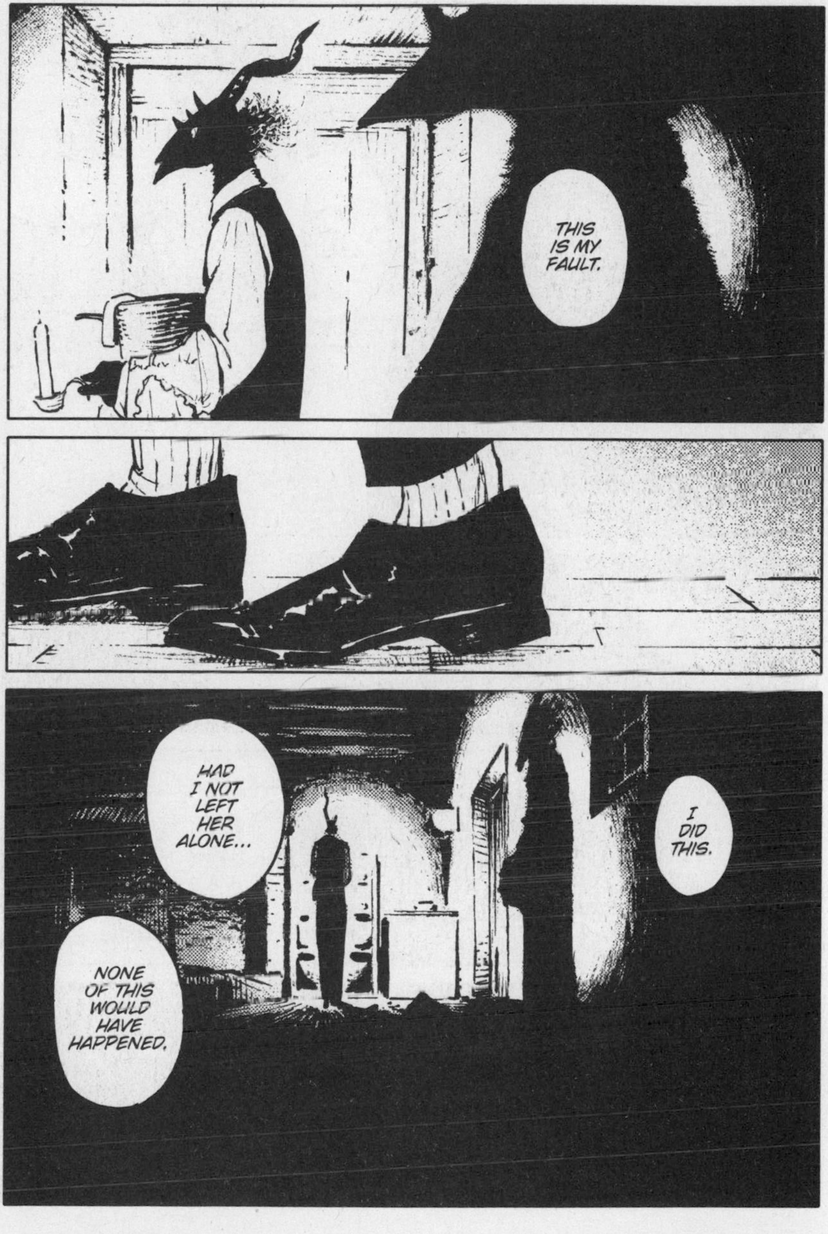
THIS IS MY FAULT.
I DID THIS.
HAD I NOT LEFT HER ALONE...
NONE OF THIS WOULD HAVE HAPPENED.

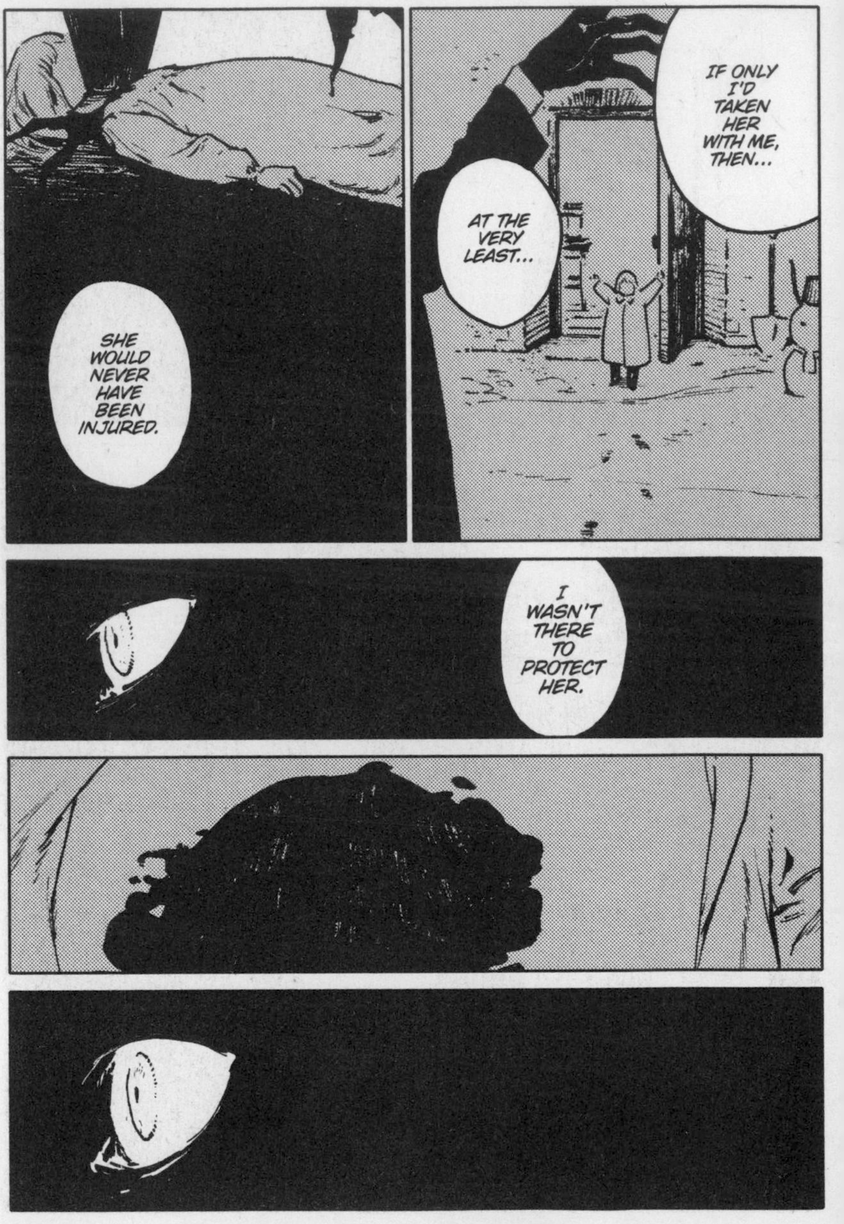
IF ONLY I'D TAKEN HER WITH ME, THEN...
AT THE VERY LEAST...
SHE WOULD NEVER HAVE BEEN INJURED.
I WASN'T THERE TO PROTECT HER.

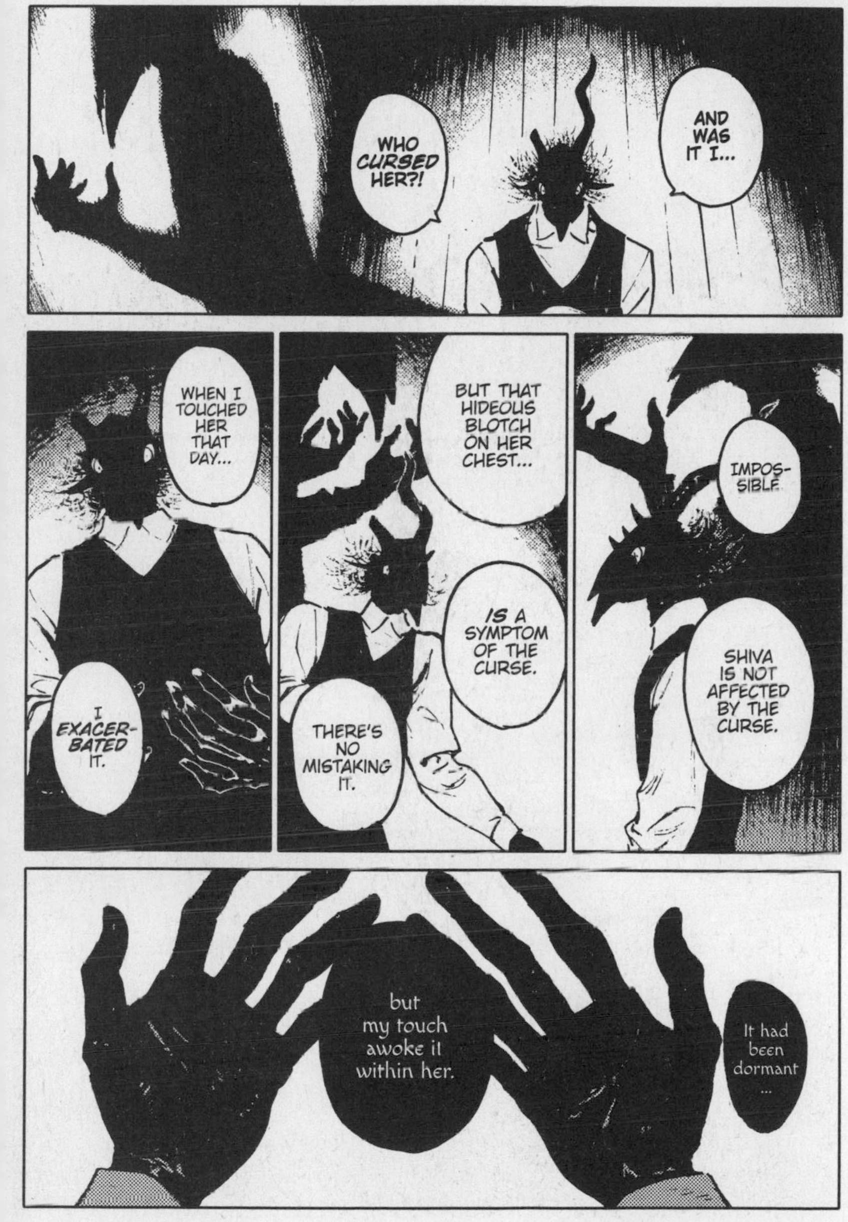
AND WAS IT I...
WHO CURSED HER?!
IMPOSSIBLE.
SHIVA IS NOT AFFECTED BY THE CURSE.
BUT THAT HIDEOUS BLOTCH ON HER CHEST...
IS A SYMPTOM OF THE CURSE.
THERE'S NO MISTAKING IT.
WHEN I TOUCHED HER THAT DAY...
I EXACERBATED IT.
It had been dormant ...
but my touch awoke it within her.

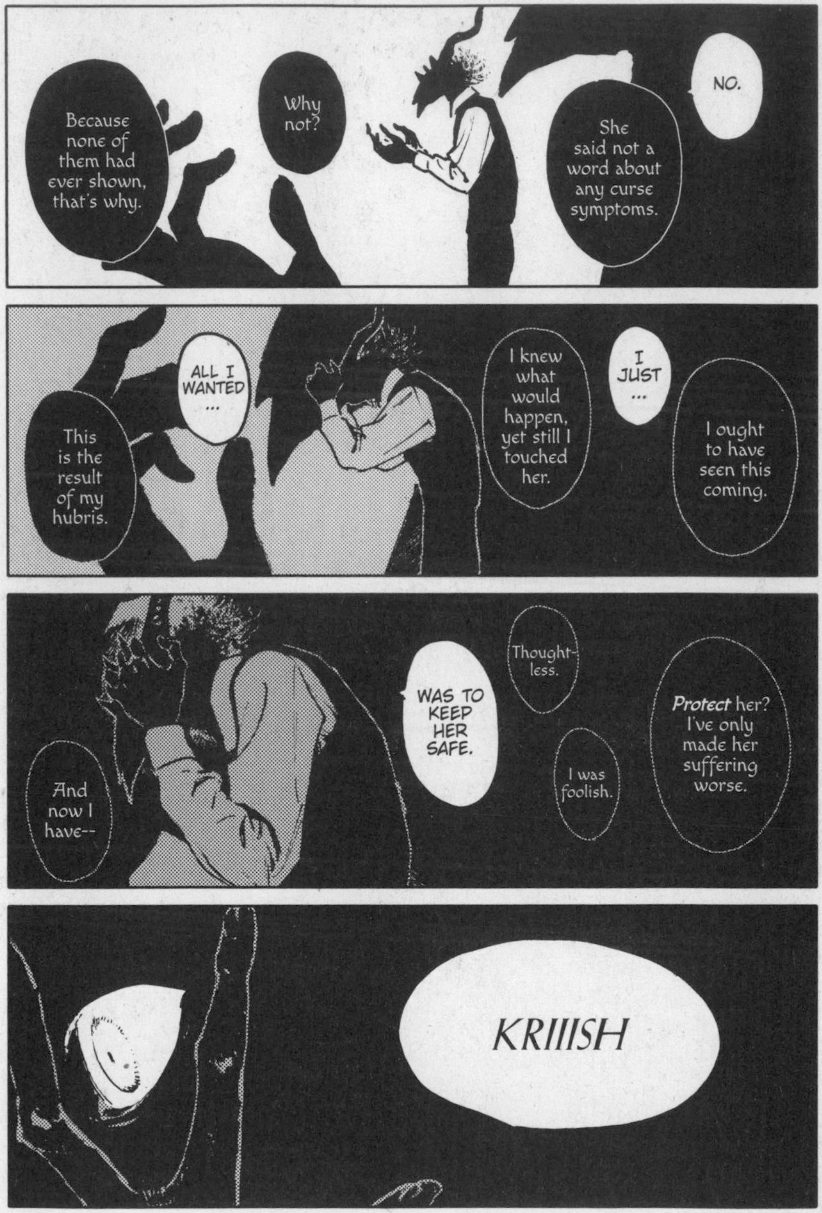
NO.
She said not a word about any curse symptoms.
Why not?
Because none of them had ever shown, that's why.
I ought to have seen this coming.
I JUST ...
I knew what would happen, yet still I touched her.
ALL I WANTED ...
This is the result of my hubris.
Protect her? I've only made her suffering worse.
Thought-less.
I was foolish.
WAS TO KEEP HER SAFE.
And now I have--
KRIIISH

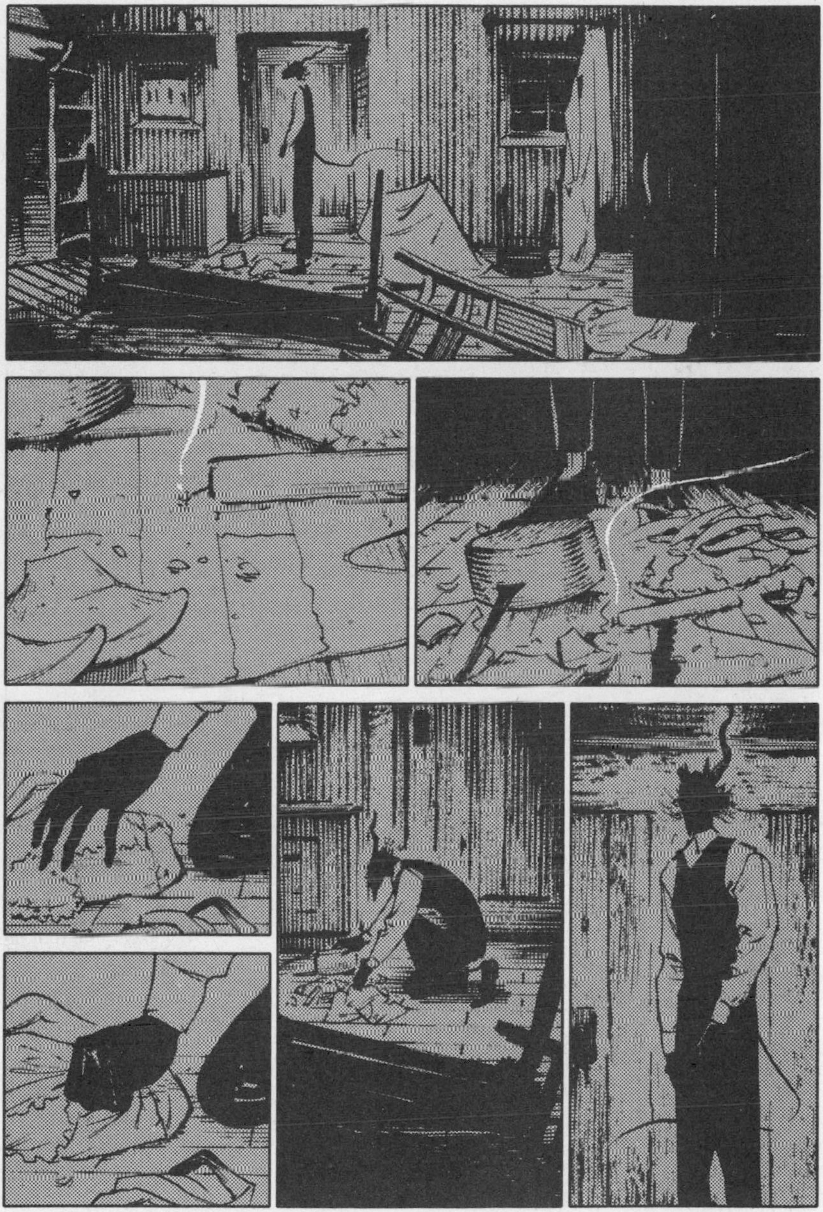

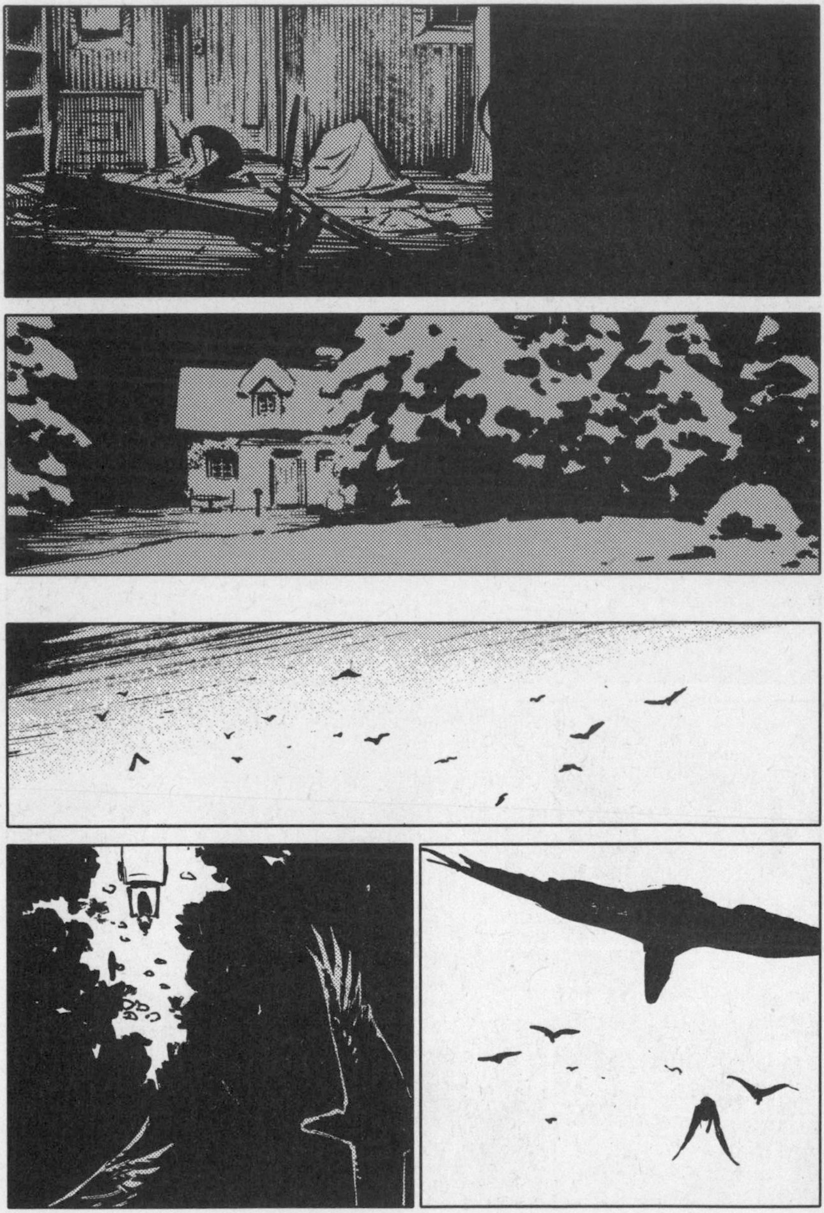

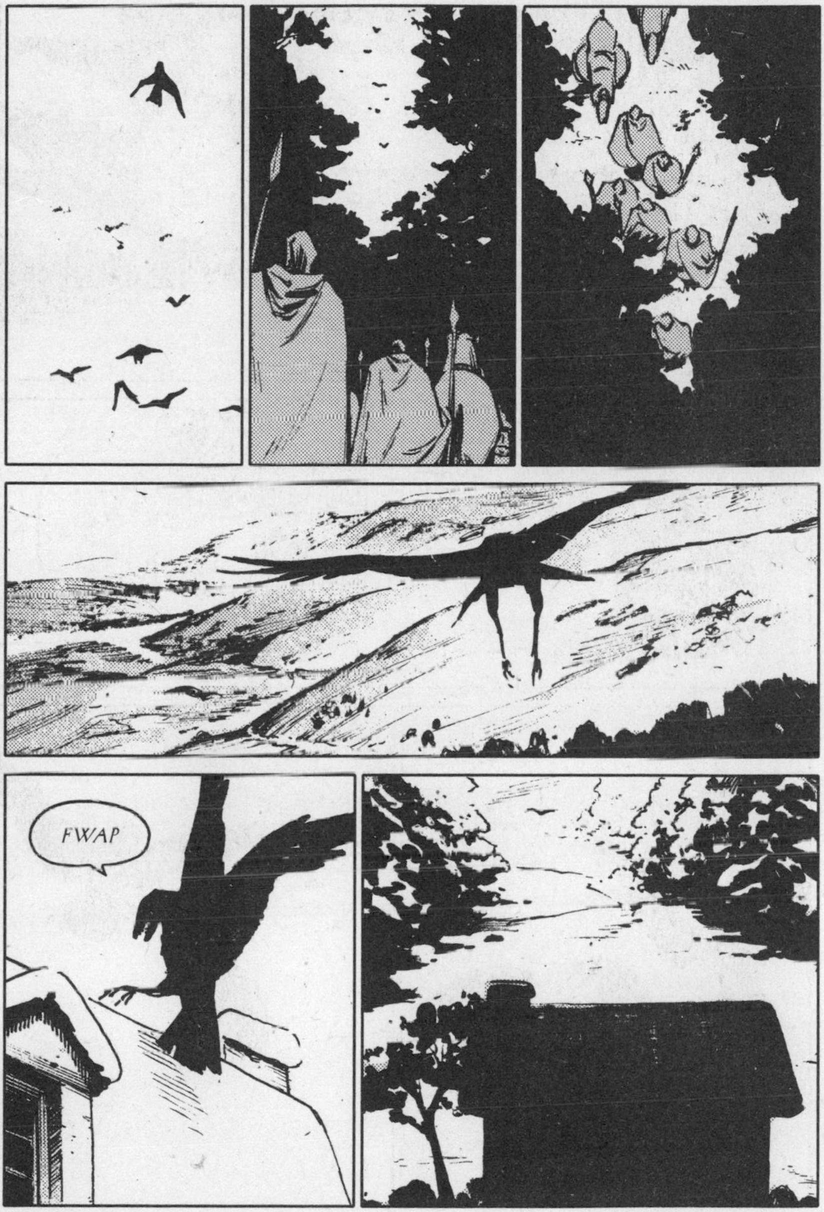
FWAP

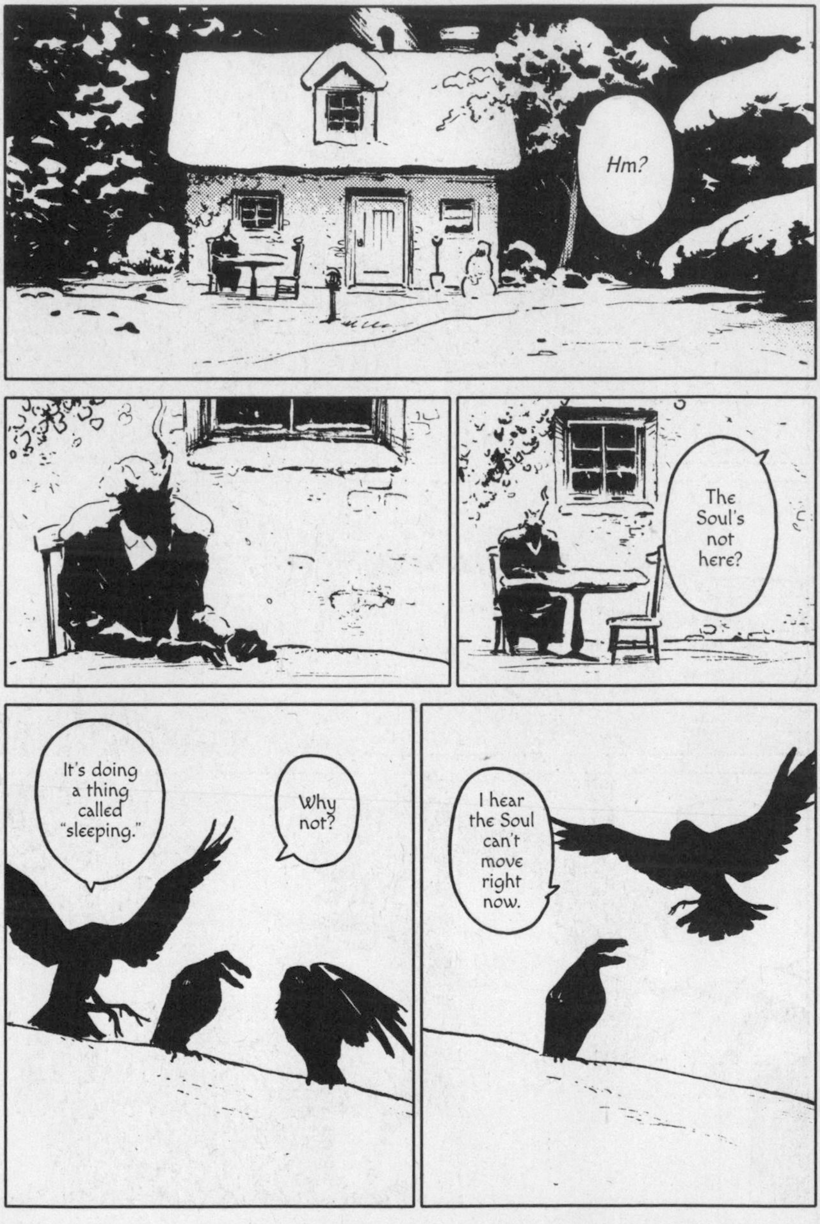
Hm?
The Soul's not here?
I hear the Soul can't move right now.
Why not?
It's doing a thing called "sleeping."

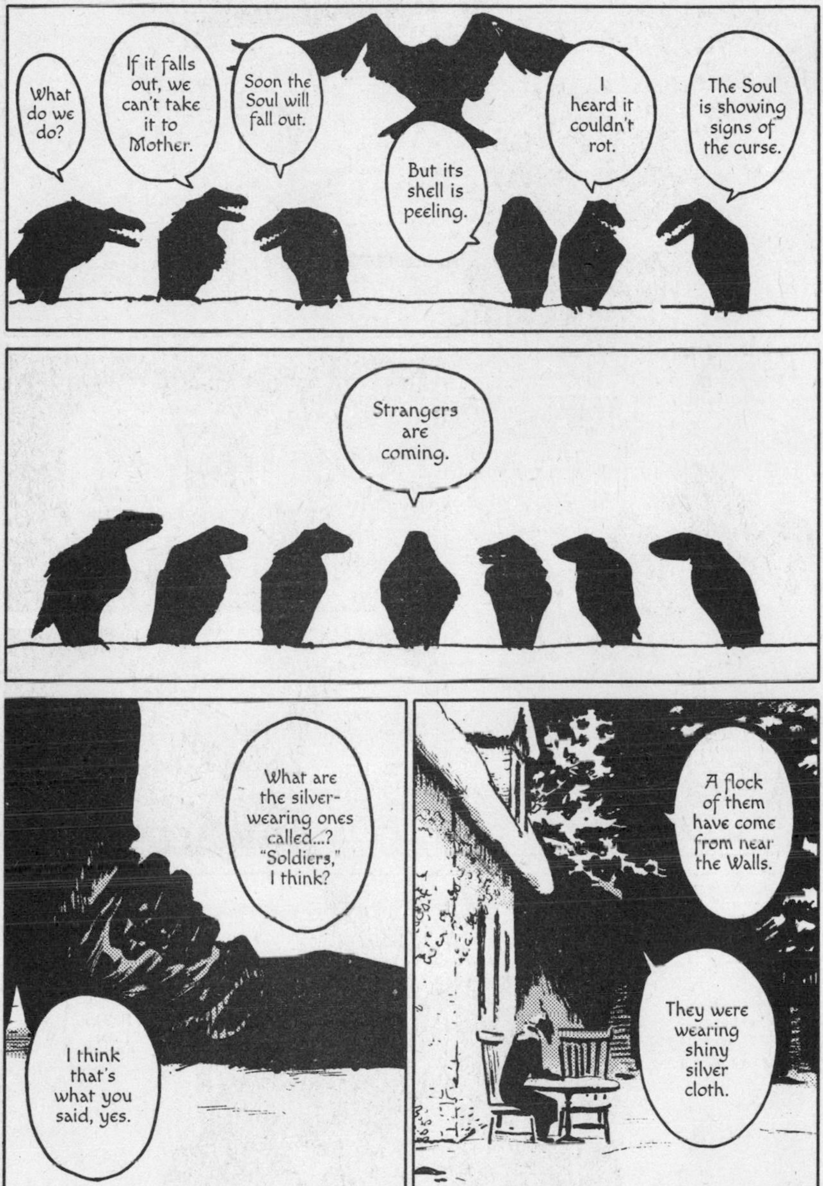
The Soul is showing signs of the curse.
I heard it couldn't rot.
But its shell is peeling.
Soon the Soul will fall out.
If it falls out, we can't take it to Mother.
What do we do?
Strangers are coming.
A flock of them have come from near the Walls.
They were wearing shiny silver cloth.
What are the silver-wearing ones called...? "Soldiers," I think?
I think that's what you said, yes.

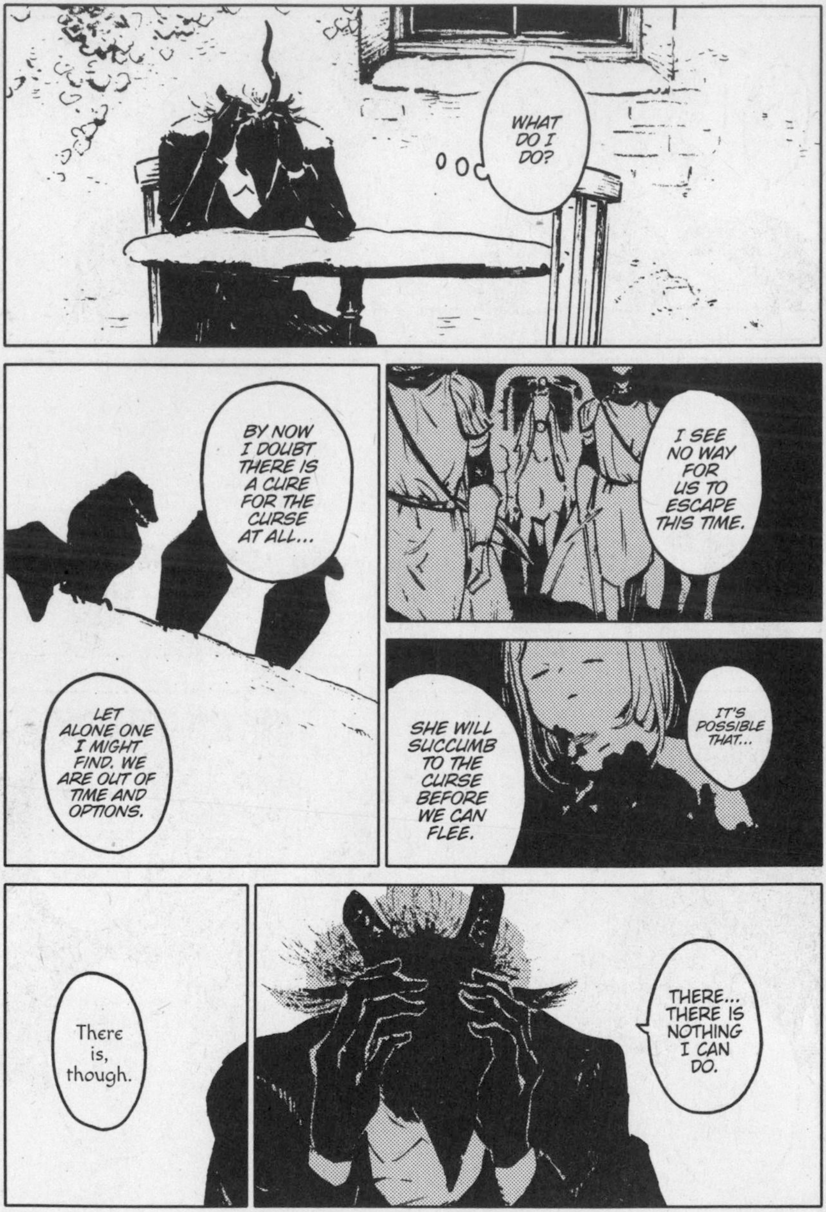
WHAT DO I DO?
I SEE NO WAY FOR US TO ESCAPE THIS TIME.
IT'S POSSIBLE THAT...
SHE WILL SUCCUMB TO THE CURSE BEFORE WE CAN FLEE.
BY NOW I DOUBT THERE IS A CURE FOR THE CURSE AT ALL...
LET ALONE ONE I MIGHT FIND. WE ARE OUT OF TIME AND OPTIONS.
THERE... THERE IS NOTHING I CAN DO.
There is, though.

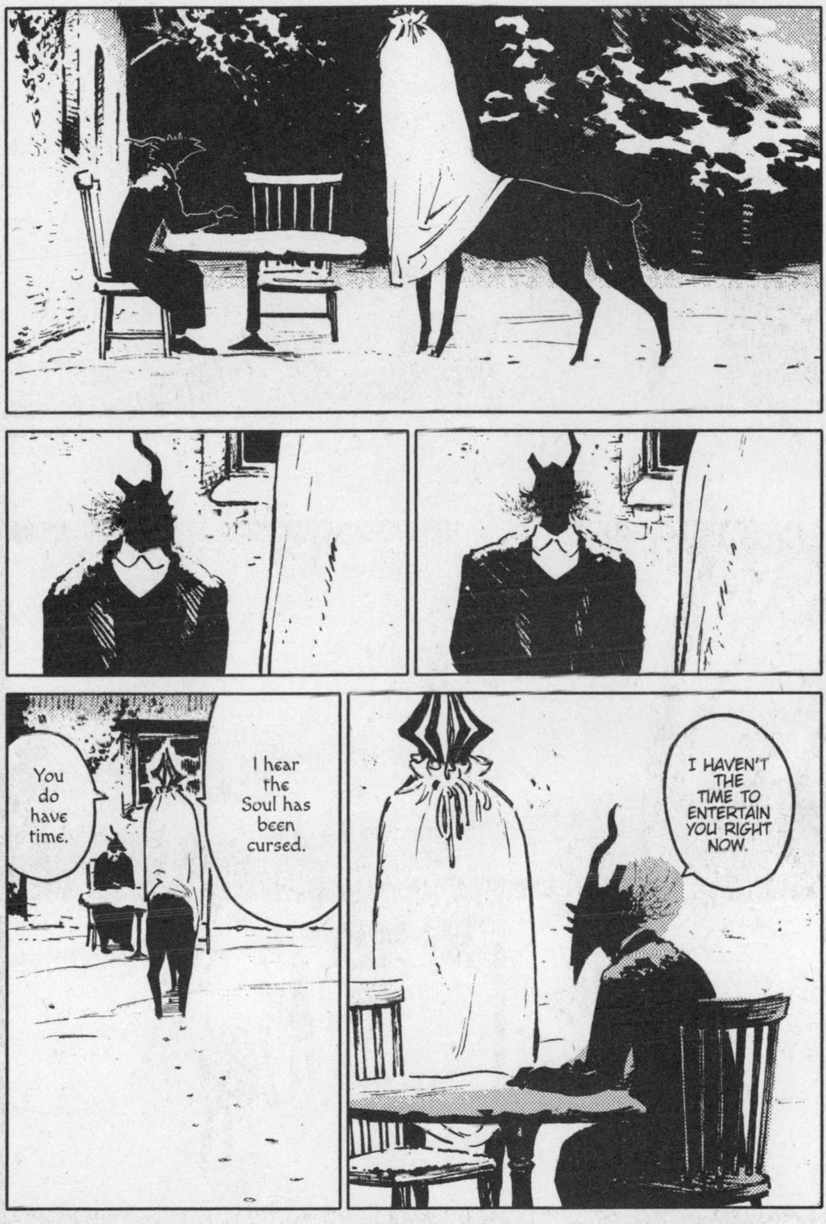
I HAVEN'T THE TIME TO ENTERTAIN YOU RIGHT NOW.
I hear the Soul has been cursed.
You do have time.

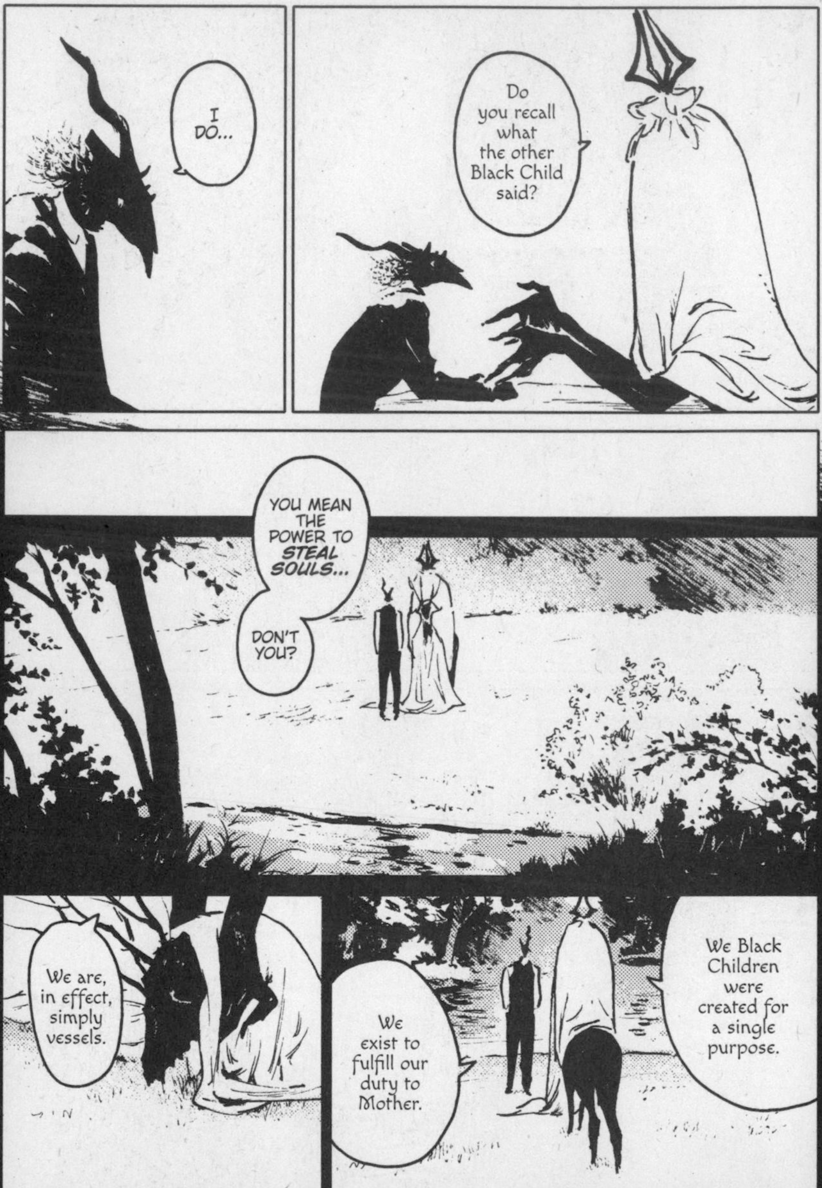
Do you recall what the other Black Child said?
I DO...
YOU MEAN THE POWER TO STEAL SOULS...
DON'T YOU?
We Black Children were created for a single purpose.
We exist to fulfill our duty to Mother.
We are, in effect, simply vessels.

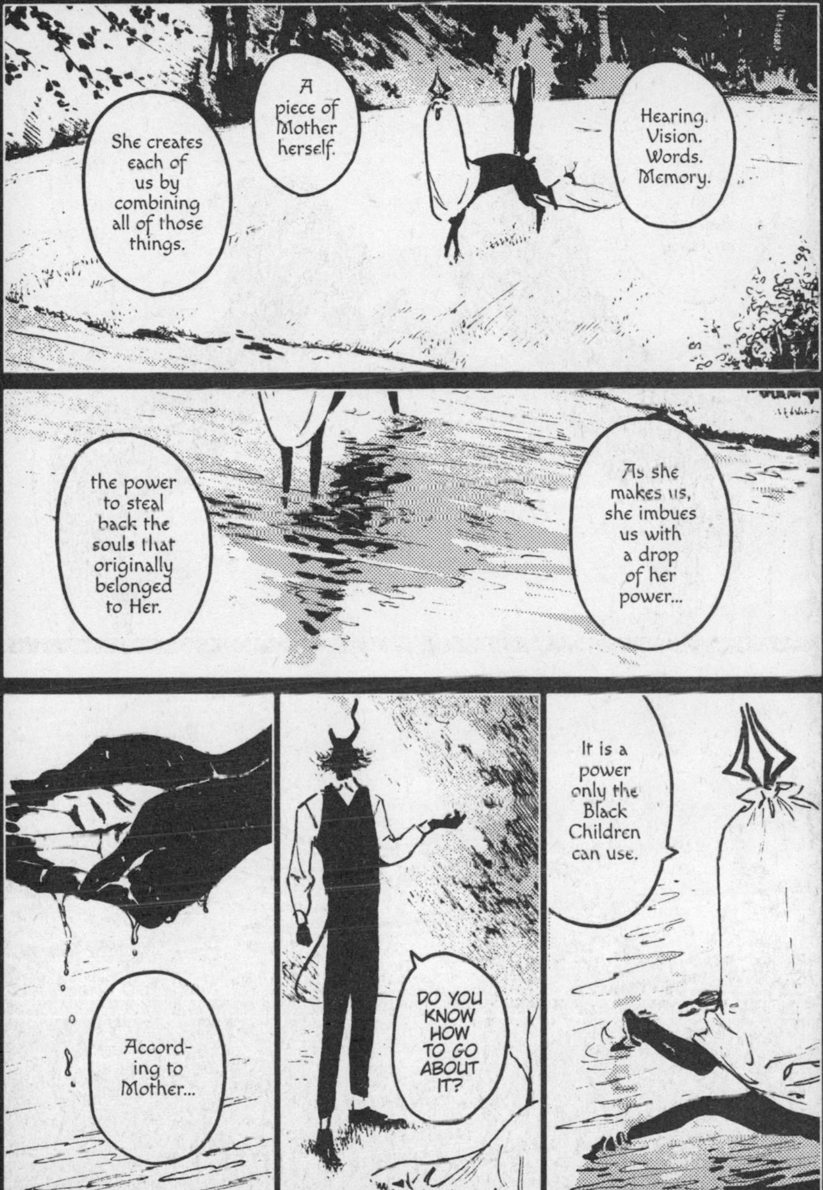
Hearing. Vision. Words. Memory.
A piece of Mother herself.
She creates each of us by combining all of those things.
As she makes us, she imbues us with a drop of her power...
the power to steal back the souls that originally belonged to Her.
It is a power only the Black Children can use.
DO YOU KNOW HOW TO GO ABOUT IT?
Accord-ing to Mother...

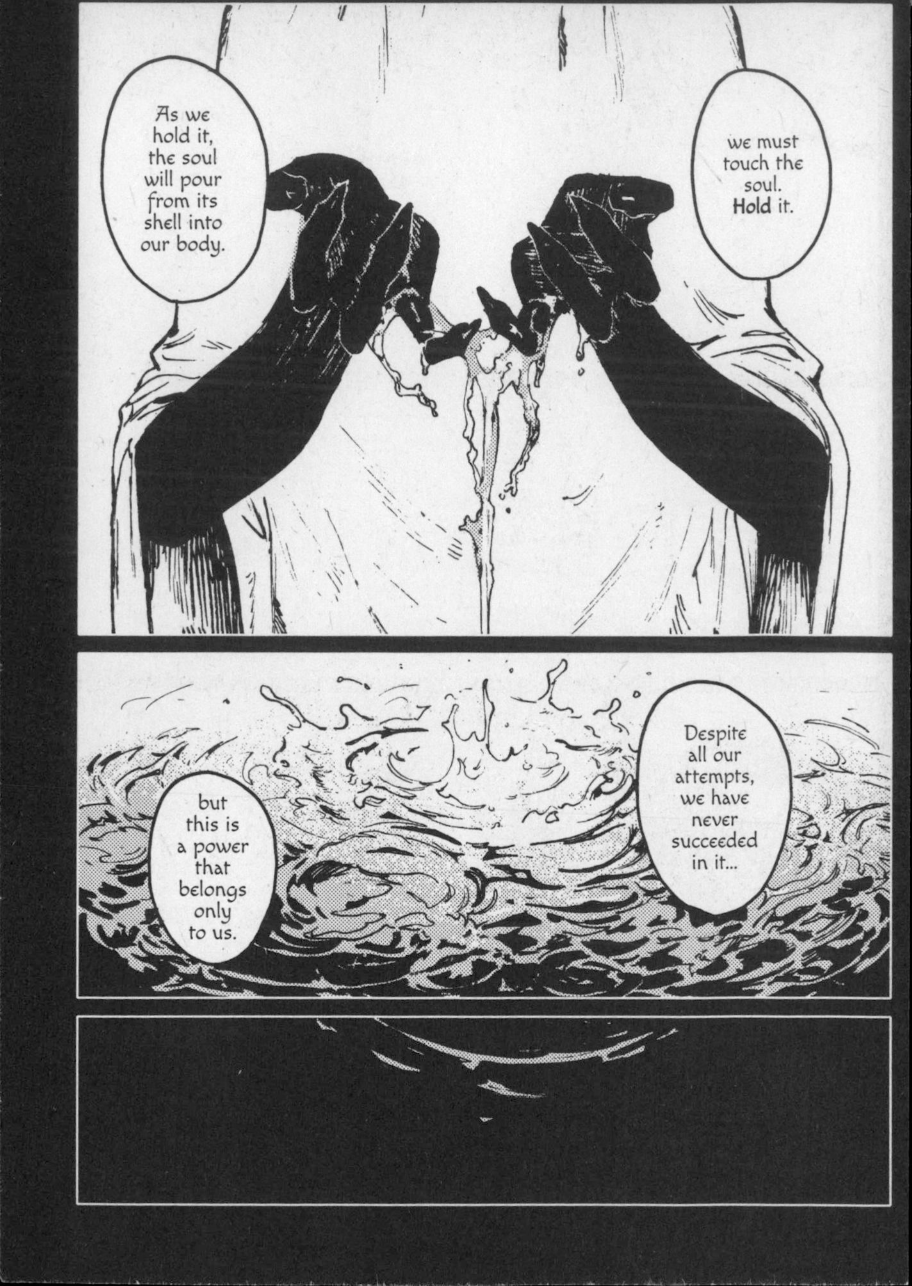
we must touch the soul. **Hold** it.
As we hold it, the soul will pour from its shell into our body.
Despite all our attempts, we have never succeeded in it...
but this is a power that belongs only to us.

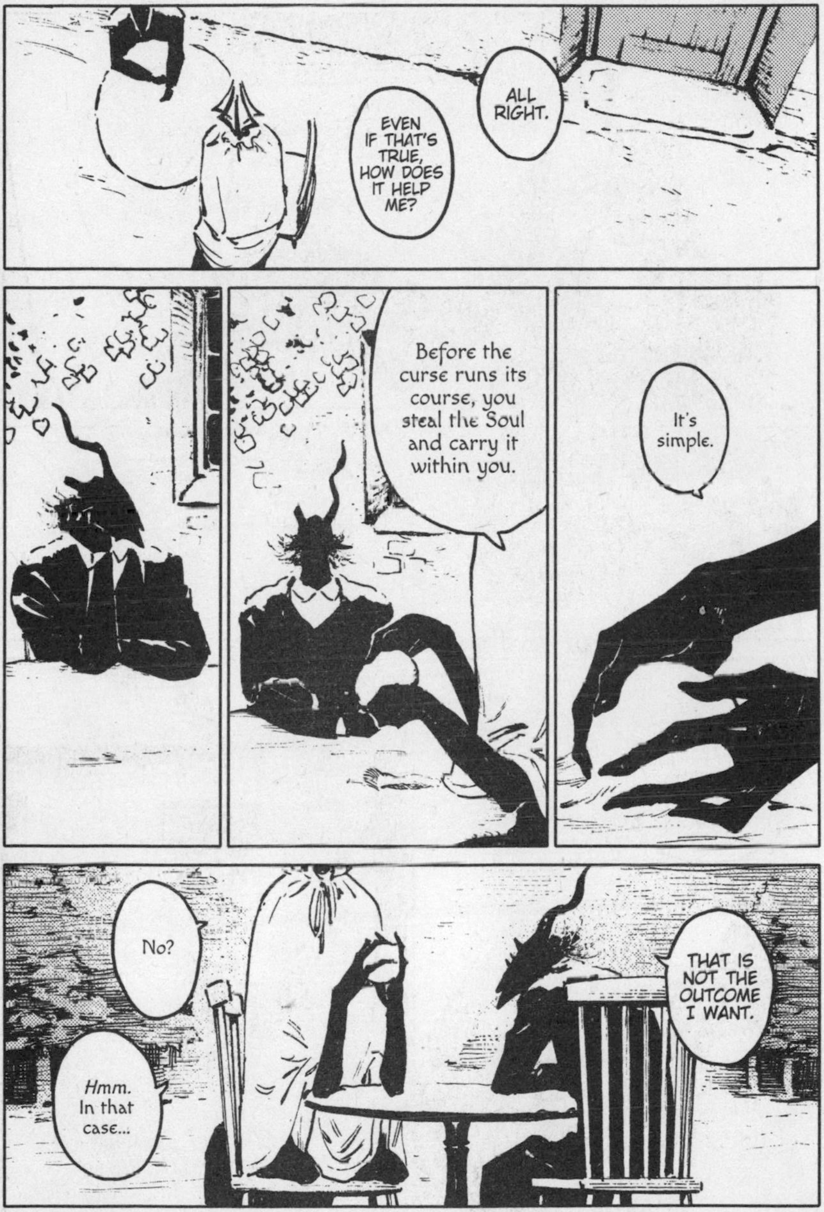
ALL RIGHT.
EVEN IF THAT'S TRUE, HOW DOES IT HELP ME?
It's simple.
Before the curse runs its course, you steal the Soul and carry it within you.
THAT IS NOT THE OUTCOME I WANT.
No?
Hmm. In that case...

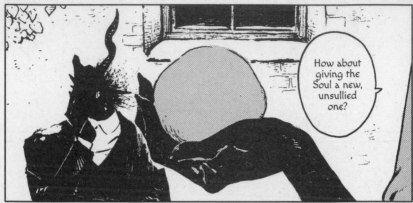

How about giving the Soul a new, unsullied one?

SKUF

Yes.

GIVE SHIVA... A NEW SOUL ...?

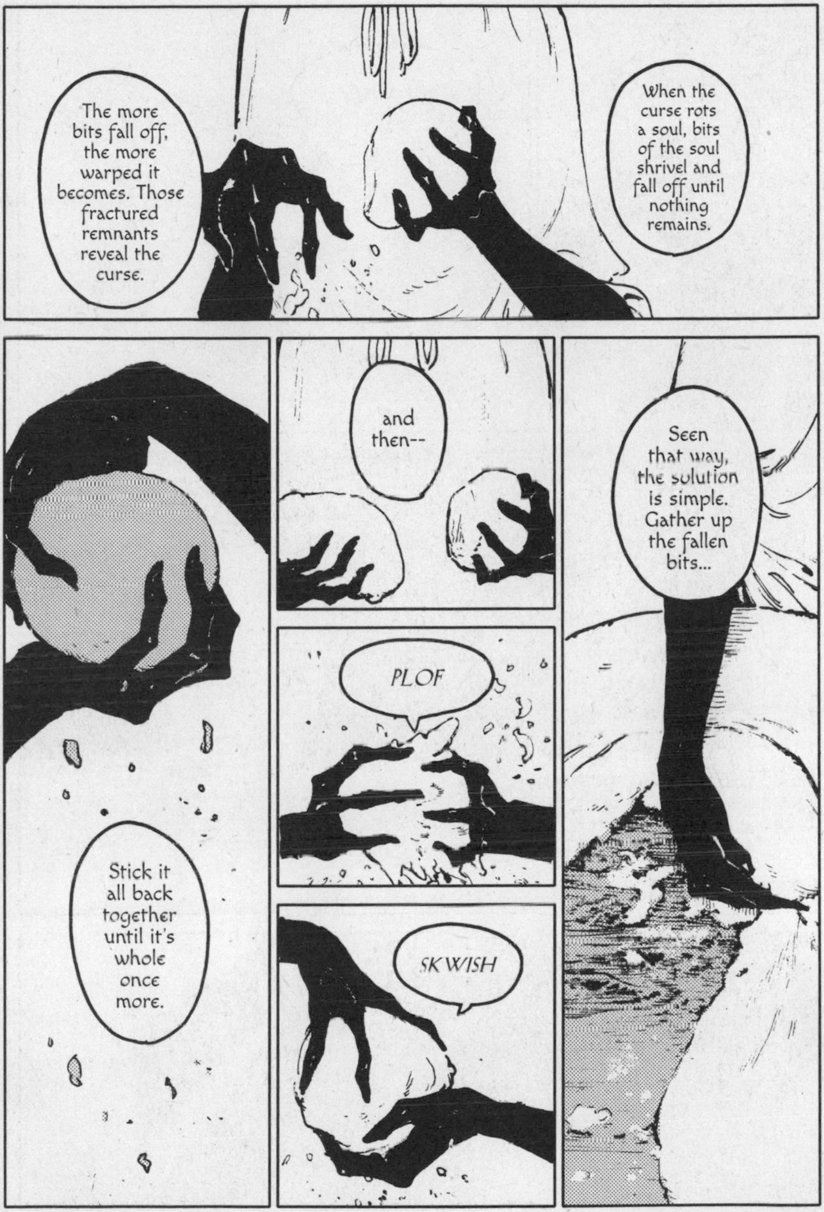
When the curse rots a soul, bits of the soul shrivel and fall off until nothing remains.
The more bits fall off, the more warped it becomes. Those fractured remnants reveal the curse.
Seen that way, the solution is simple. Gather up the fallen bits...
and then--
PLOF
SKWISH
Stick it all back together until it's whole once more.

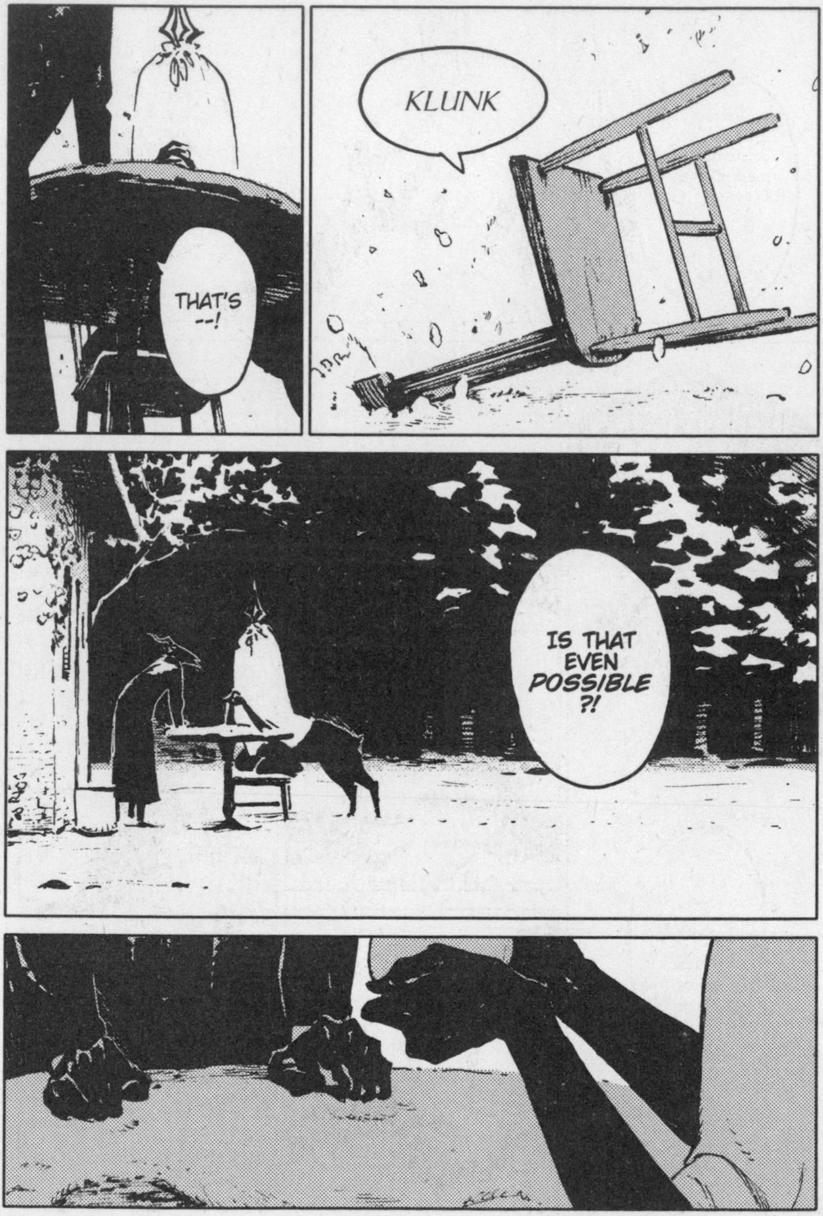
KLUNK
THAT'S --!
IS THAT EVEN POSSIBLE ?!

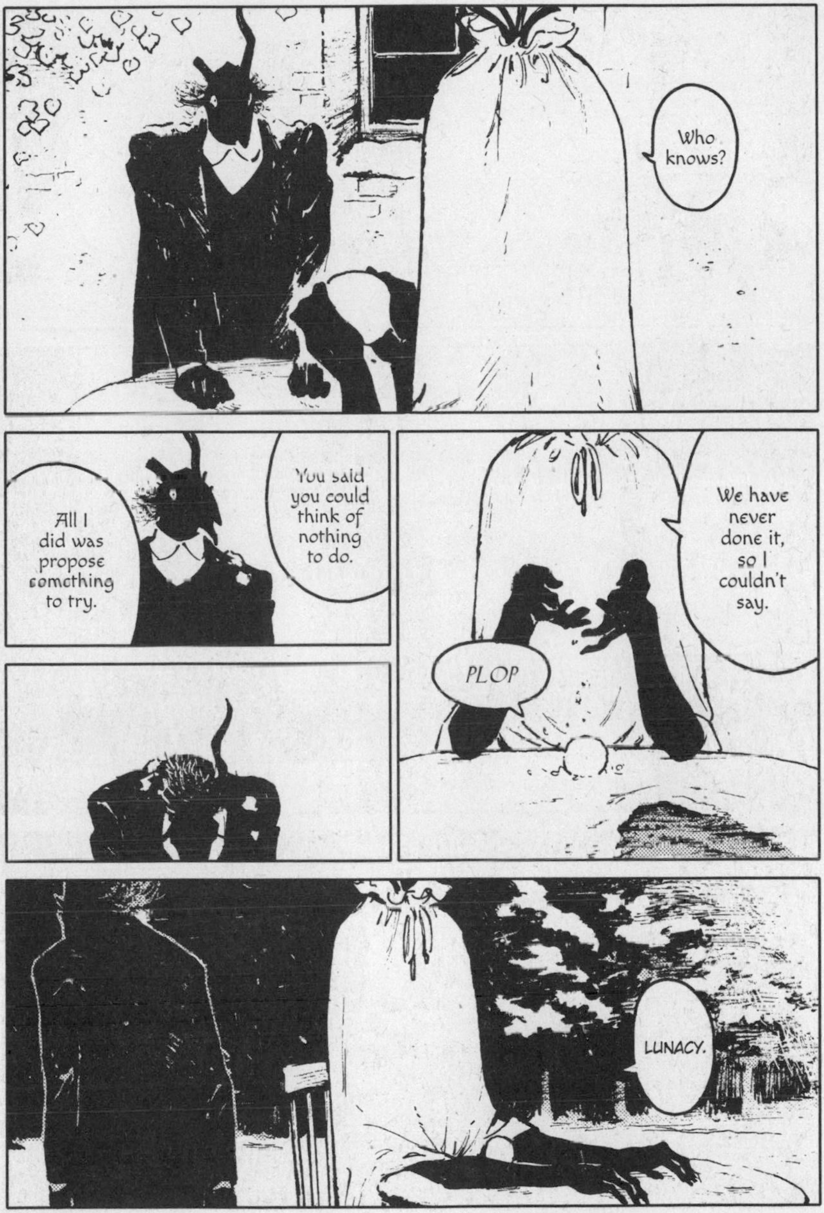
Who knows?
We have never done it, so I couldn't say.
PLOP
You said you could think of nothing to do.
All I did was propose something to try.
LUNACY.

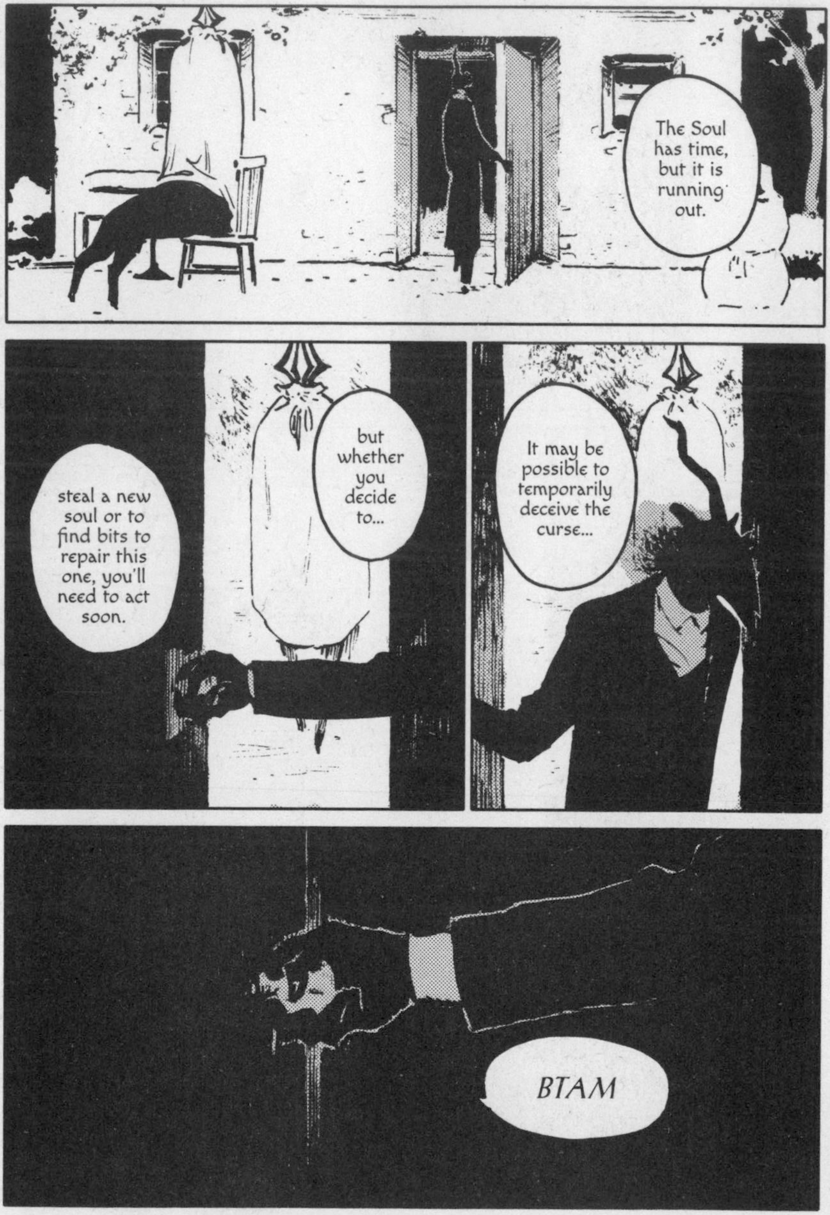
The Soul has time, but it is running out.
It may be possible to temporarily deceive the curse...
but whether you decide to...
steal a new soul or to find bits to repair this one, you'll need to act soon.
BTAM

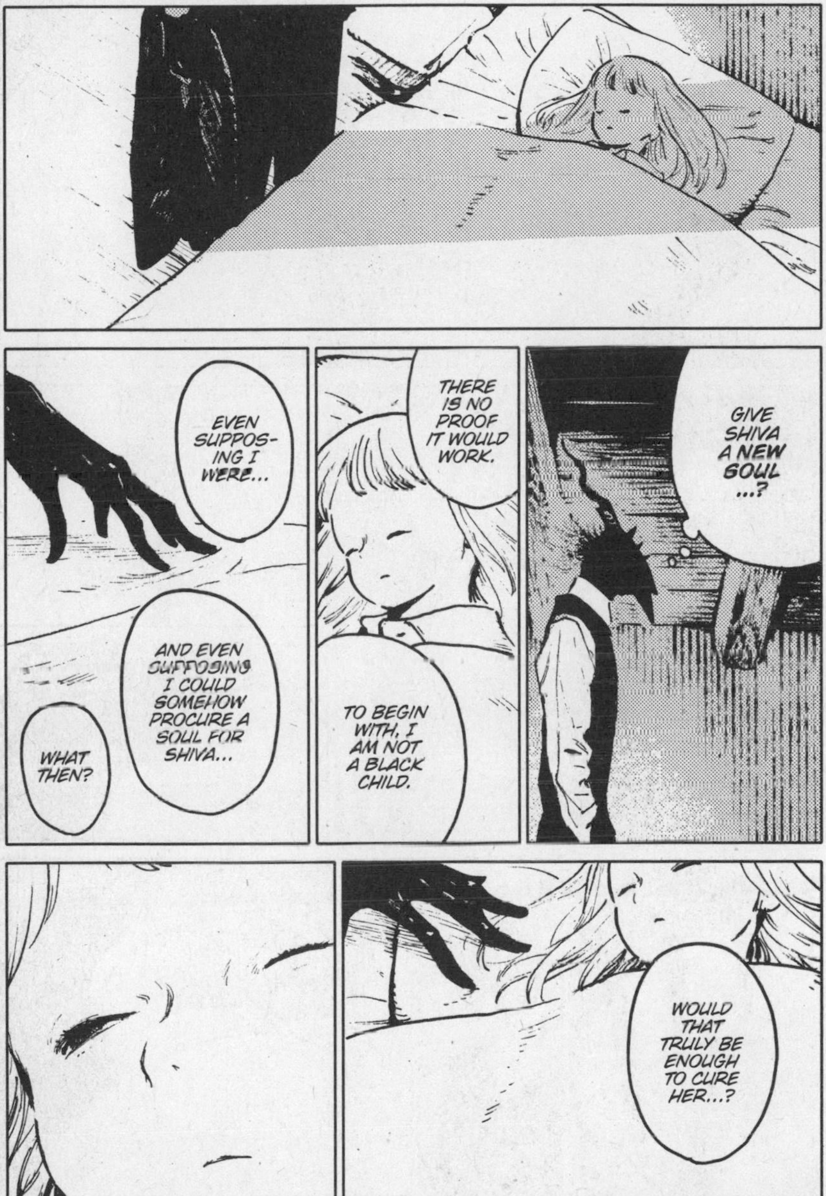
GIVE SHIVA A NEW SOUL ...?
THERE IS NO PROOF IT WOULD WORK.
TO BEGIN WITH, I AM NOT A BLACK CHILD.
EVEN SUPPOSING I WERE...
AND EVEN SUPPOSING I COULD SOMEHOW PROCURE A SOUL FOR SHIVA...
WHAT THEN?
WOULD THAT TRULY BE ENOUGH TO CURE HER...?

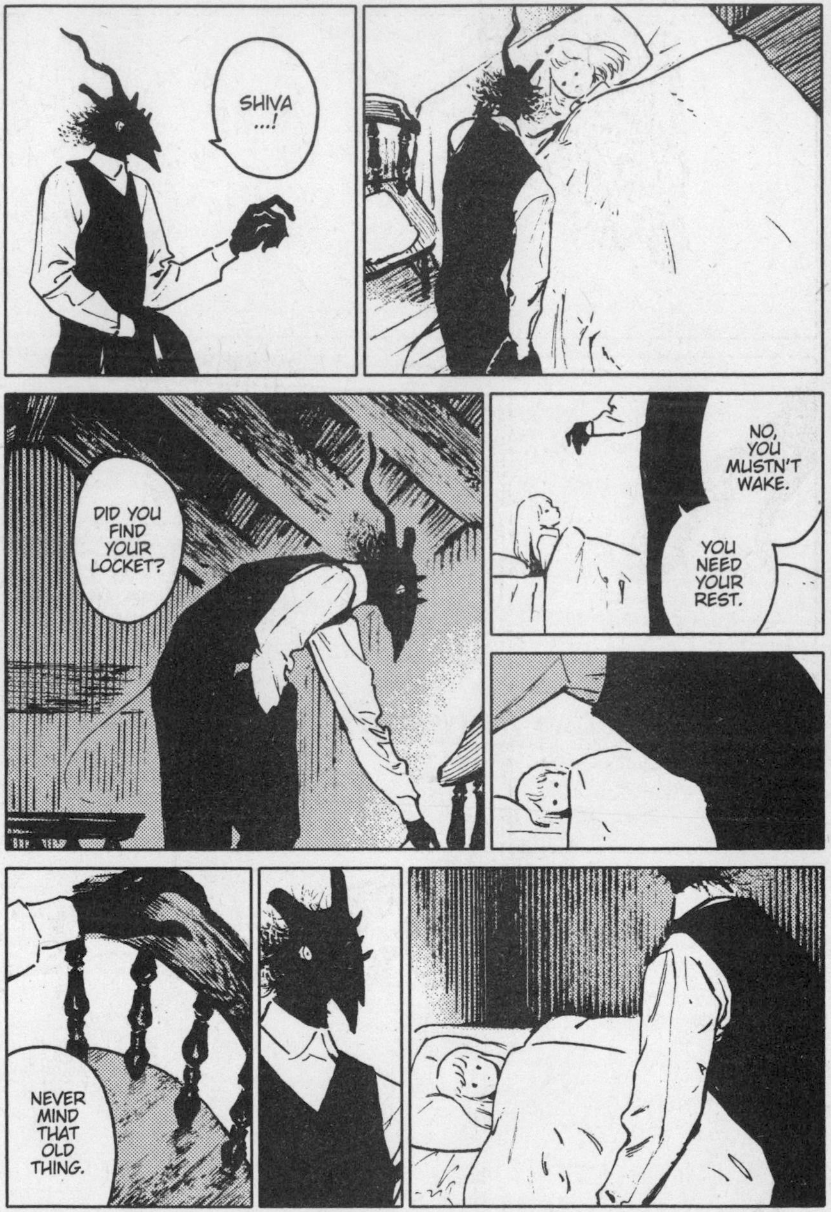
SHIVA ...!
NO, YOU MUSTN'T WAKE.
YOU NEED YOUR REST.
DID YOU FIND YOUR LOCKET?
NEVER MIND THAT OLD THING.

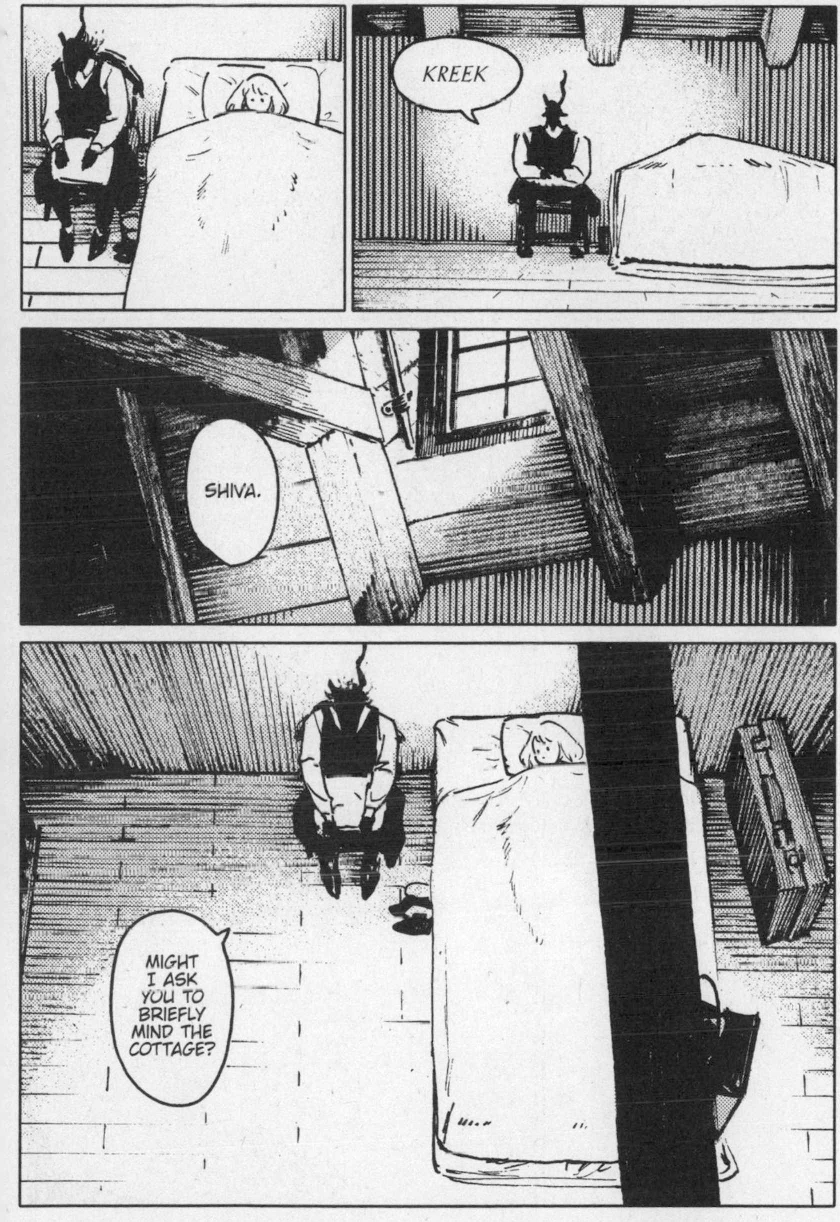
KREEK
SHIVA.
MIGHT I ASK YOU TO BRIEFLY MIND THE COTTAGE?

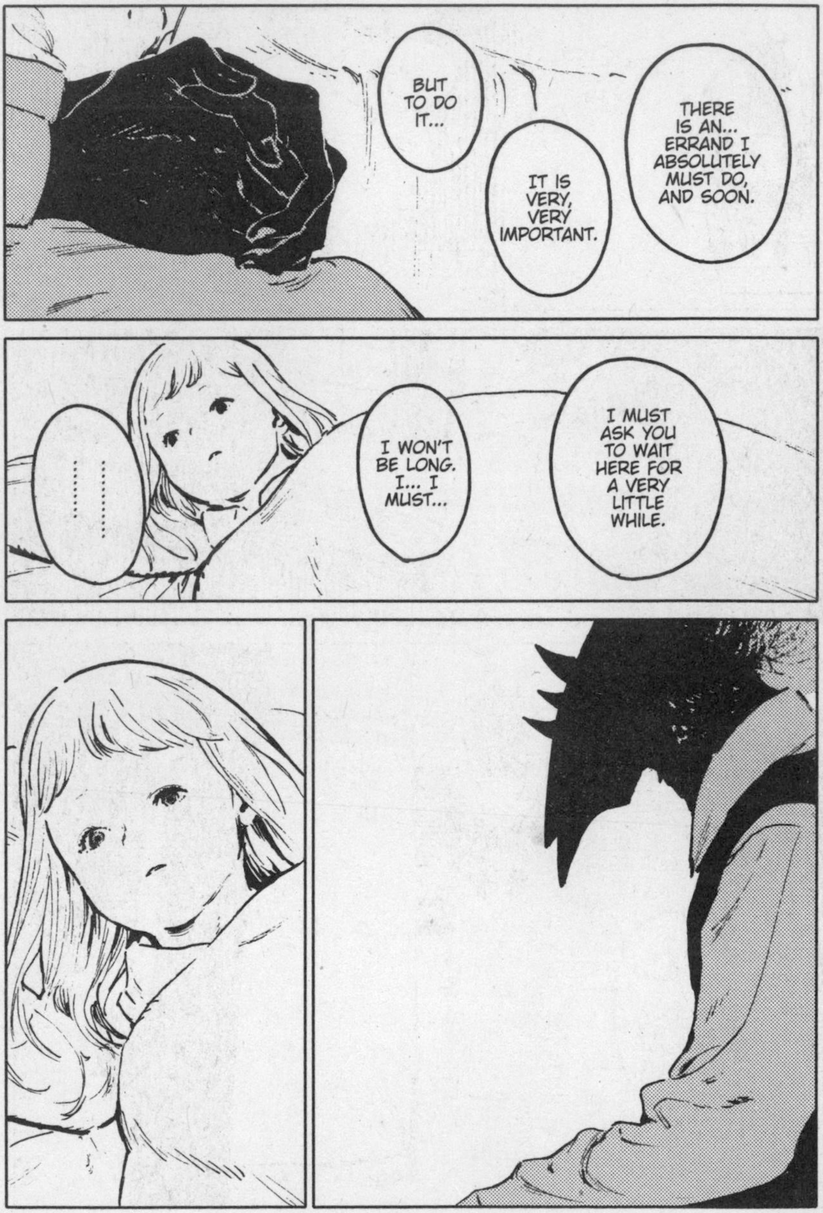
THERE IS AN... ERRAND I ABSOLUTELY MUST DO, AND SOON.
IT IS VERY, VERY IMPORTANT.
BUT TO DO IT...
I MUST ASK YOU TO WAIT HERE FOR A VERY LITTLE WHILE.
I WON'T BE LONG. I... I MUST...
......

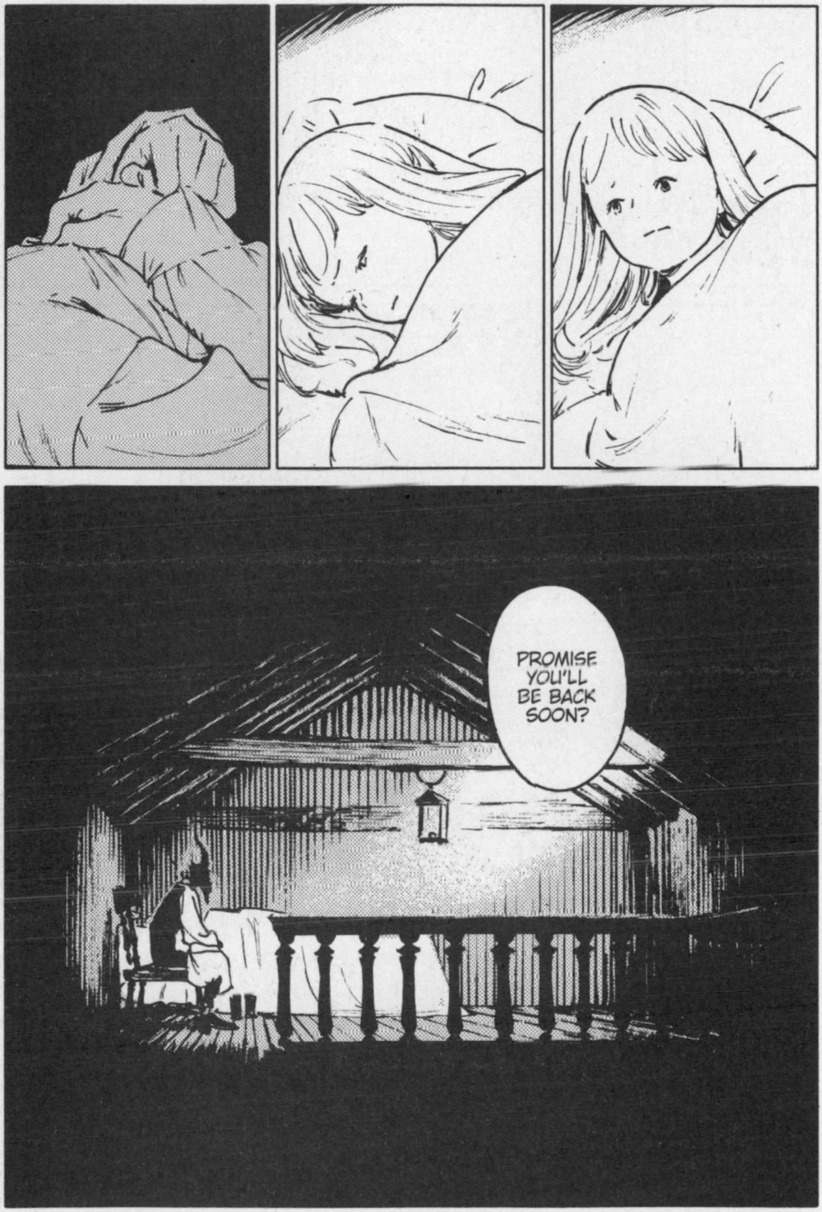
PROMISE YOU'LL BE BACK SOON?

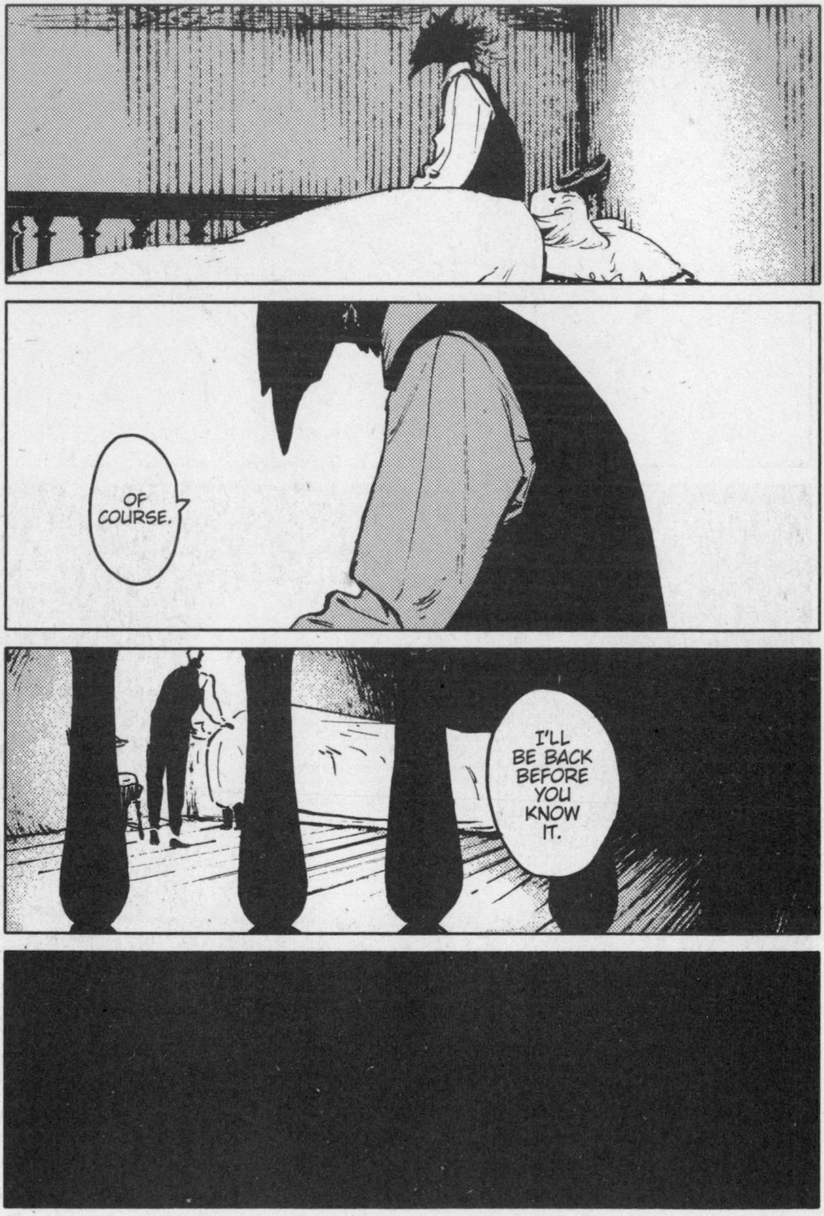
OF COURSE.
I'LL BE BACK BEFORE YOU KNOW IT.

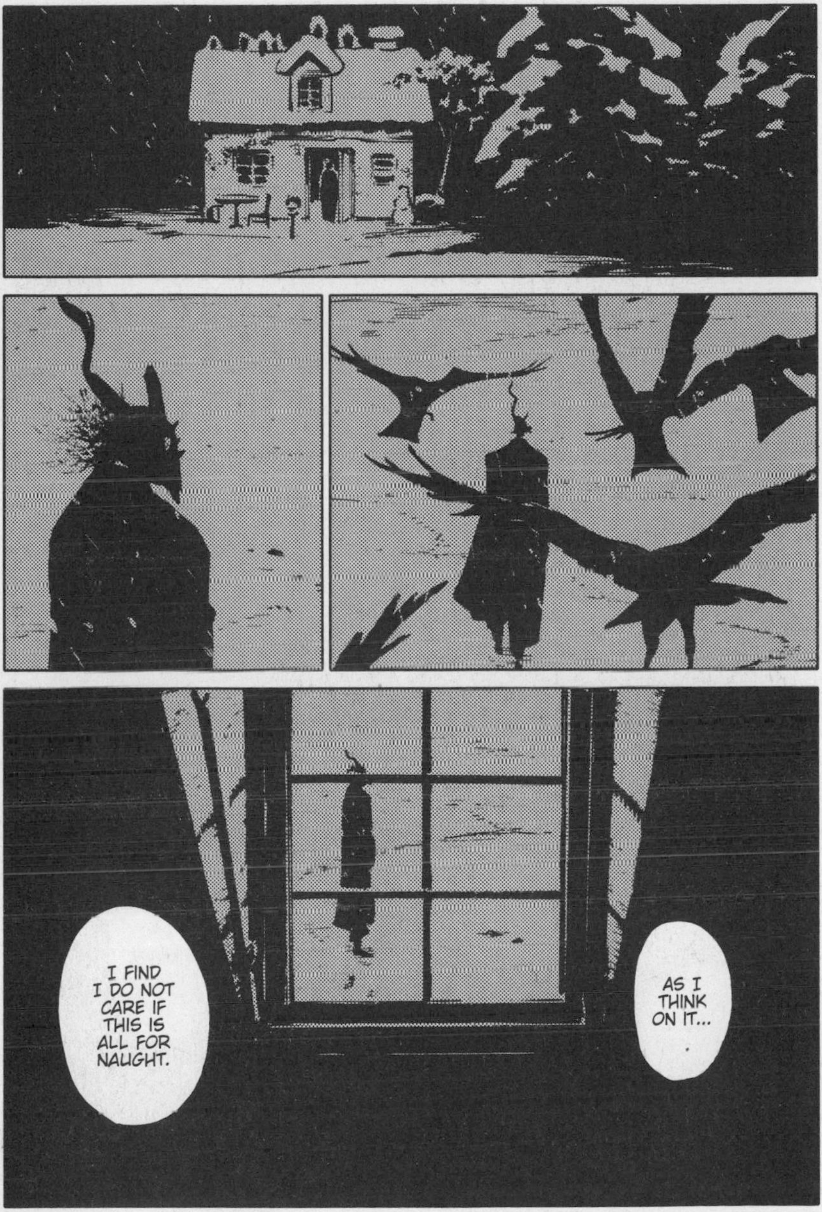
AS I THINK ON IT...
I FIND I DO NOT CARE IF THIS IS ALL FOR NAUGHT.

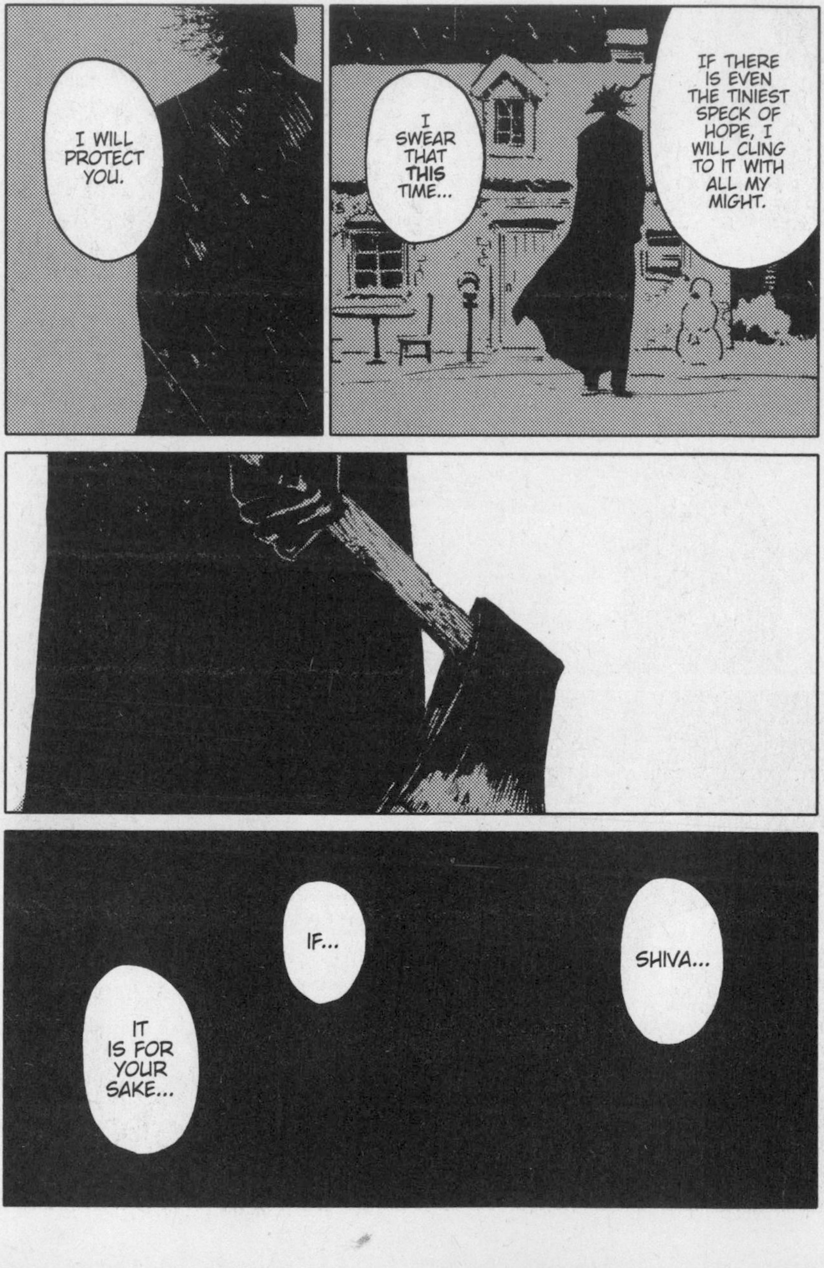
IF THERE IS EVEN THE TINIEST SPECK OF HOPE, I WILL CLING TO IT WITH ALL MY MIGHT.
I SWEAR THAT THIS TIME...
I WILL PROTECT YOU.
SHIVA...
IF...
IT IS FOR YOUR SAKE...

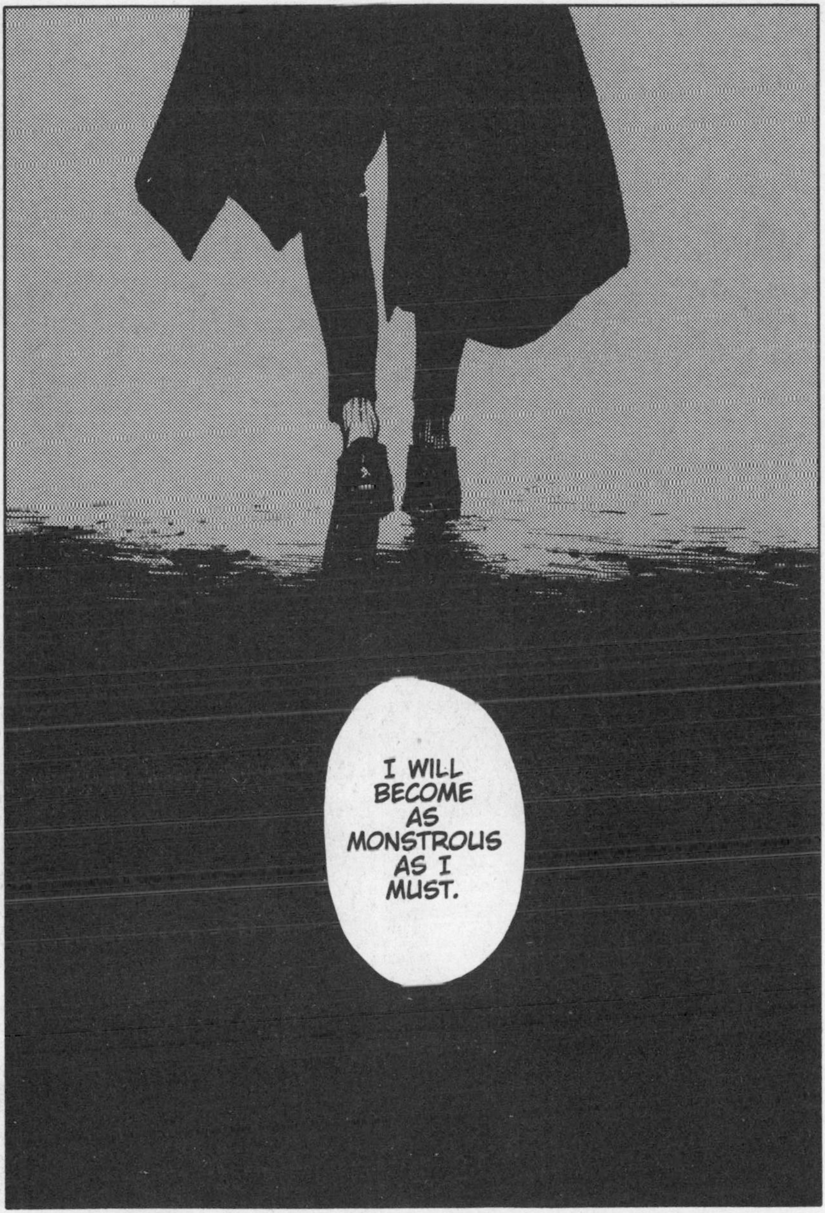
I WILL BECOME AS MONSTROUS AS I MUST.

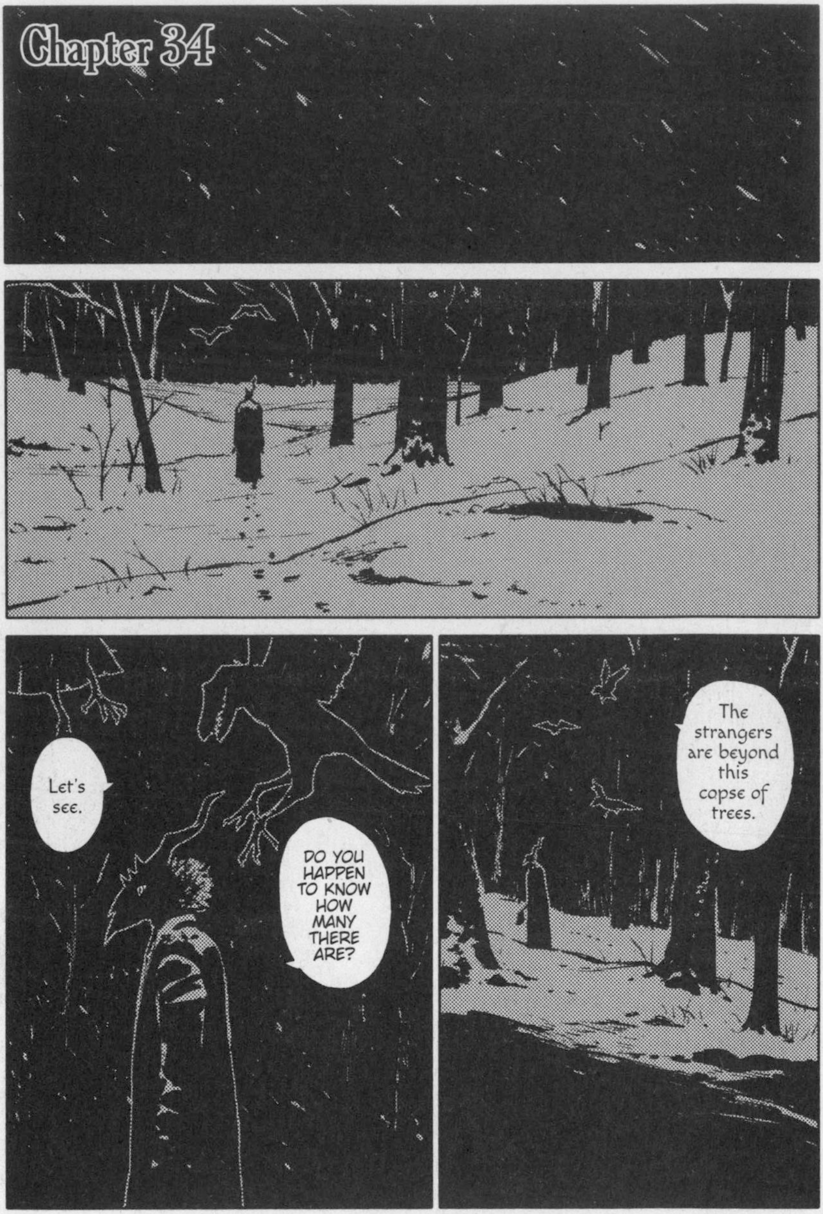
Chapter 34
The strangers are beyond this copse of trees.
DO YOU HAPPEN TO KNOW HOW MANY THERE ARE?
Let's see.

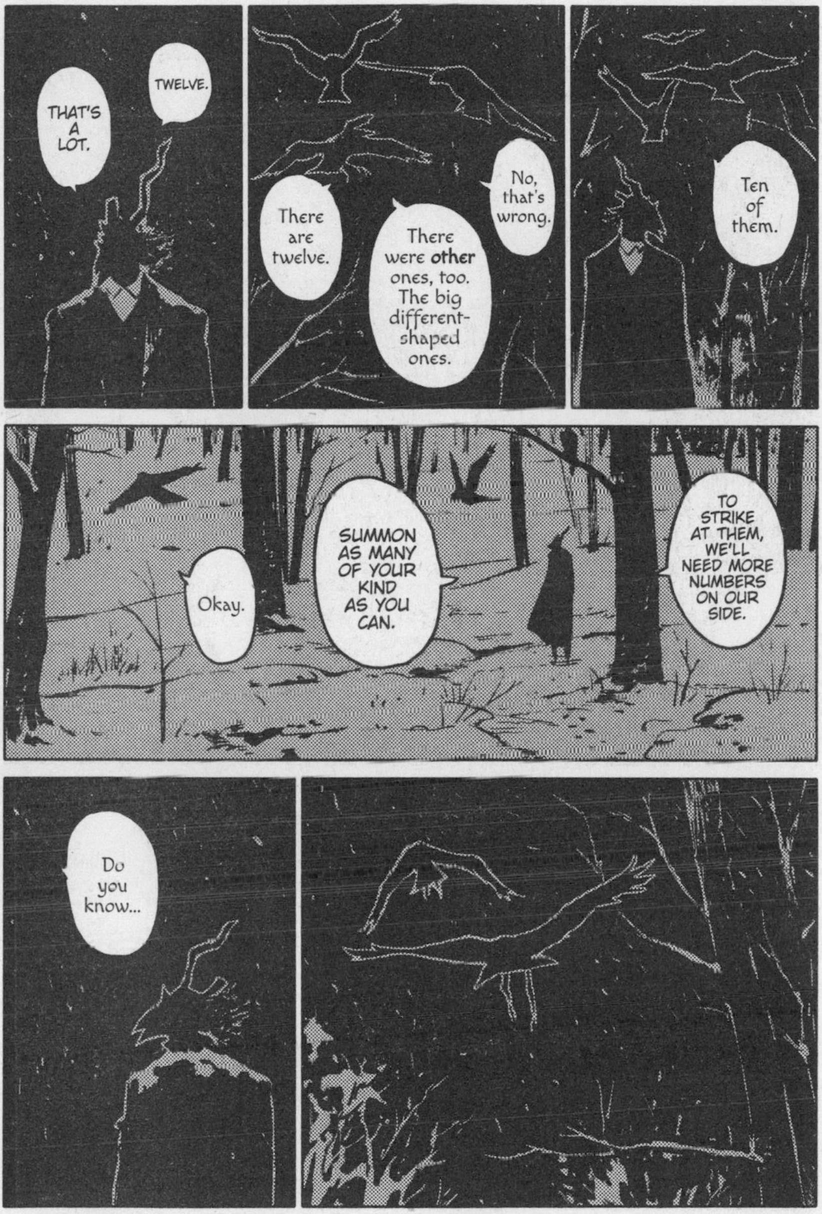
Ten of them.
No, that's wrong.
There were **other** ones, too. The big different-shaped ones.
There are twelve.
TWELVE.
THAT'S A LOT.
TO STRIKE AT THEM, WE'LL NEED MORE NUMBERS ON OUR SIDE.
SUMMON AS MANY OF YOUR KIND AS YOU CAN.
Okay.
Do you know...

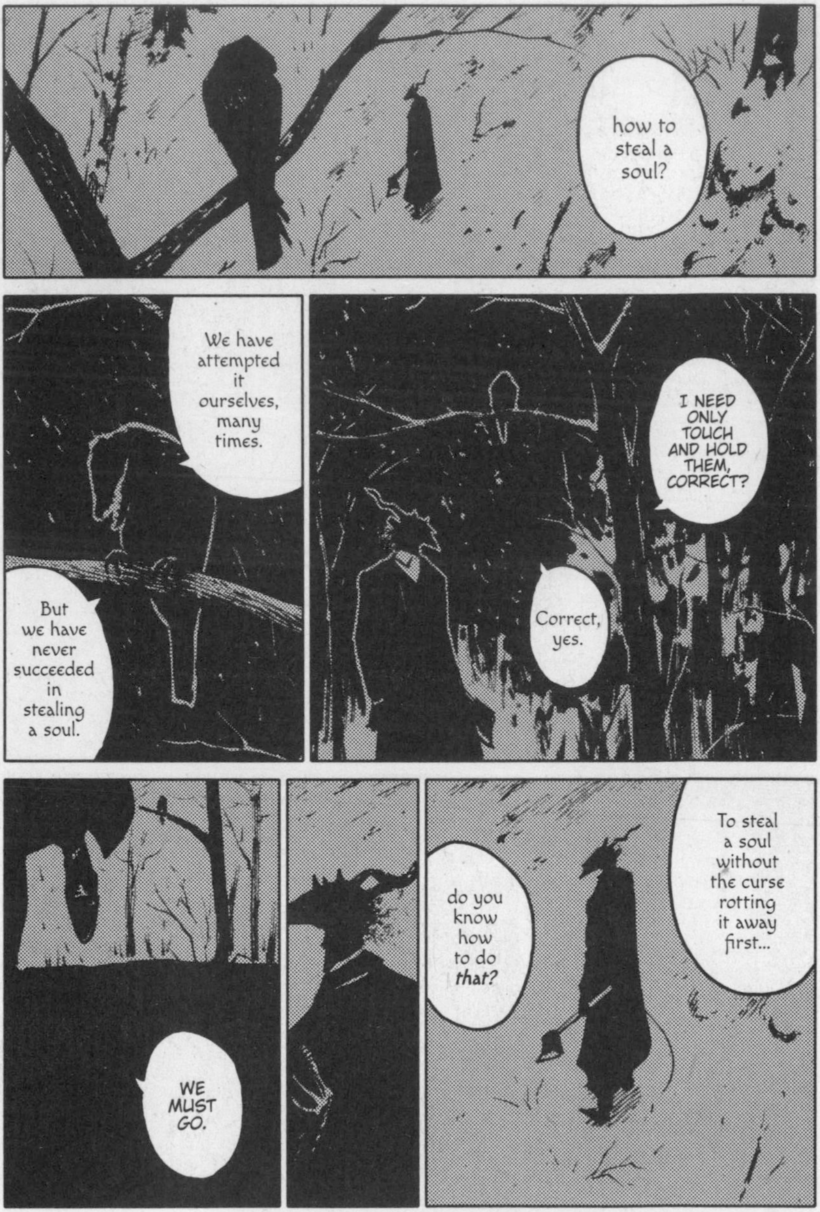
how to steal a soul?
I NEED ONLY TOUCH AND HOLD THEM, CORRECT?
Correct, yes.
We have attempted it ourselves, many times.
But we have never succeeded in stealing a soul.
To steal a soul without the curse rotting it away first...
do you know how to do *that?*
WE MUST GO.

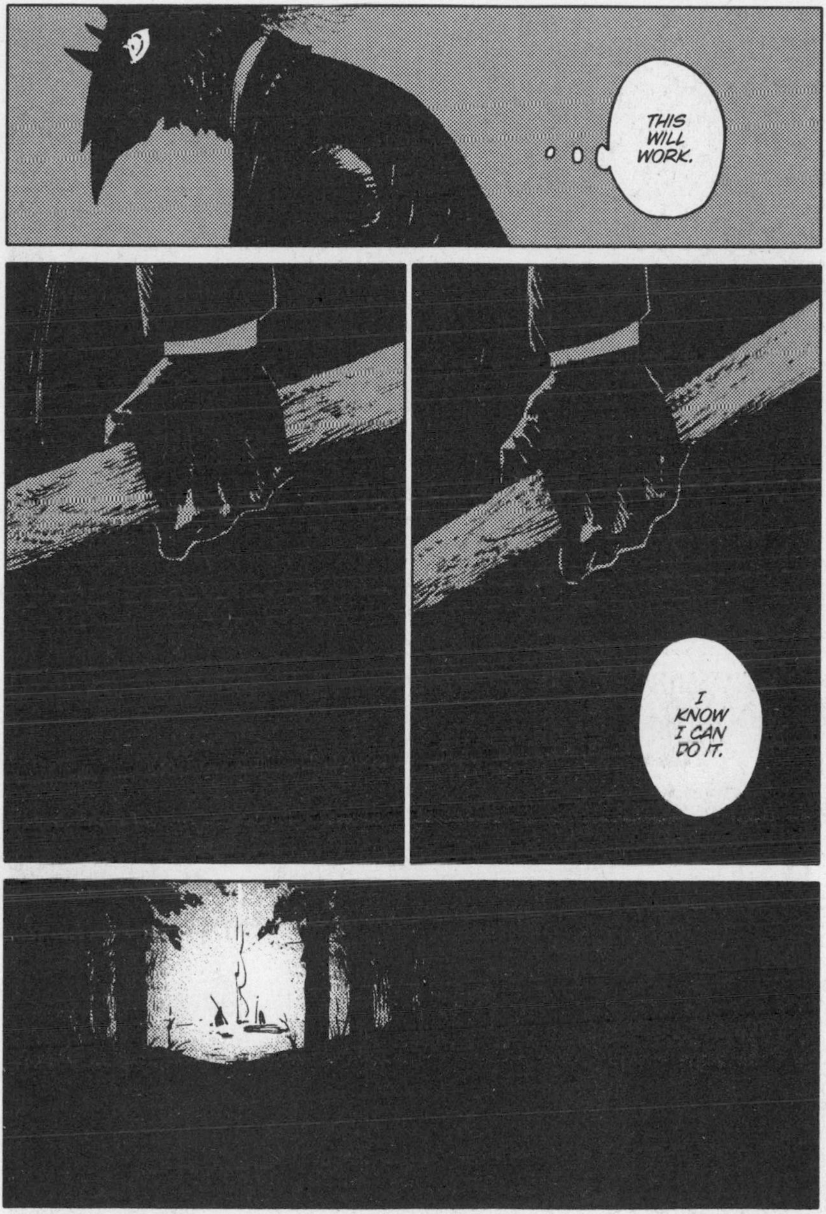
THIS WILL WORK.
I KNOW I CAN DO IT.

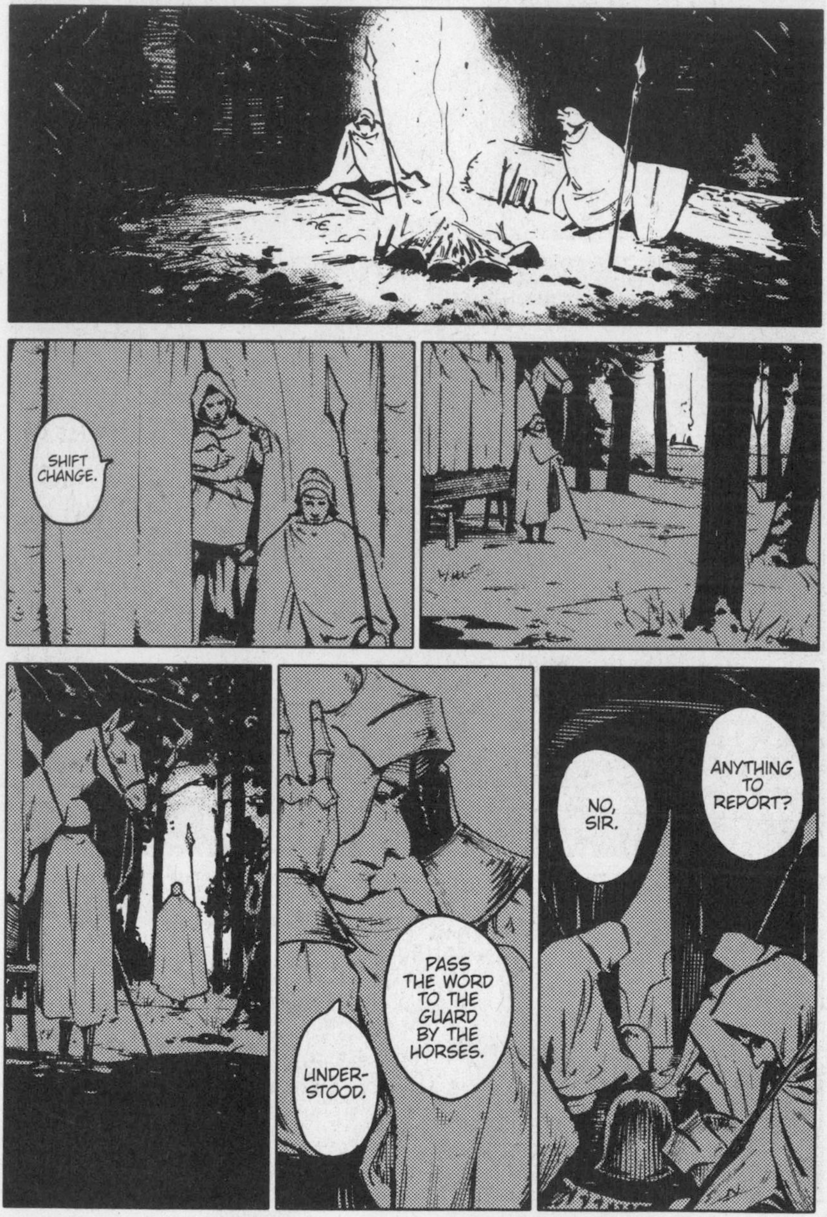
SHIFT CHANGE.
ANYTHING TO REPORT?
NO, SIR.
PASS THE WORD TO THE GUARD BY THE HORSES.
UNDER-STOOD.

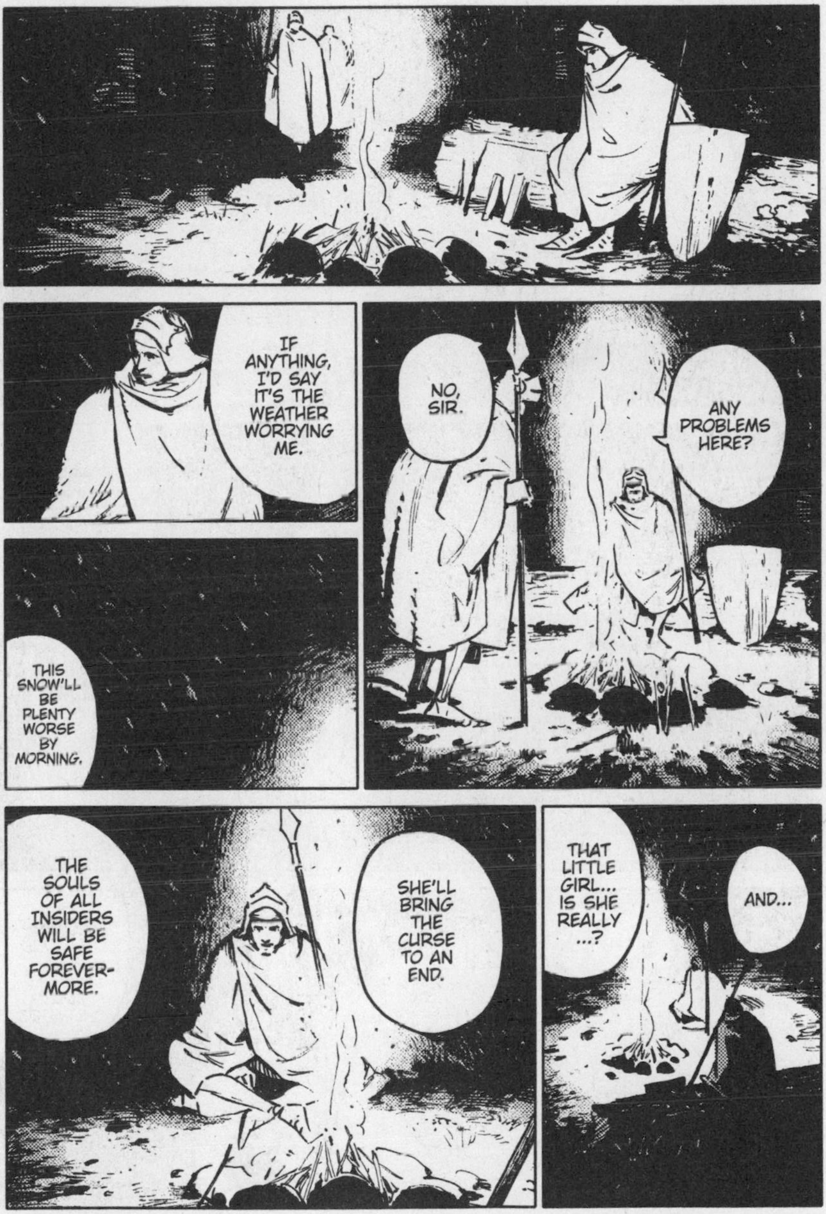
ANY PROBLEMS HERE?
NO, SIR.
IF ANYTHING, I'D SAY IT'S THE WEATHER WORRYING ME.
THIS SNOW'LL BE PLENTY WORSE BY MORNING.
AND...
THAT LITTLE GIRL... IS SHE REALLY ...?
SHE'LL BRING THE CURSE TO AN END.
THE SOULS OF ALL INSIDERS WILL BE SAFE FOREVER-MORE.

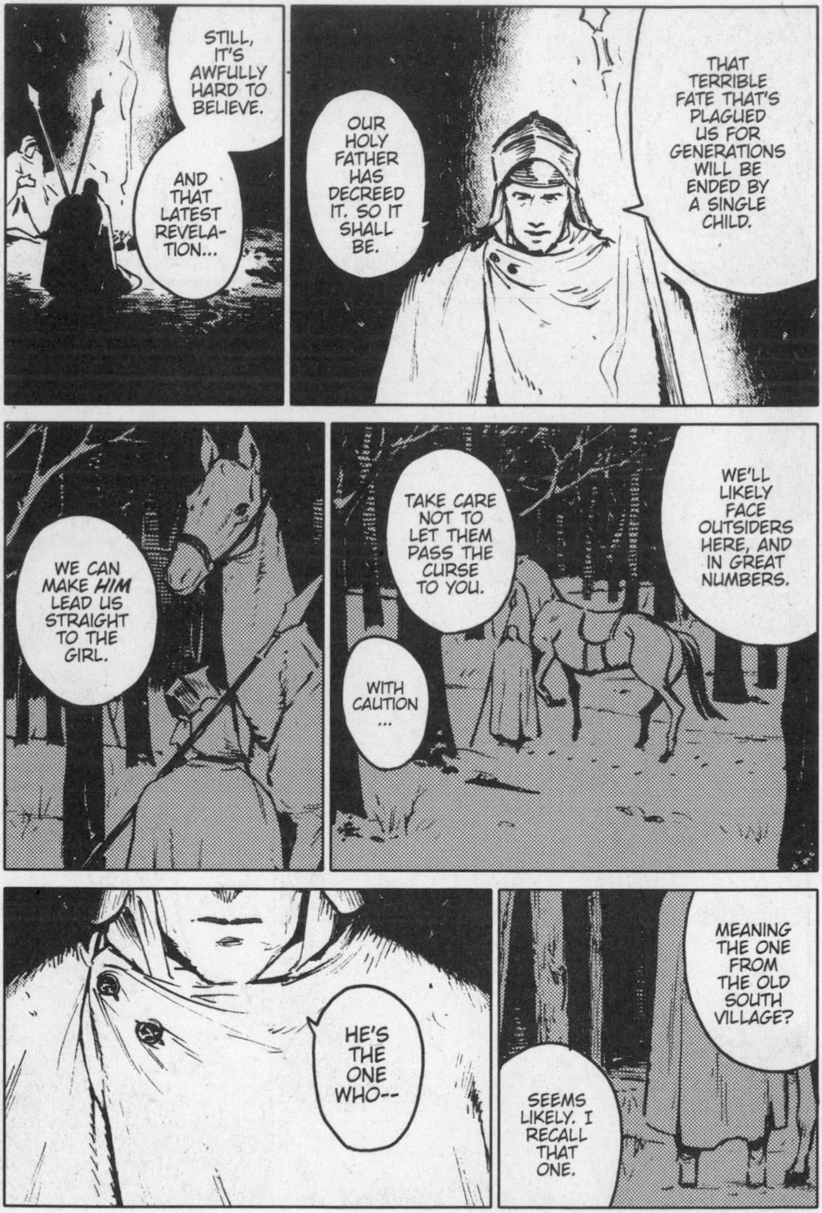
THAT TERRIBLE FATE THAT'S PLAGUED US FOR GENERATIONS WILL BE ENDED BY A SINGLE CHILD.
OUR HOLY FATHER HAS DECREED IT. SO IT SHALL BE.
STILL, IT'S AWFULLY HARD TO BELIEVE.
AND THAT LATEST REVELATION...
WE'LL LIKELY FACE OUTSIDERS HERE, AND IN GREAT NUMBERS.
TAKE CARE NOT TO LET THEM PASS THE CURSE TO YOU.
WITH CAUTION...
WE CAN MAKE *HIM* LEAD US STRAIGHT TO THE GIRL.
MEANING THE ONE FROM THE OLD SOUTH VILLAGE?
SEEMS LIKELY. I RECALL THAT ONE.
HE'S THE ONE WHO--

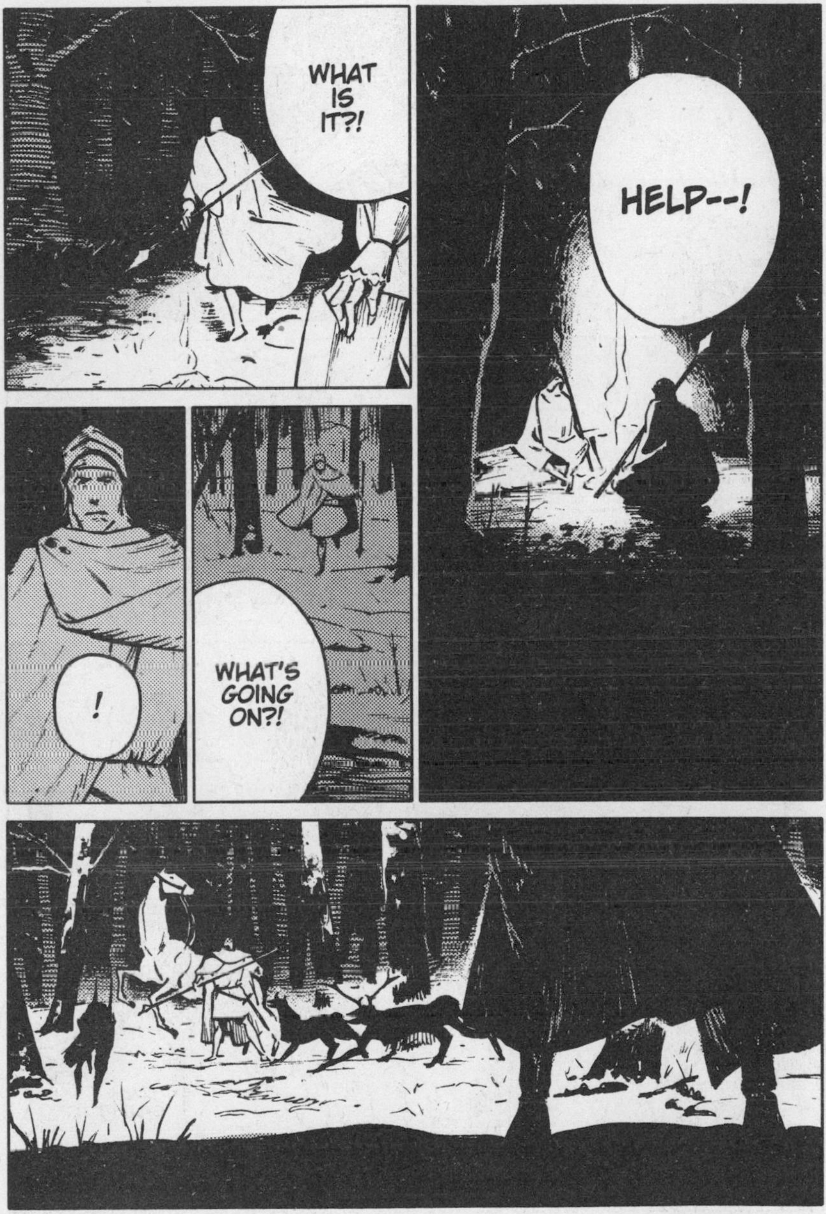
HELP--!
WHAT IS IT?!
WHAT'S GOING ON?!
!

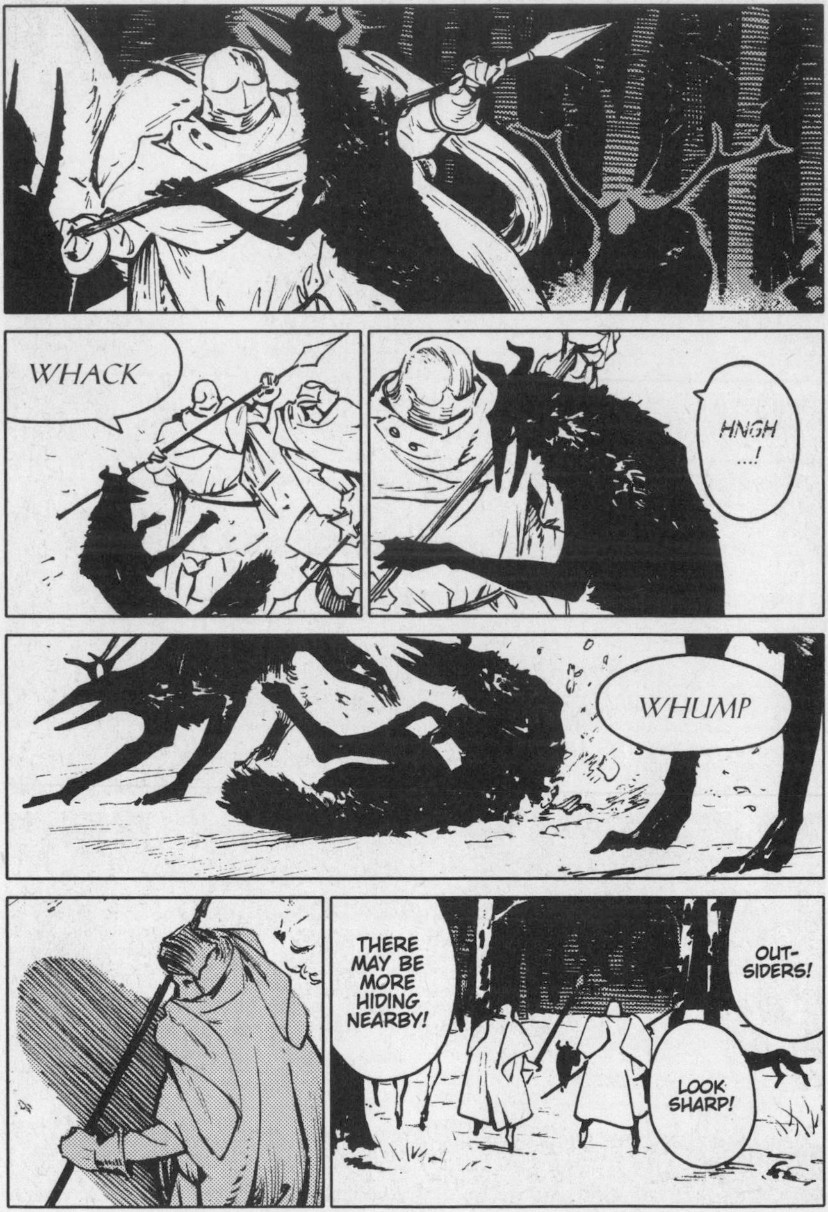
HNGH ...!
WHACK
WHUMP
OUT-SIDERS!
THERE MAY BE MORE HIDING NEARBY!
LOOK SHARP!

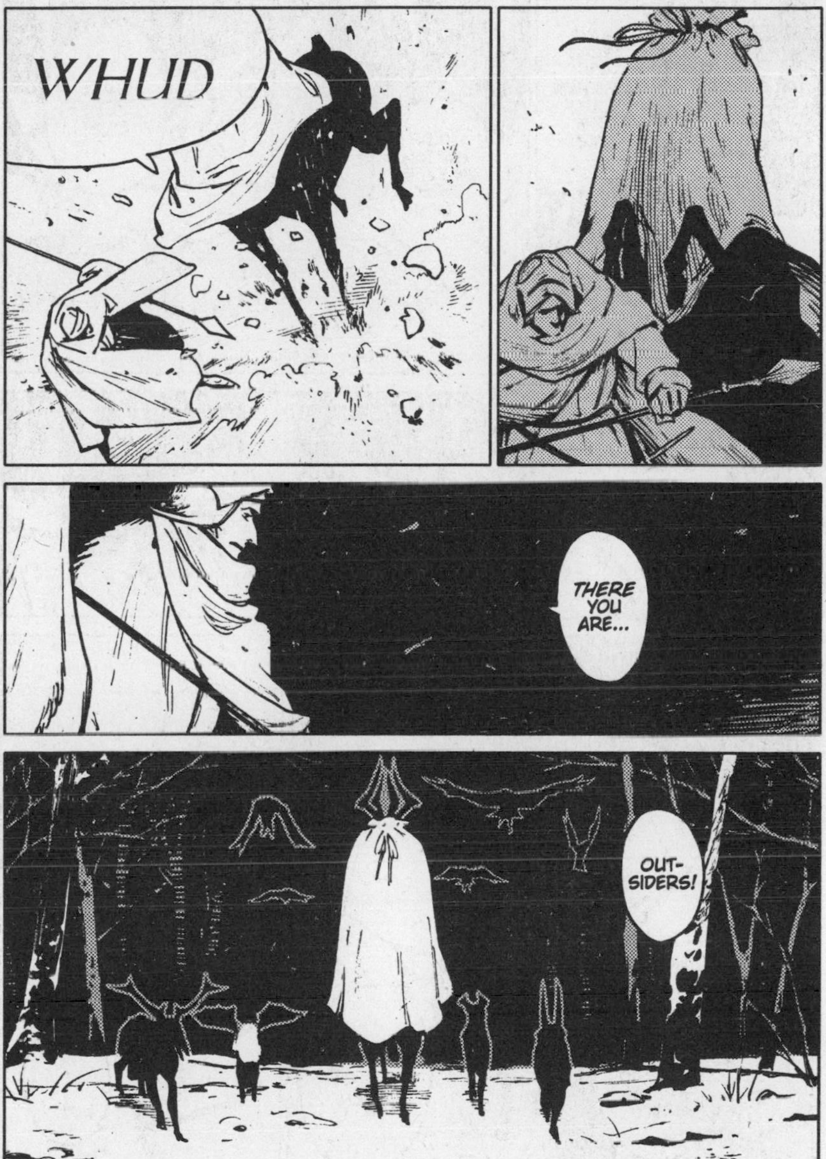
WHUD
THERE YOU ARE...
OUT-SIDERS!

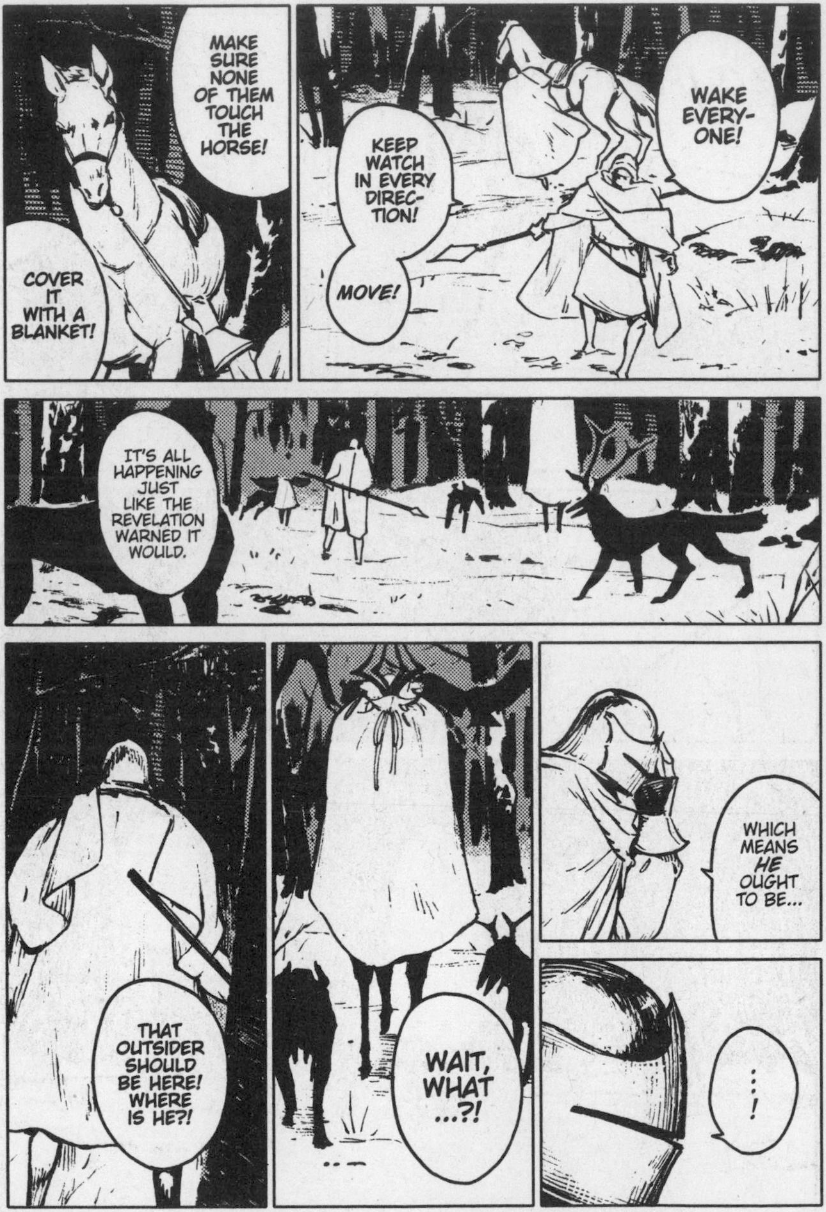
WAKE EVERY-ONE!
KEEP WATCH IN EVERY DIRECTION!
MOVE!
MAKE SURE NONE OF THEM TOUCH THE HORSE!
COVER IT WITH A BLANKET!
IT'S ALL HAPPENING JUST LIKE THE REVELATION WARNED IT WOULD.
WHICH MEANS *HE* OUGHT TO BE...
...!
WAIT, WHAT ...?!
THAT OUTSIDER SHOULD BE HERE! WHERE IS HE?!

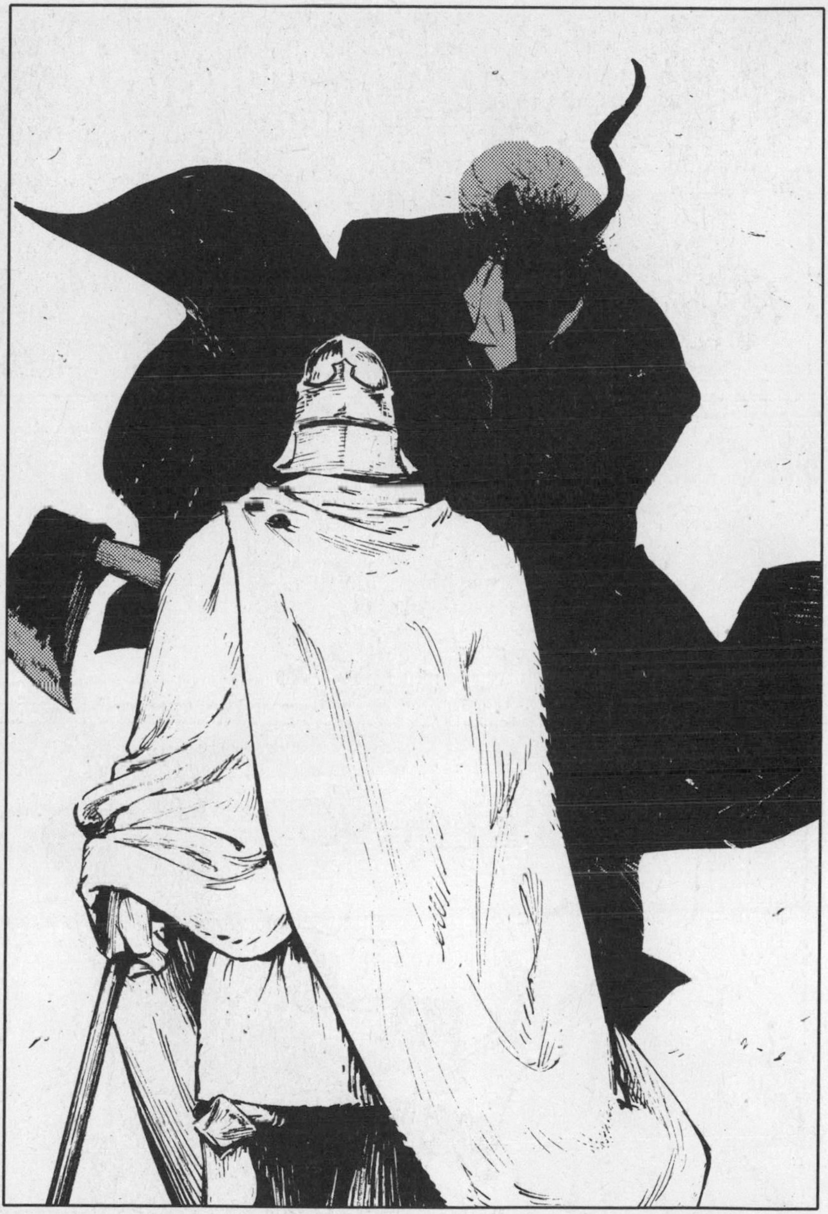

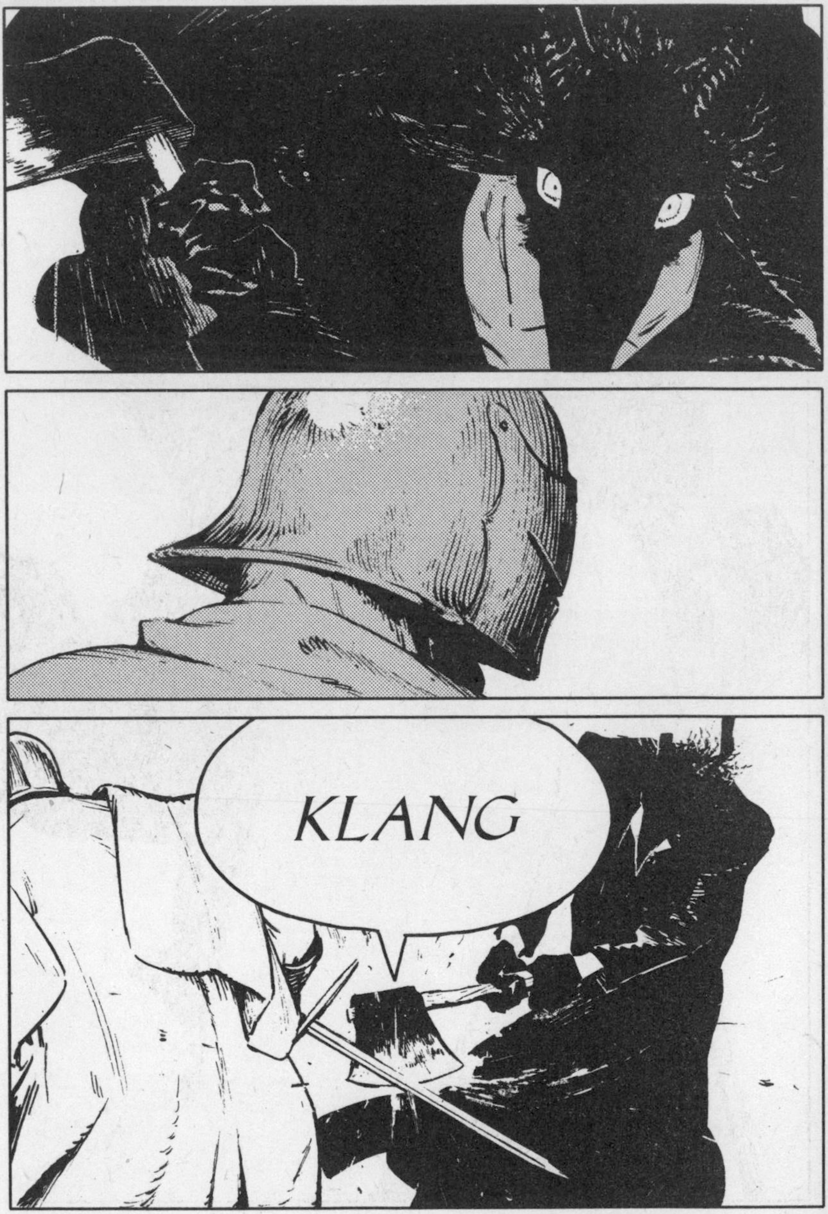
KLANG

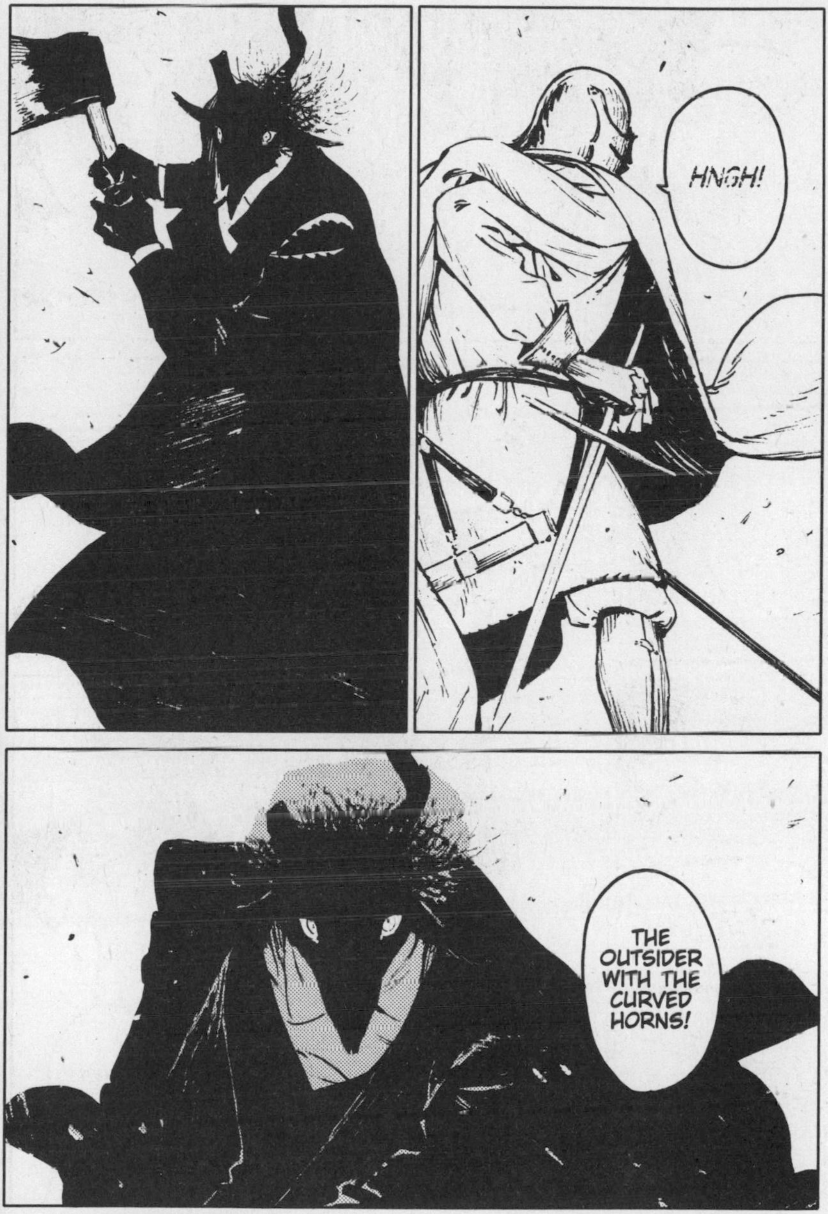
HNGH!
THE OUTSIDER WITH THE CURVED HORNS!

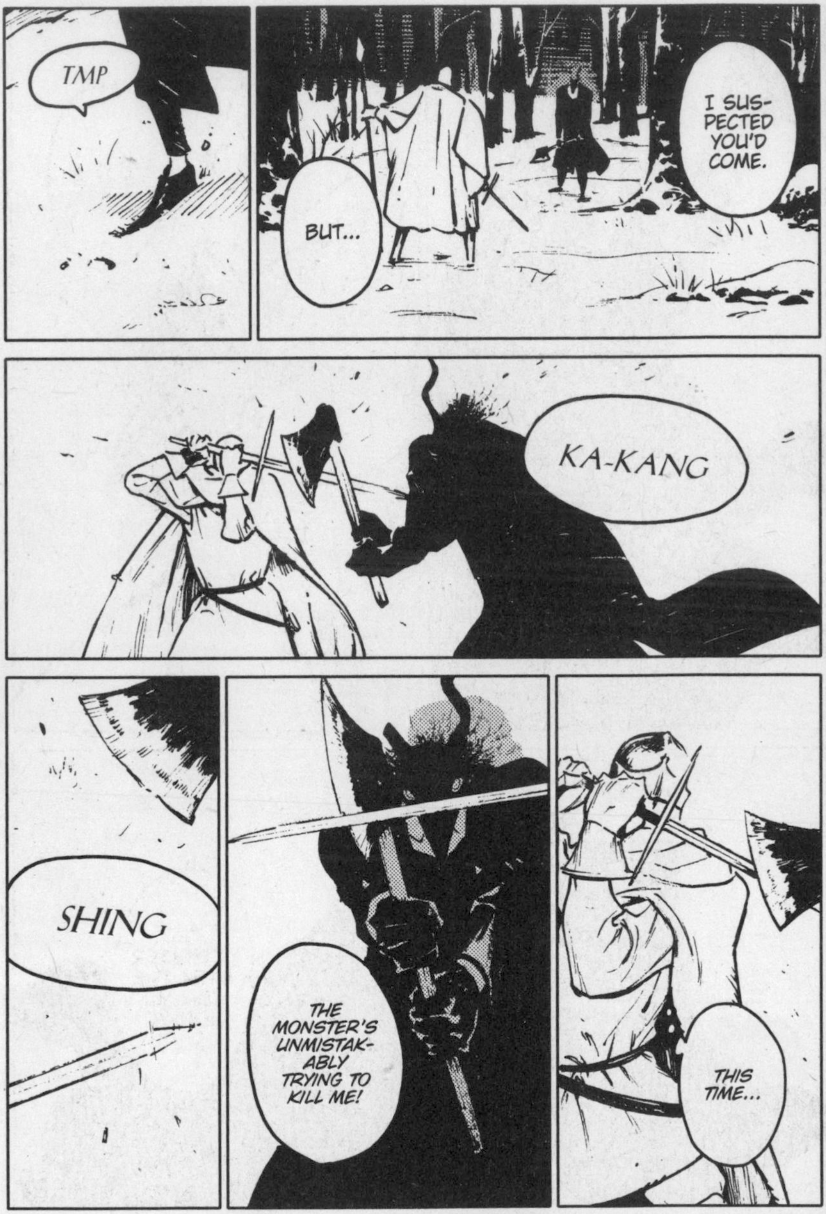
I SUS-PECTED YOU'D COME.
BUT...
TMP
KA-KANG
THIS TIME...
THE MONSTER'S UNMISTAK-ABLY TRYING TO KILL ME!
SHING

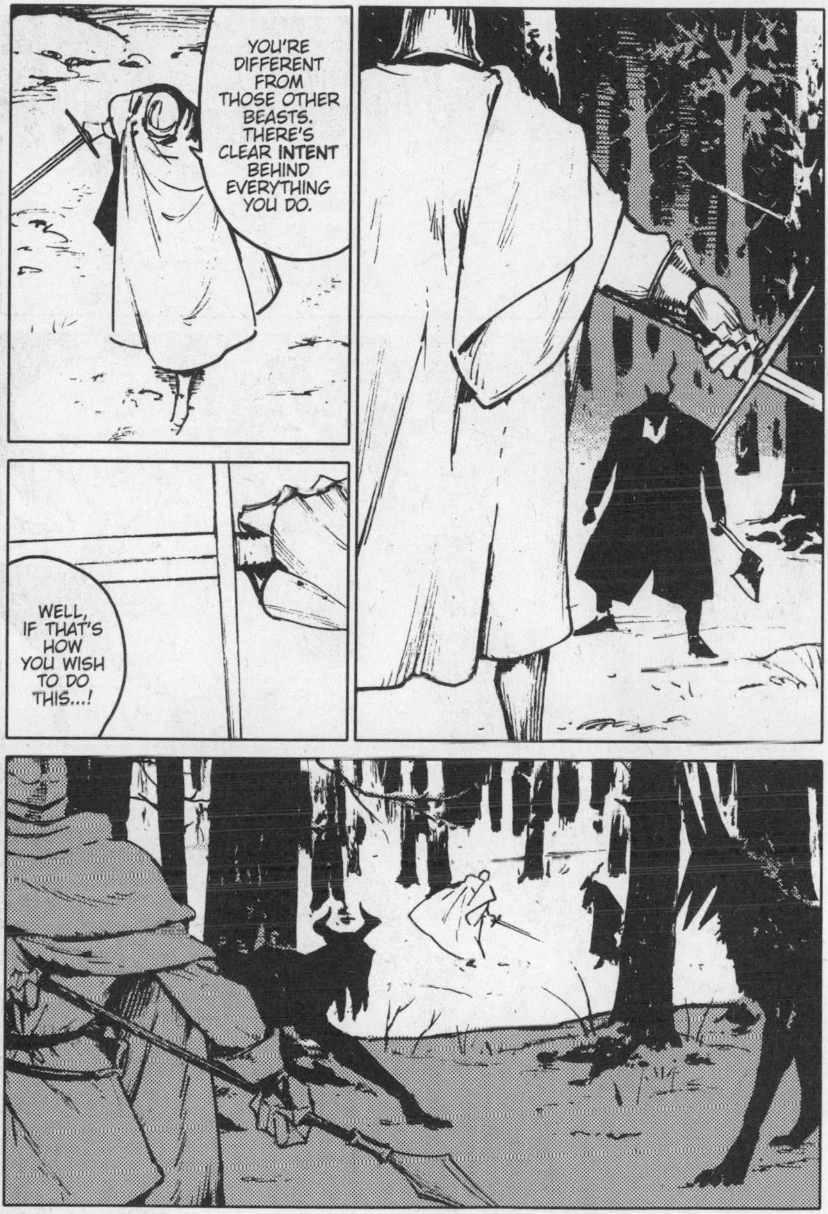
YOU'RE DIFFERENT FROM THOSE OTHER BEASTS. THERE'S CLEAR INTENT BEHIND EVERYTHING YOU DO.
WELL, IF THAT'S HOW YOU WISH TO DO THIS...!

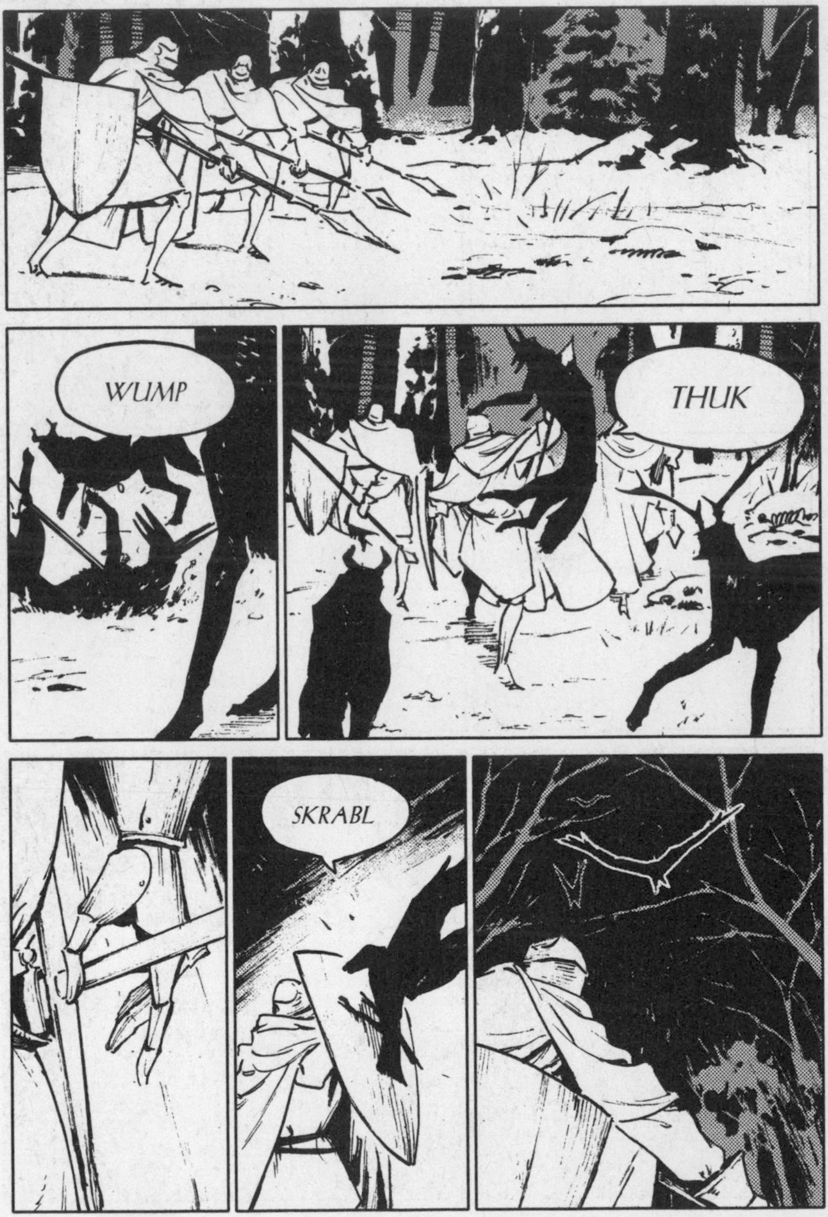
THUK
WUMP
SKRABL

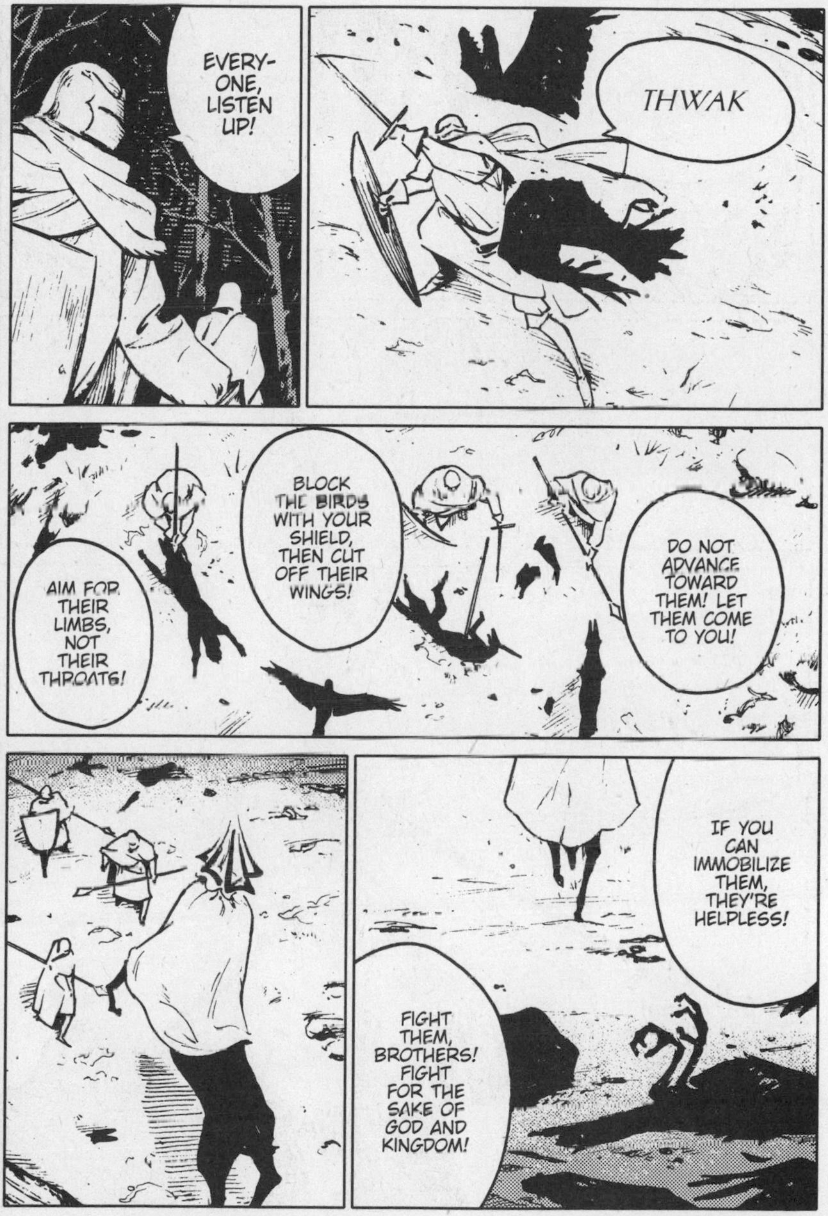
THWAK
EVERY-ONE, LISTEN UP!
DO NOT ADVANCE TOWARD THEM! LET THEM COME TO YOU!
BLOCK THE BIRDS WITH YOUR SHIELD, THEN CUT OFF THEIR WINGS!
AIM FOR THEIR LIMBS, NOT THEIR THROATS!
IF YOU CAN IMMOBILIZE THEM, THEY'RE HELPLESS!
FIGHT THEM, BROTHERS! FIGHT FOR THE SAKE OF GOD AND KINGDOM!

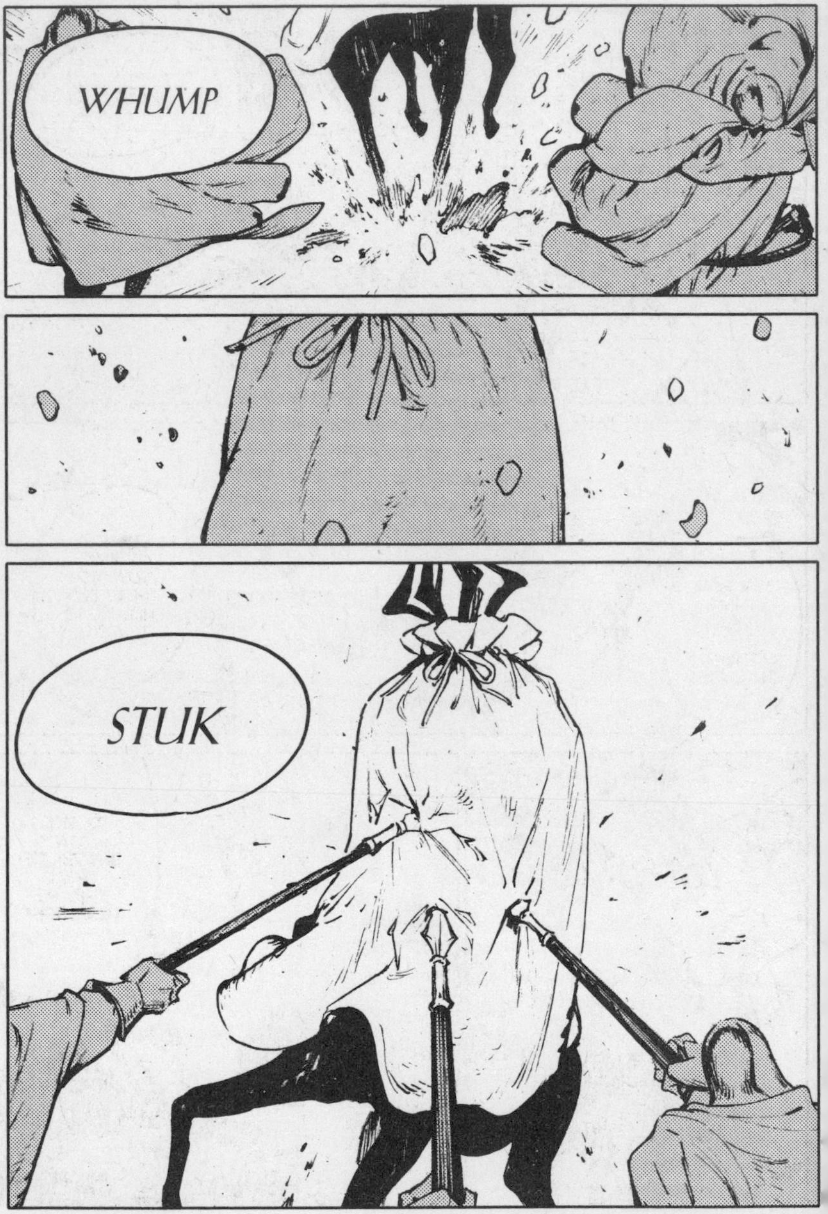
WHUMP
STUK

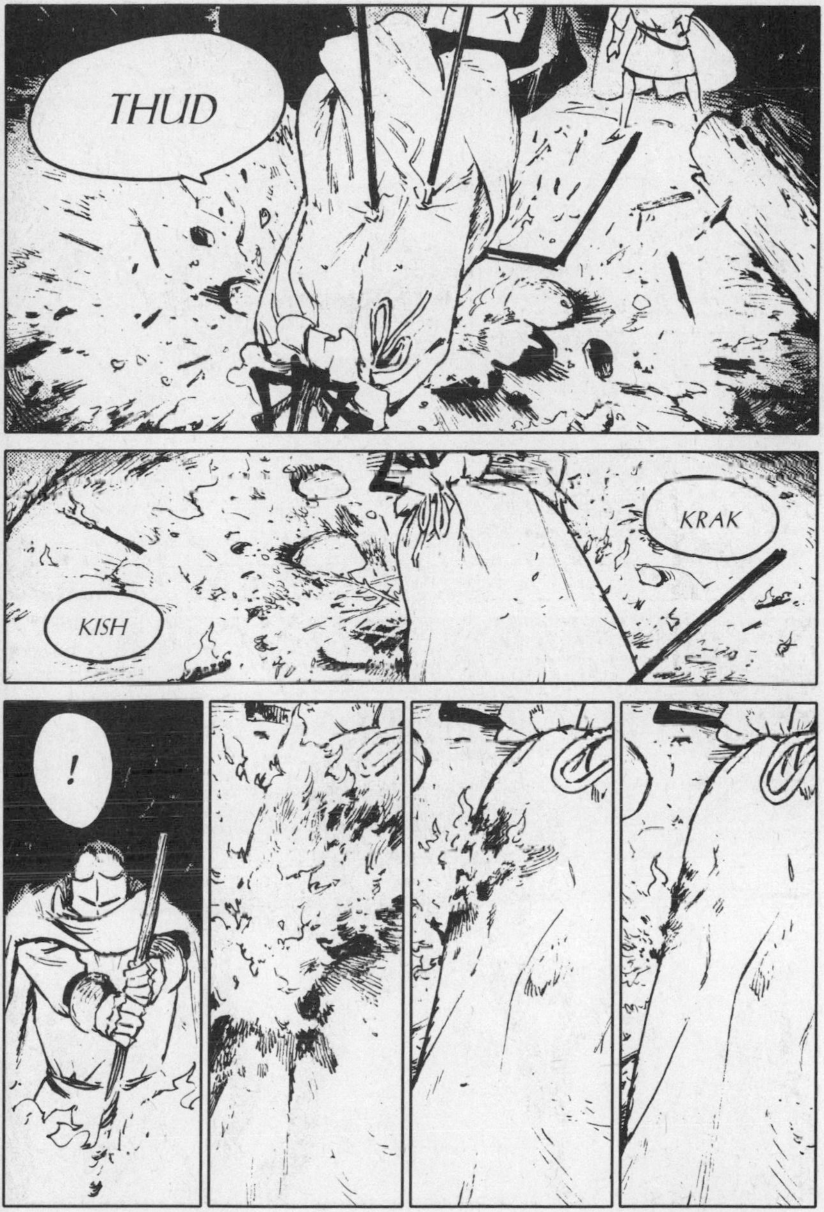
THUD
KRAK
KISH
!

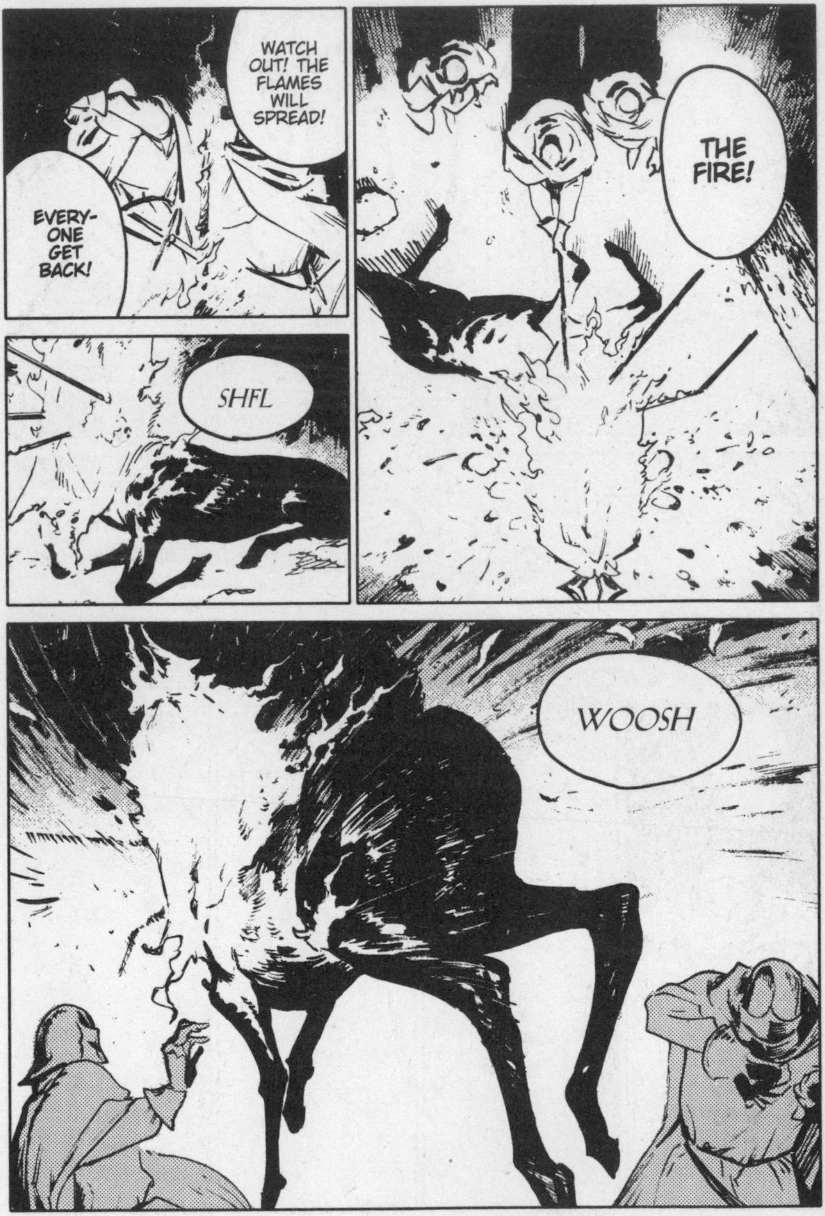
THE FIRE!
WATCH OUT! THE FLAMES WILL SPREAD!
EVERY-ONE GET BACK!
SHFL
WOOSH

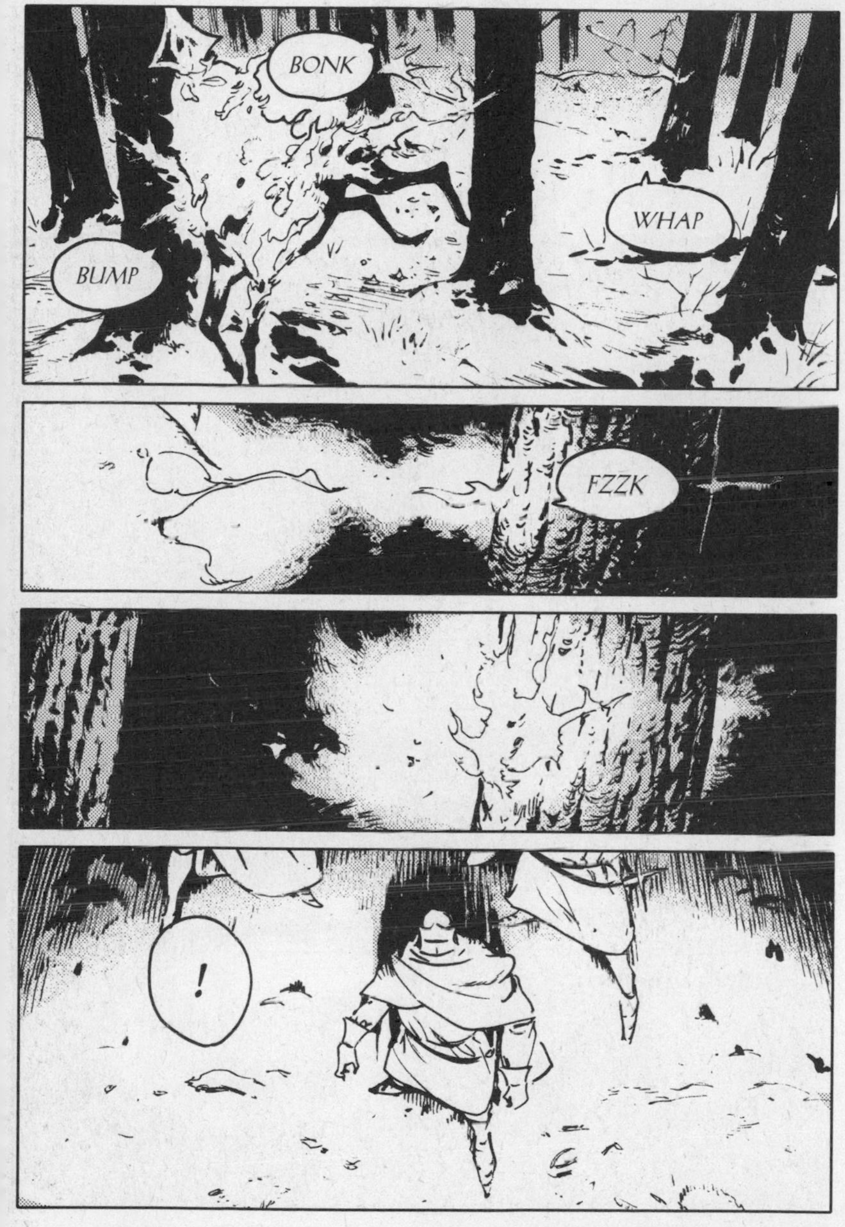
BONK
WHAP
BUMP
FZZK
!

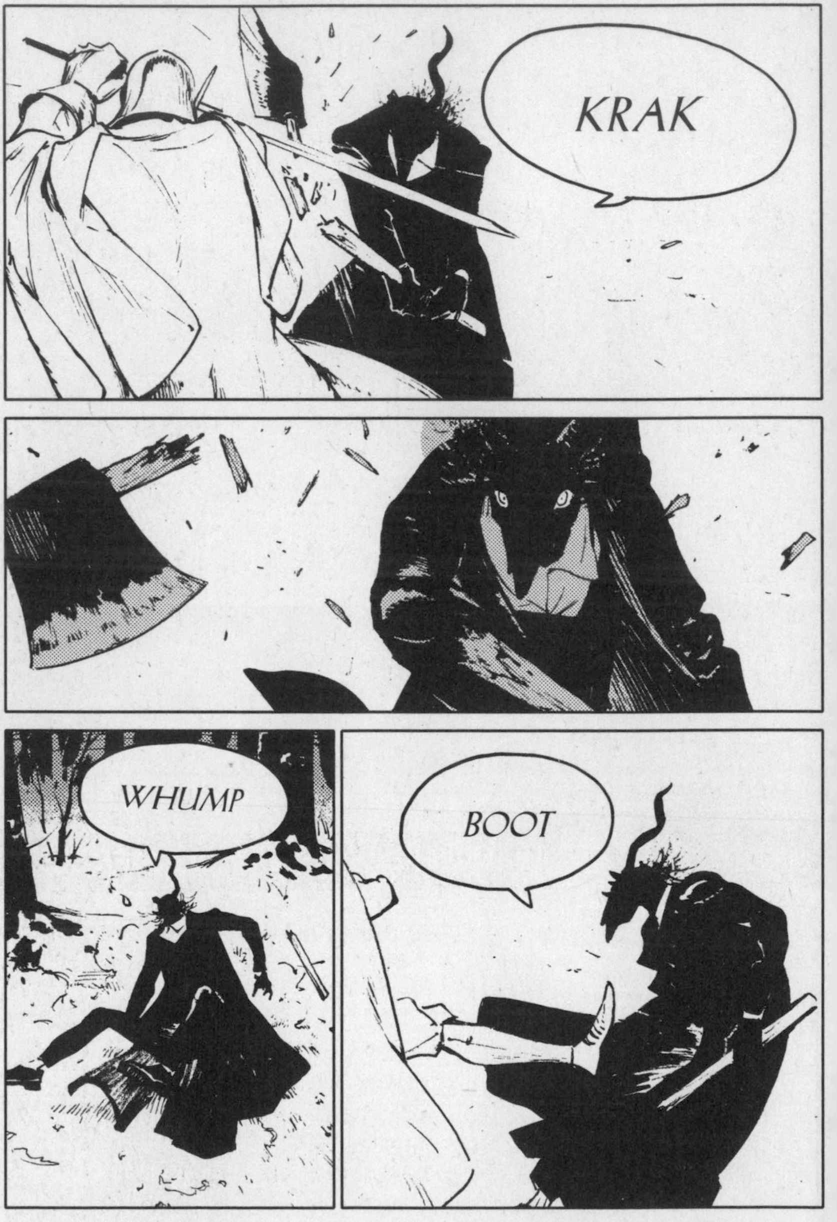
KRAK
BOOT
WHUMP

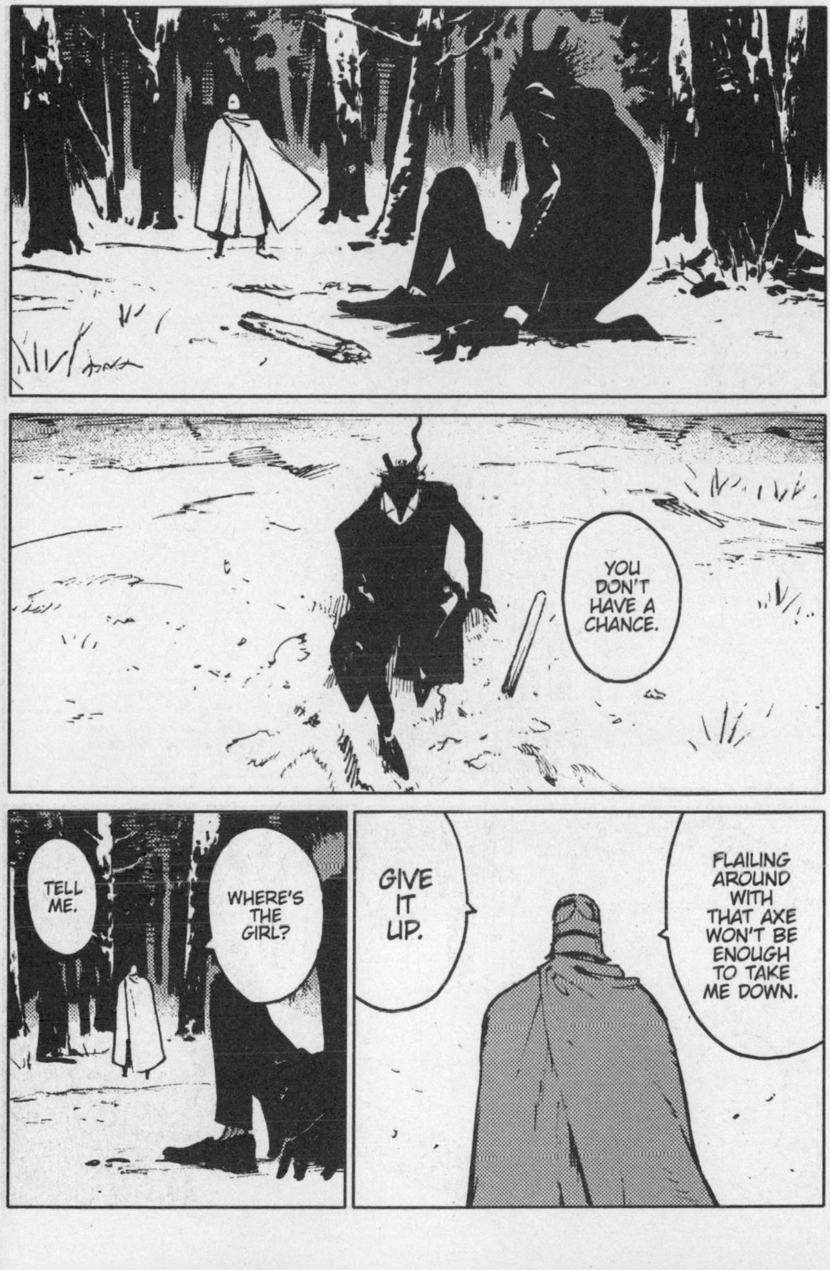
YOU DON'T HAVE A CHANCE.
FLAILING AROUND WITH THAT AXE WON'T BE ENOUGH TO TAKE ME DOWN.
GIVE IT UP.
WHERE'S THE GIRL?
TELL ME.

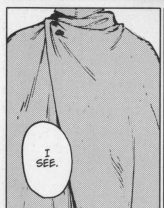

I
SEE.

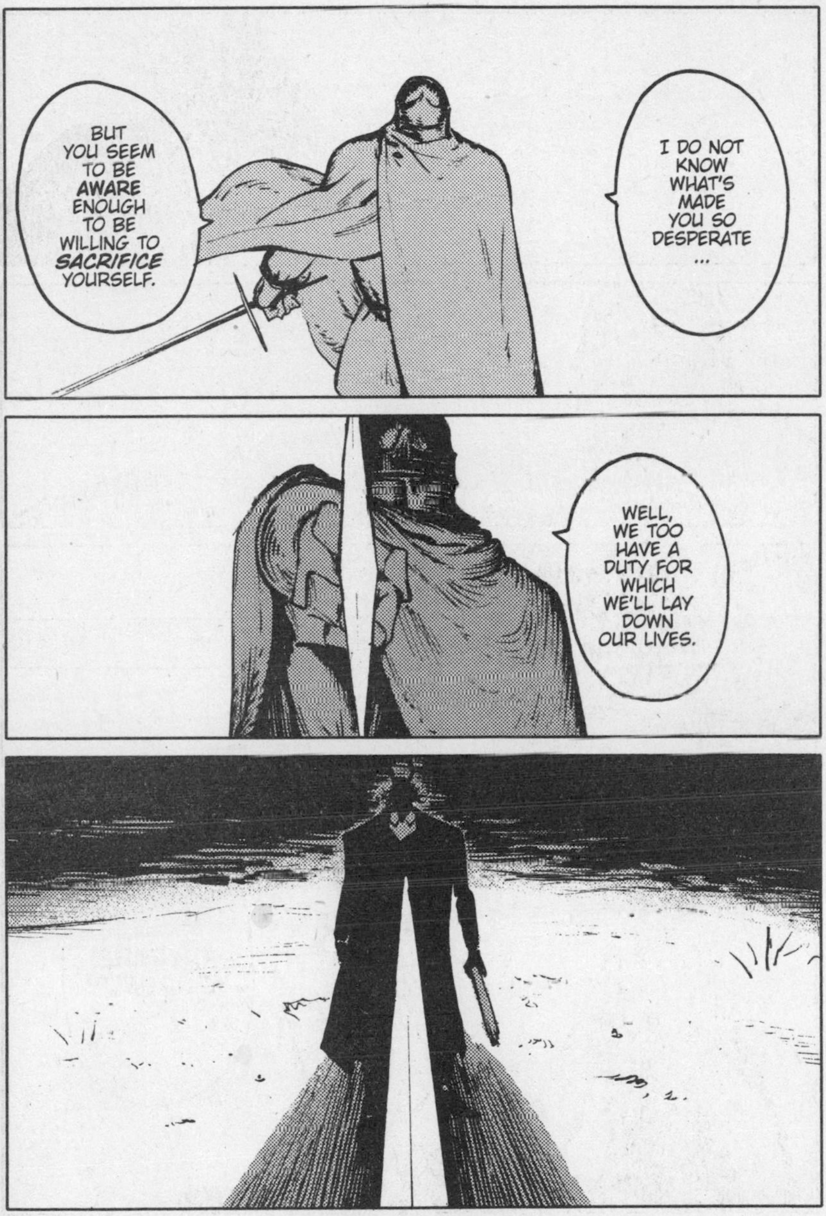
I DO NOT KNOW WHAT'S MADE YOU SO DESPERATE ...
BUT YOU SEEM TO BE AWARE ENOUGH TO BE WILLING TO SACRIFICE YOURSELF.
WELL, WE TOO HAVE A DUTY FOR WHICH WE'LL LAY DOWN OUR LIVES.

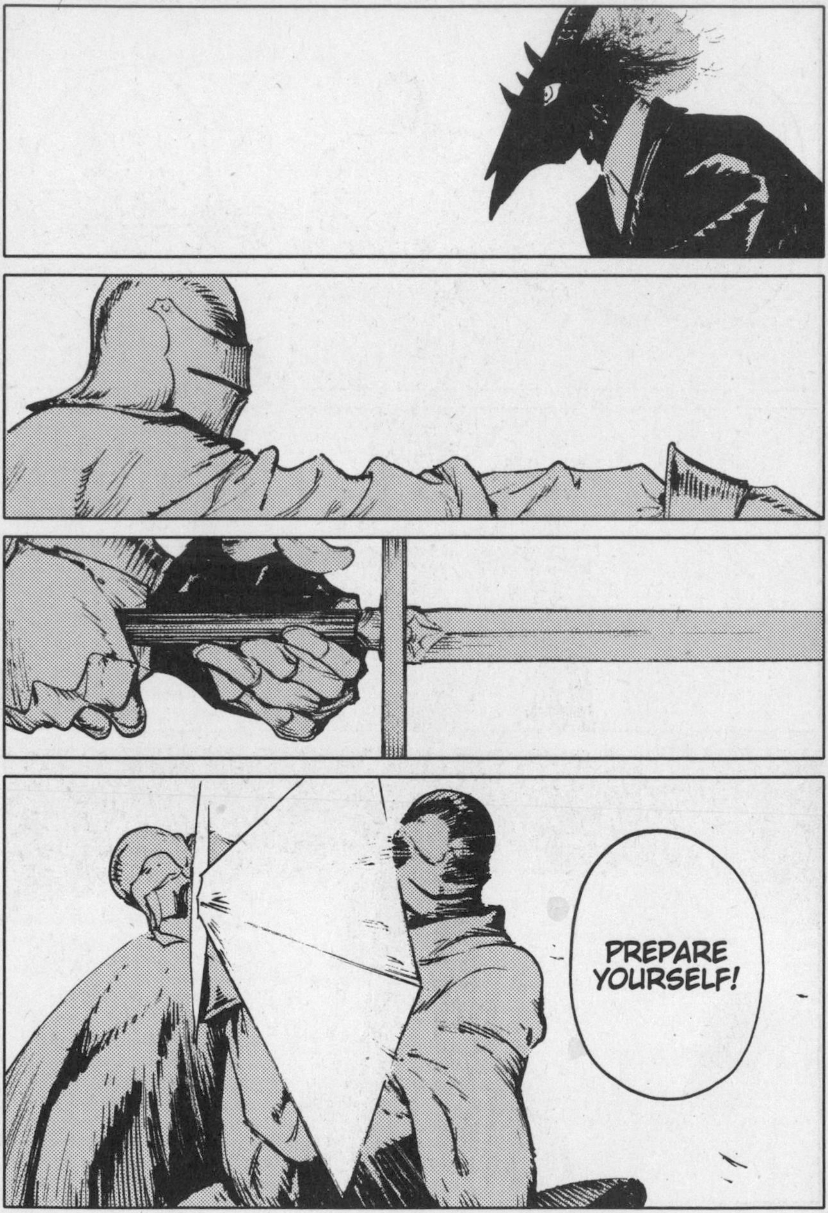
PREPARE YOURSELF!

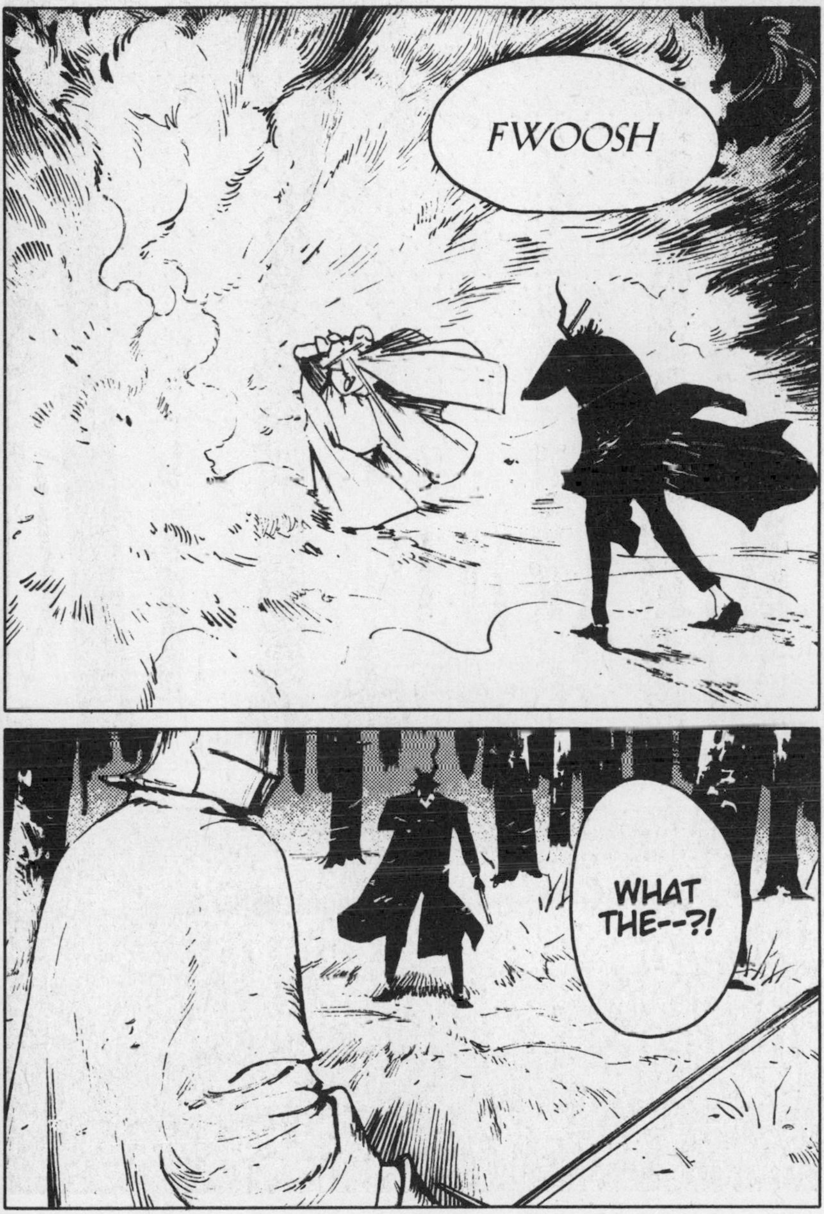
FWOOSH
WHAT THE--?!

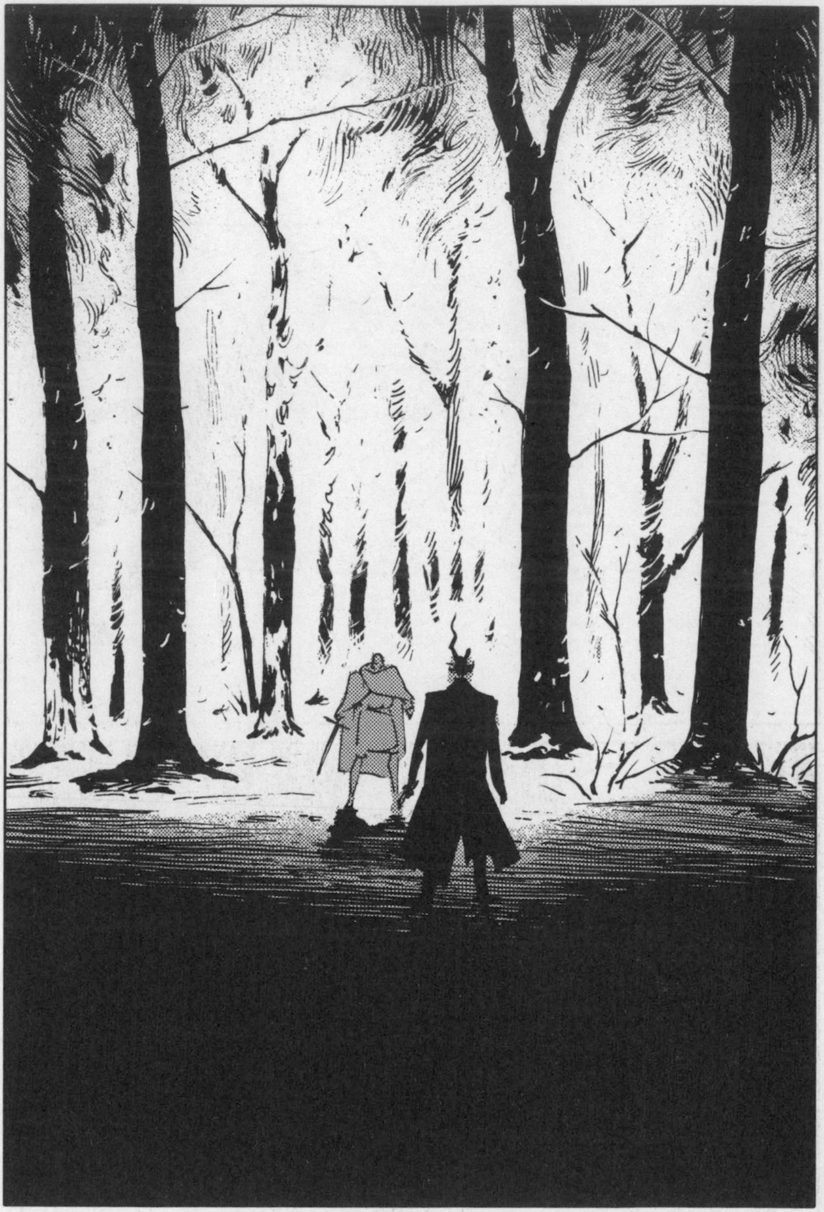

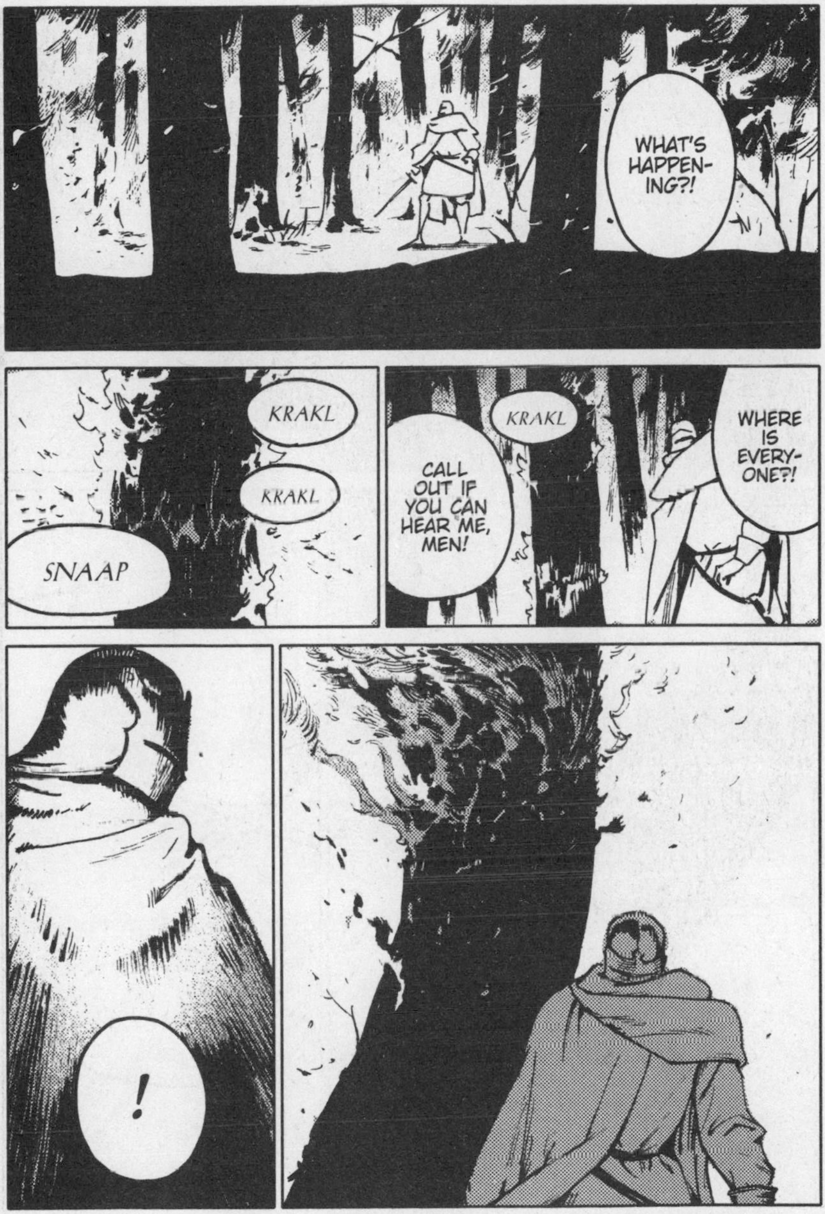
WHAT'S HAPPENING?!
WHERE IS EVERYONE?!
KRAKL
CALL OUT IF YOU CAN HEAR ME, MEN!
KRAKL
KRAKL
SNAAP
!

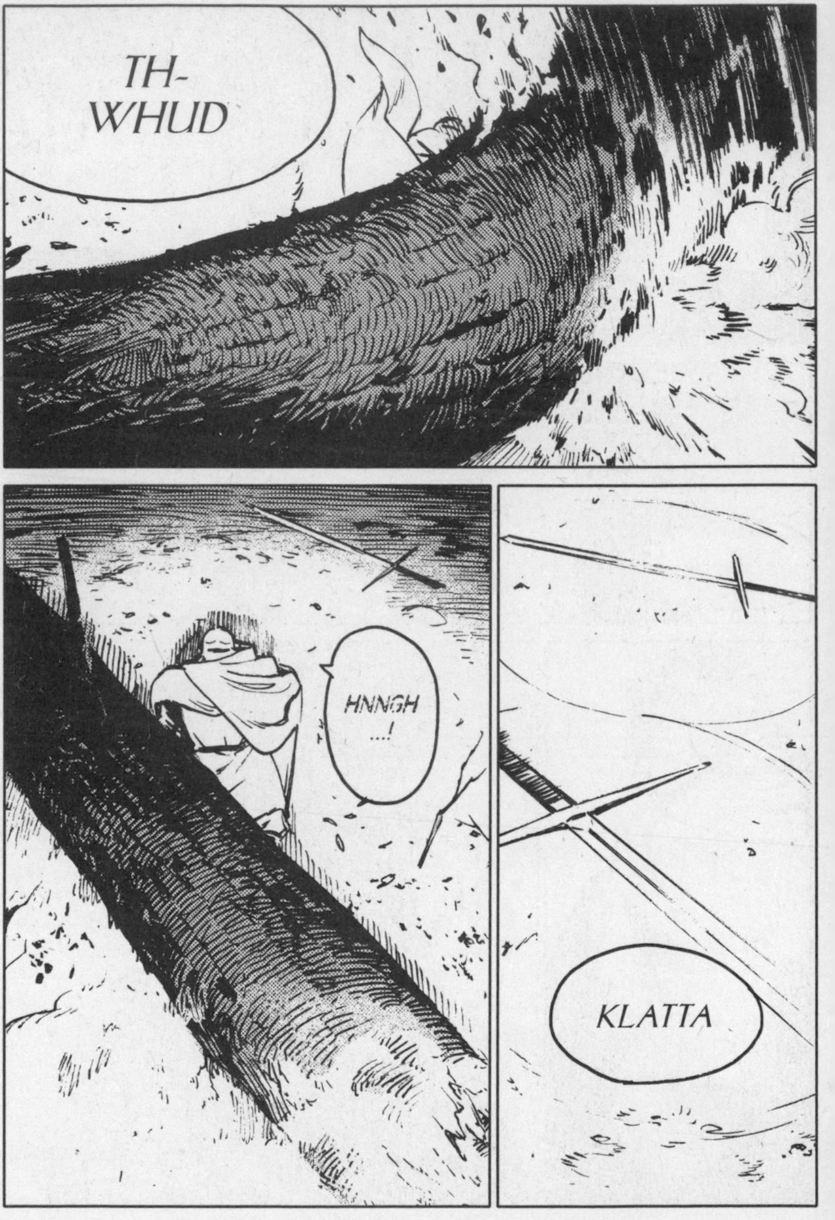
TH-
WHUD
KLATTA
HNNGH
...!

TUG

TUG

MY...
MY
LEG...

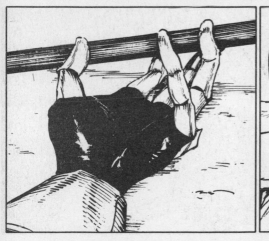

HNN!

STOMP

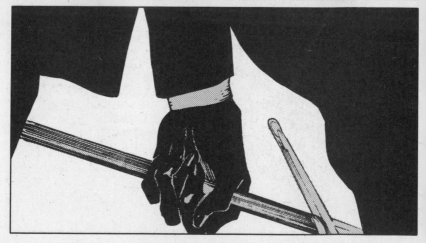

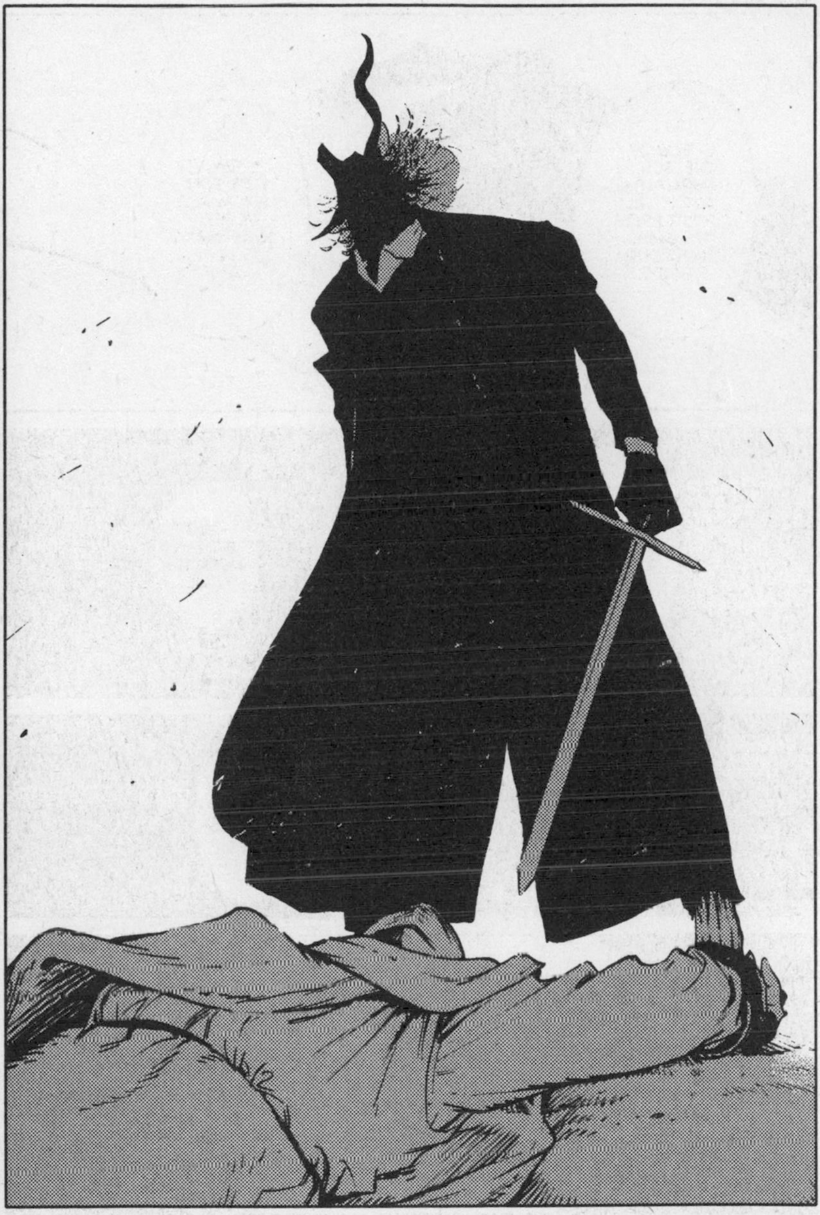

Chapter 35

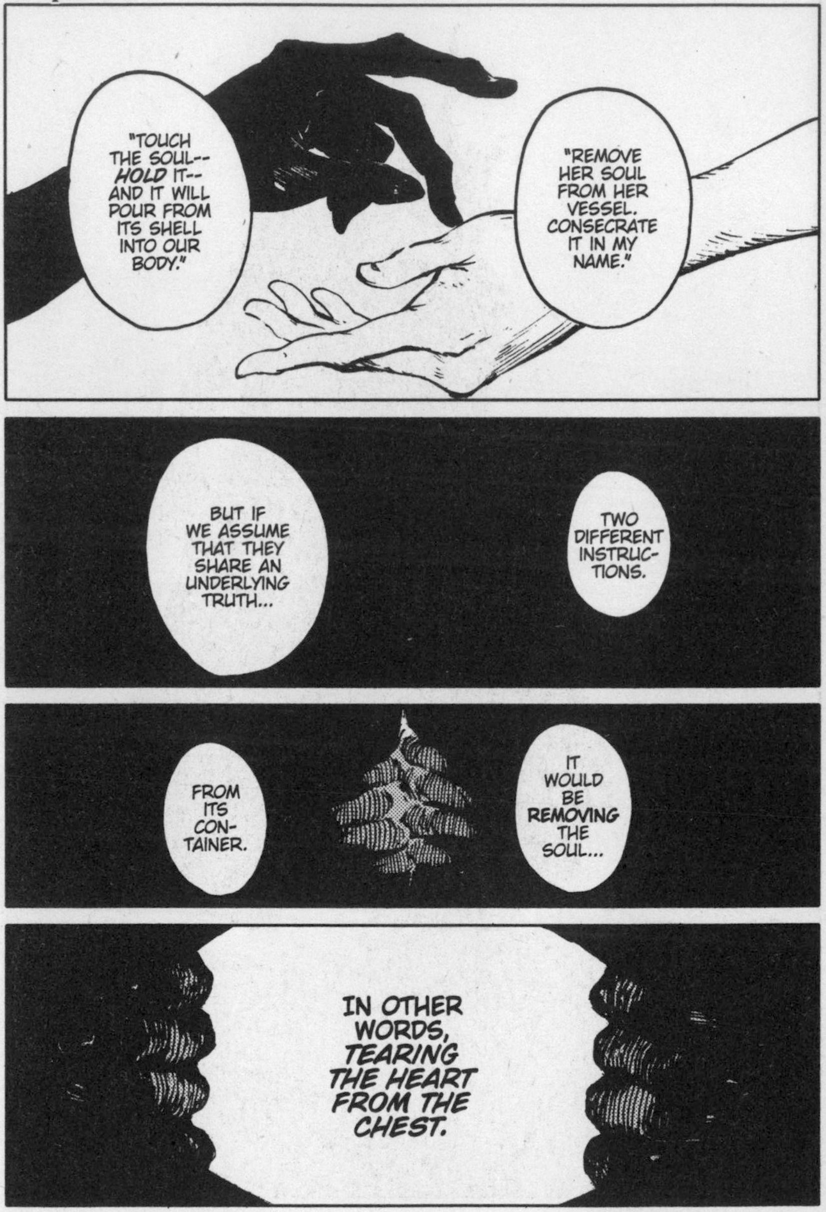
"REMOVE HER SOUL FROM HER VESSEL. CONSECRATE IT IN MY NAME."
"TOUCH THE SOUL--*HOLD* IT--AND IT WILL POUR FROM ITS SHELL INTO OUR BODY."
TWO DIFFERENT INSTRUC-TIONS.
BUT IF WE ASSUME THAT THEY SHARE AN UNDERLYING TRUTH...
IT WOULD BE **REMOVING** THE SOUL...
FROM ITS CON-TAINER.
IN OTHER WORDS, *TEARING THE HEART FROM THE CHEST.*

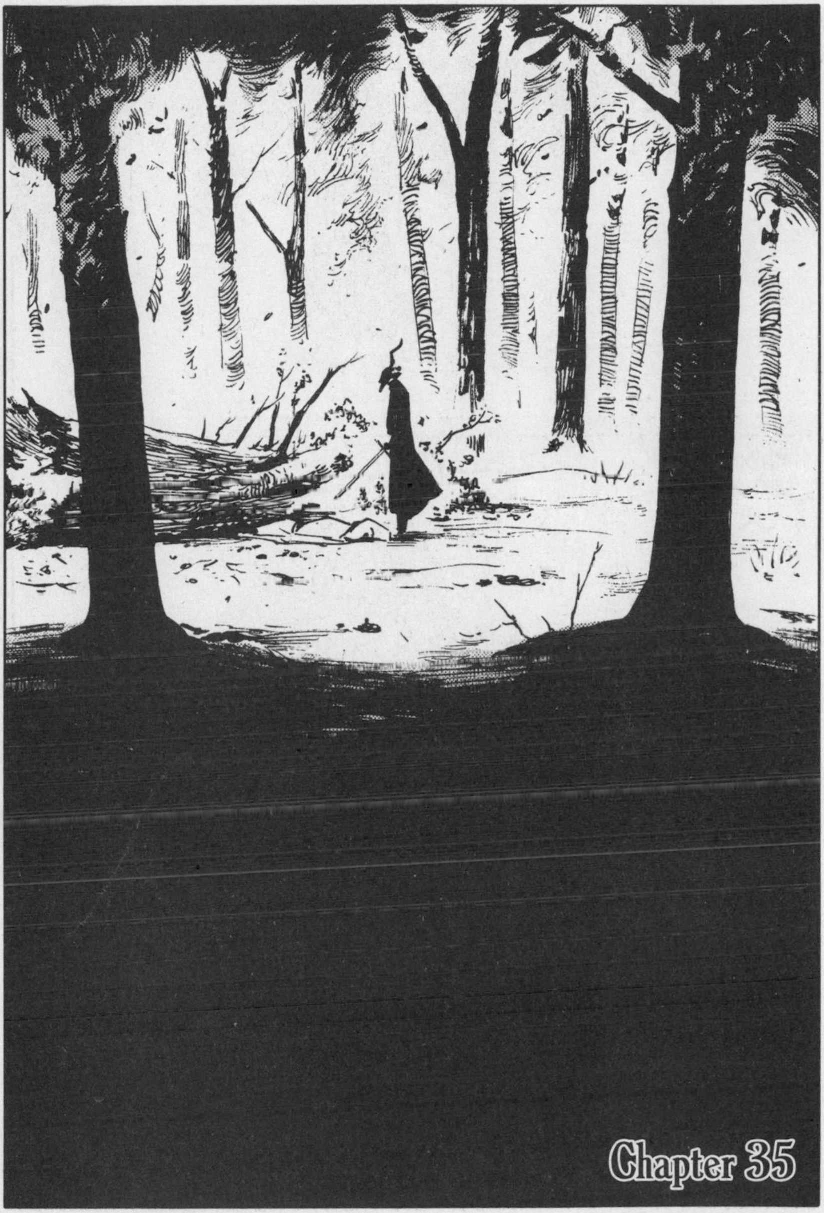
Chapter 35

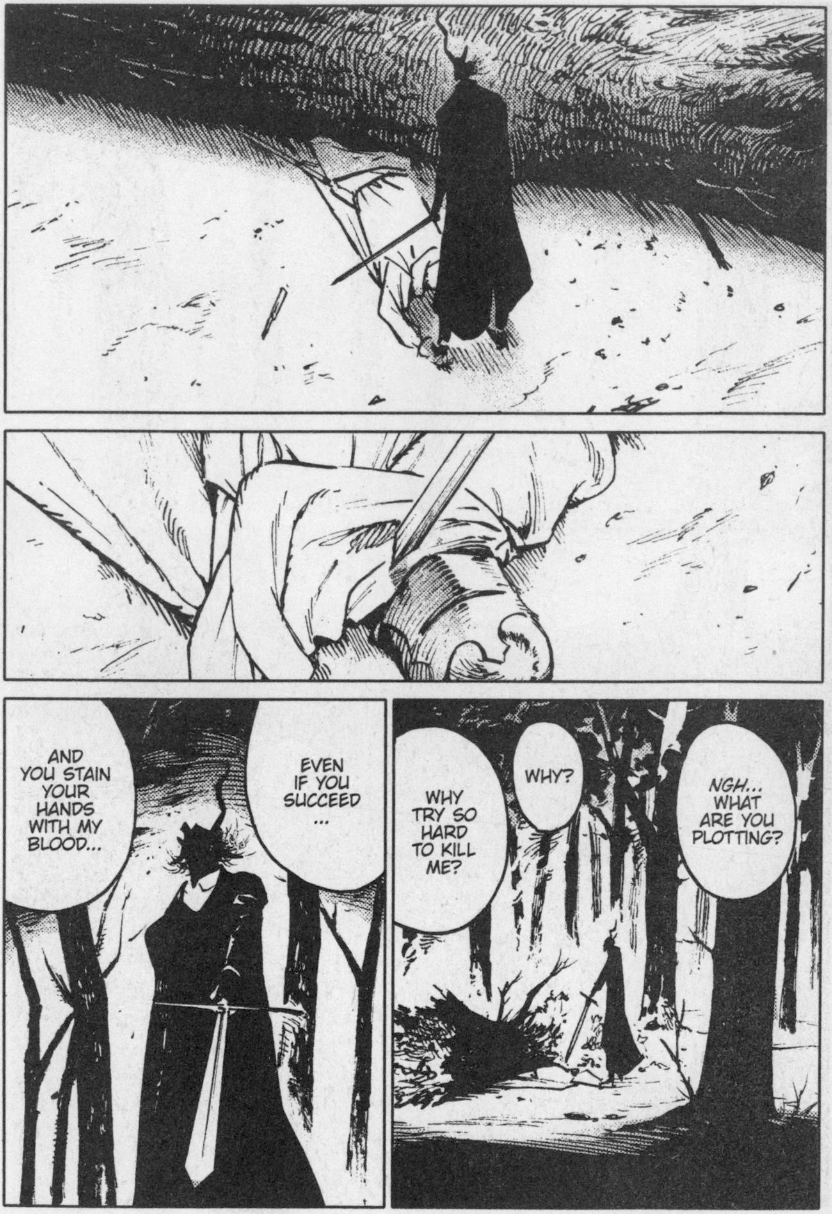
NGH... WHAT ARE YOU PLOTTING?
WHY?
WHY TRY SO HARD TO KILL ME?
EVEN IF YOU SUCCEED ...
AND YOU STAIN YOUR HANDS WITH MY BLOOD...

WHAT
COULD
YOU
POSSIBLY
GAIN?

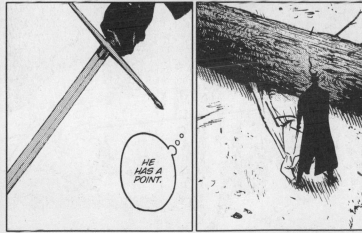

HE
HAS A
POINT.

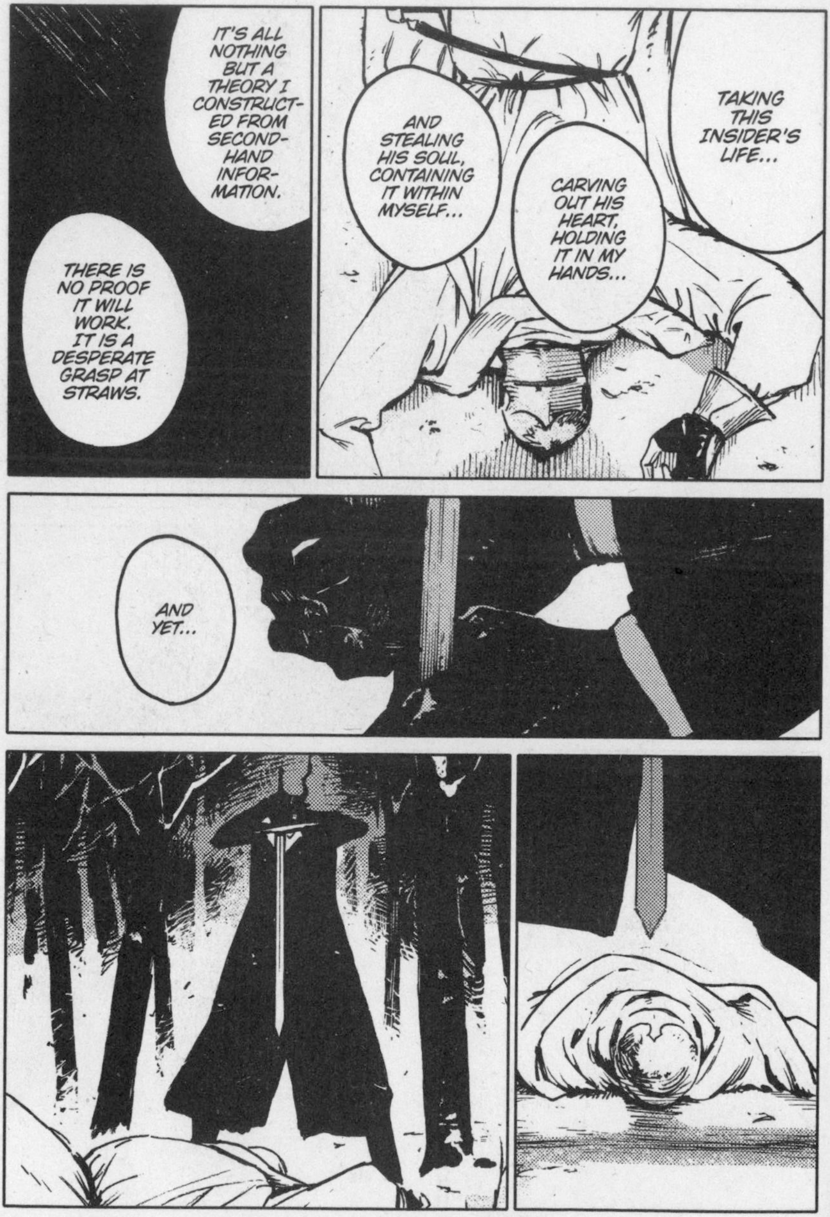
TAKING THIS INSIDER'S LIFE...
CARVING OUT HIS HEART, HOLDING IT IN MY HANDS...
AND STEALING HIS SOUL, CONTAINING IT WITHIN MYSELF...
IT'S ALL NOTHING BUT A THEORY I CONSTRUCTED FROM SECOND-HAND INFORMATION.
THERE IS NO PROOF IT WILL WORK. IT IS A DESPERATE GRASP AT STRAWS.
AND YET...

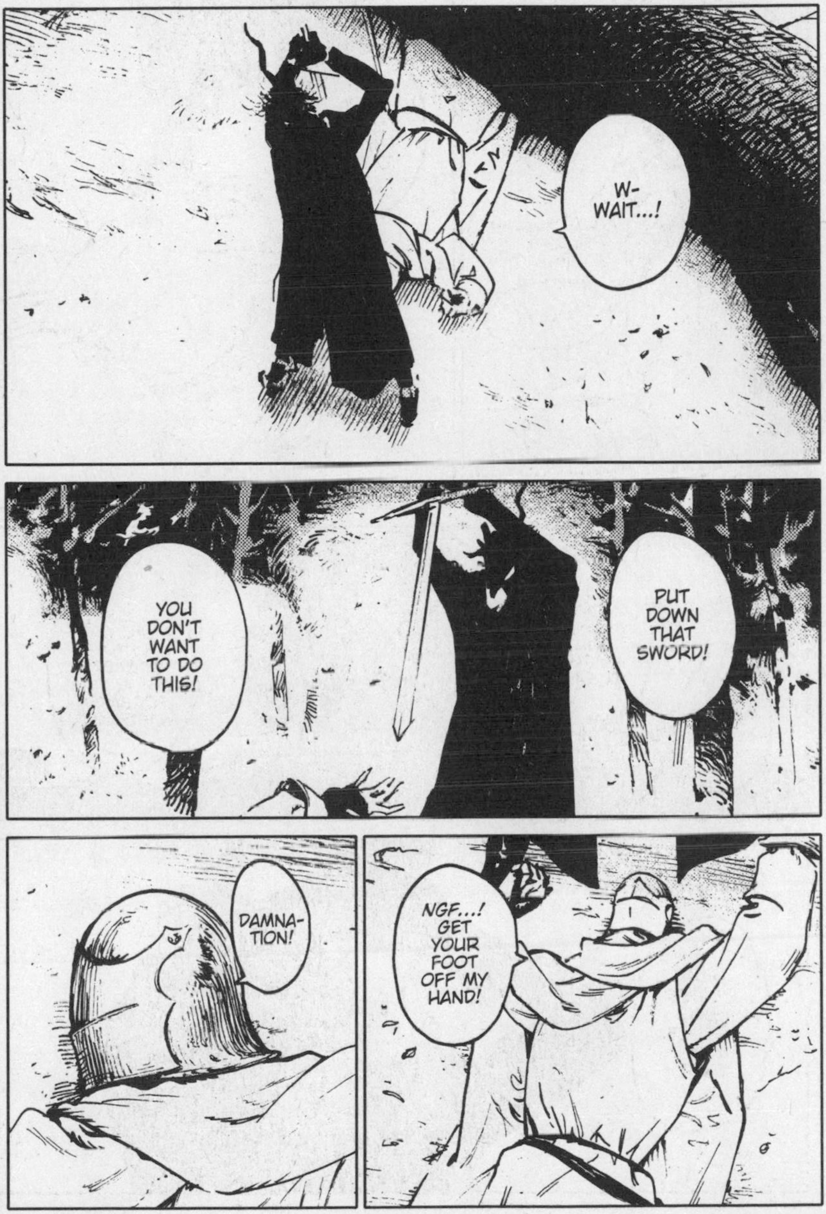
W-WAIT...!
PUT DOWN THAT SWORD!
YOU DON'T WANT TO DO THIS!
NGF...! GET YOUR FOOT OFF MY HAND!
DAMNA-TION!

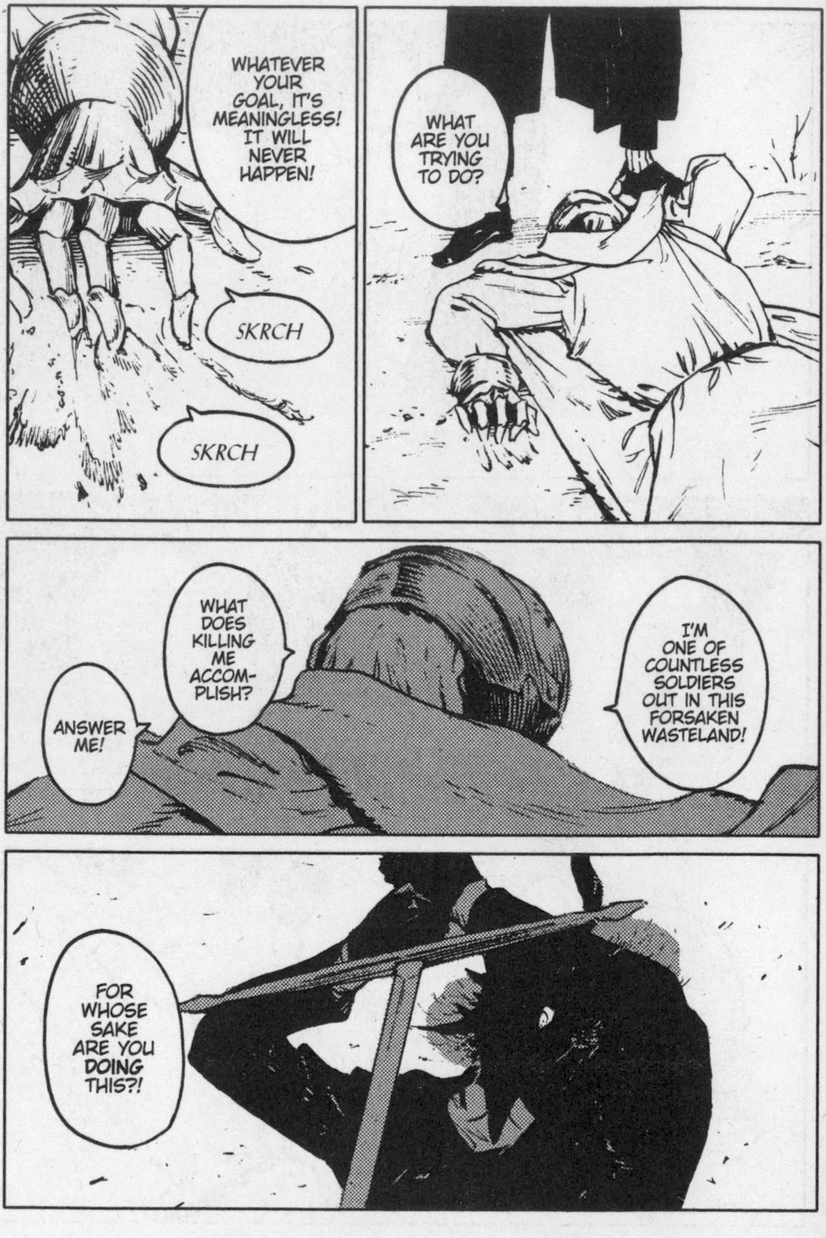
WHAT ARE YOU TRYING TO DO?
WHATEVER YOUR GOAL, IT'S MEANINGLESS! IT WILL NEVER HAPPEN!
SKRCH
SKRCH
I'M ONE OF COUNTLESS SOLDIERS OUT IN THIS FORSAKEN WASTELAND!
WHAT DOES KILLING ME ACCOM-PLISH?
ANSWER ME!
FOR WHOSE SAKE ARE YOU DOING THIS?!

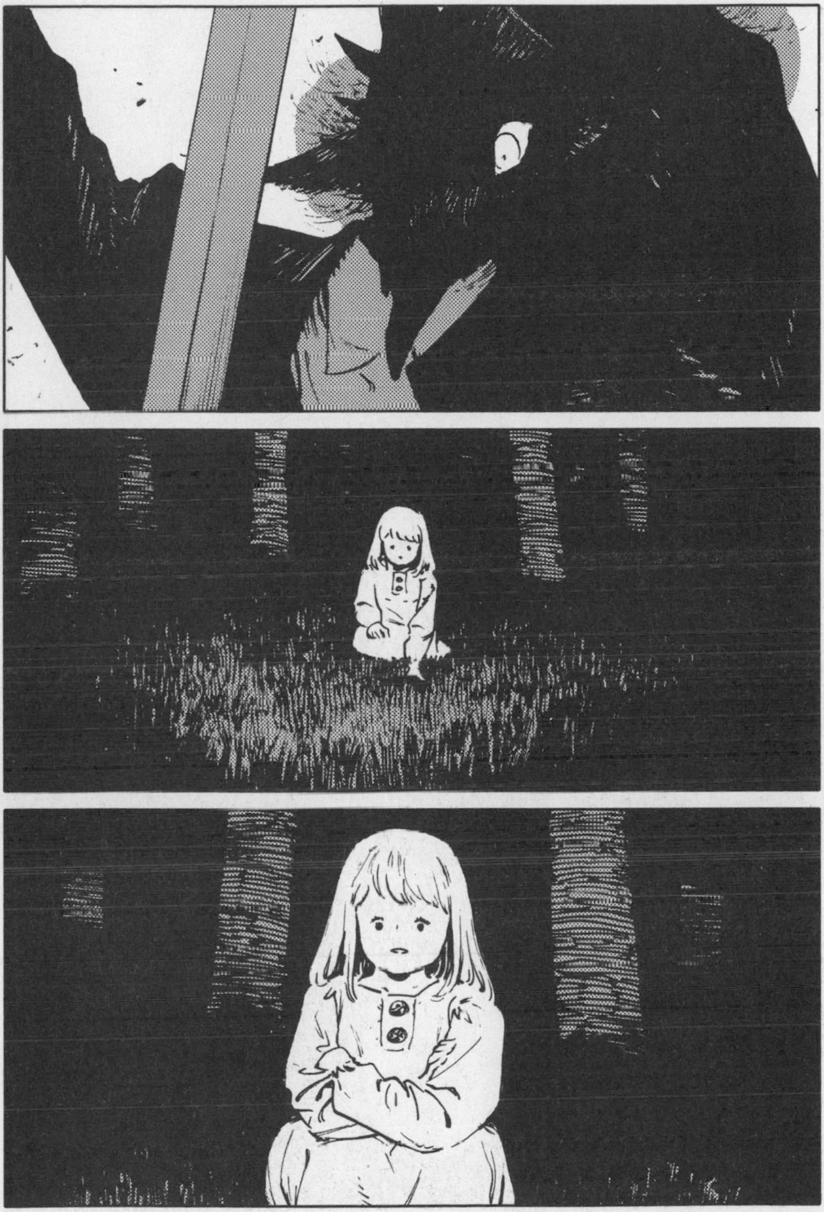

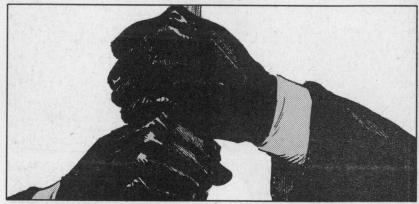

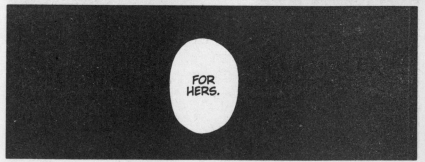

FOR HERS.

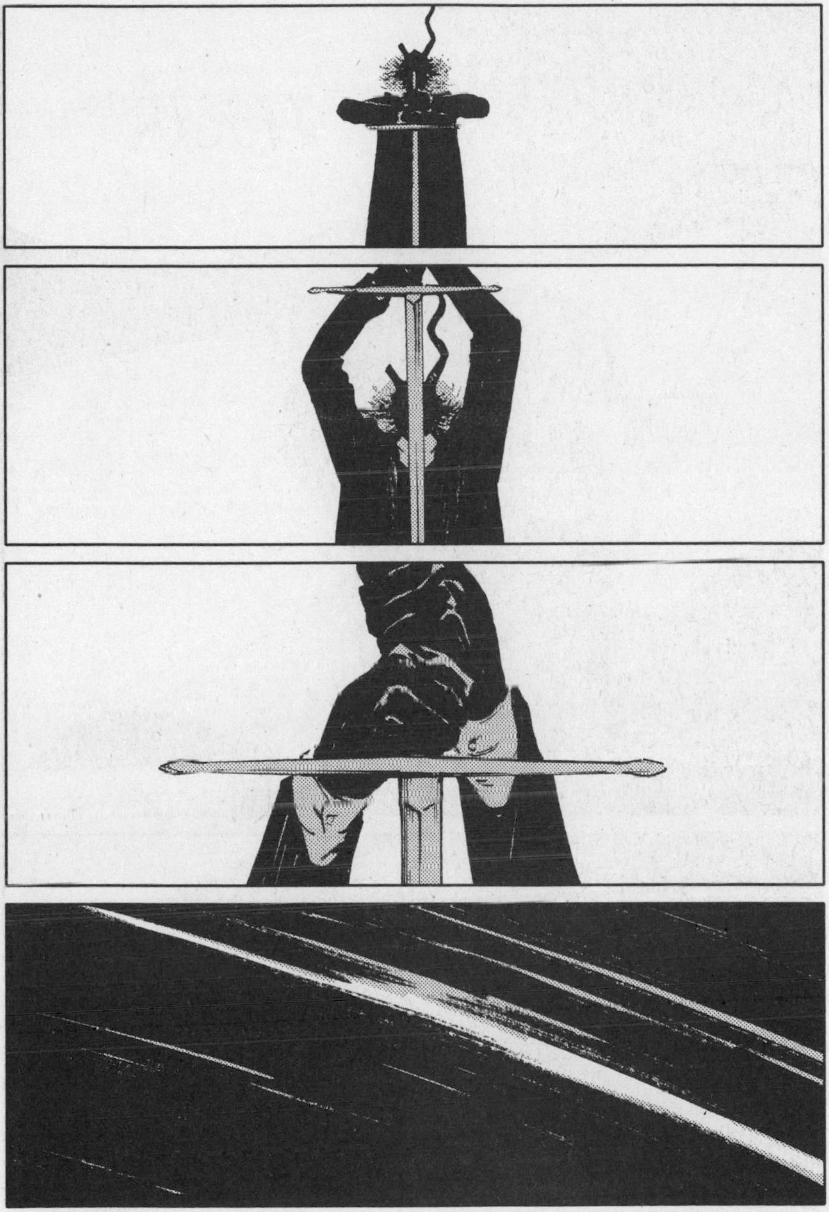

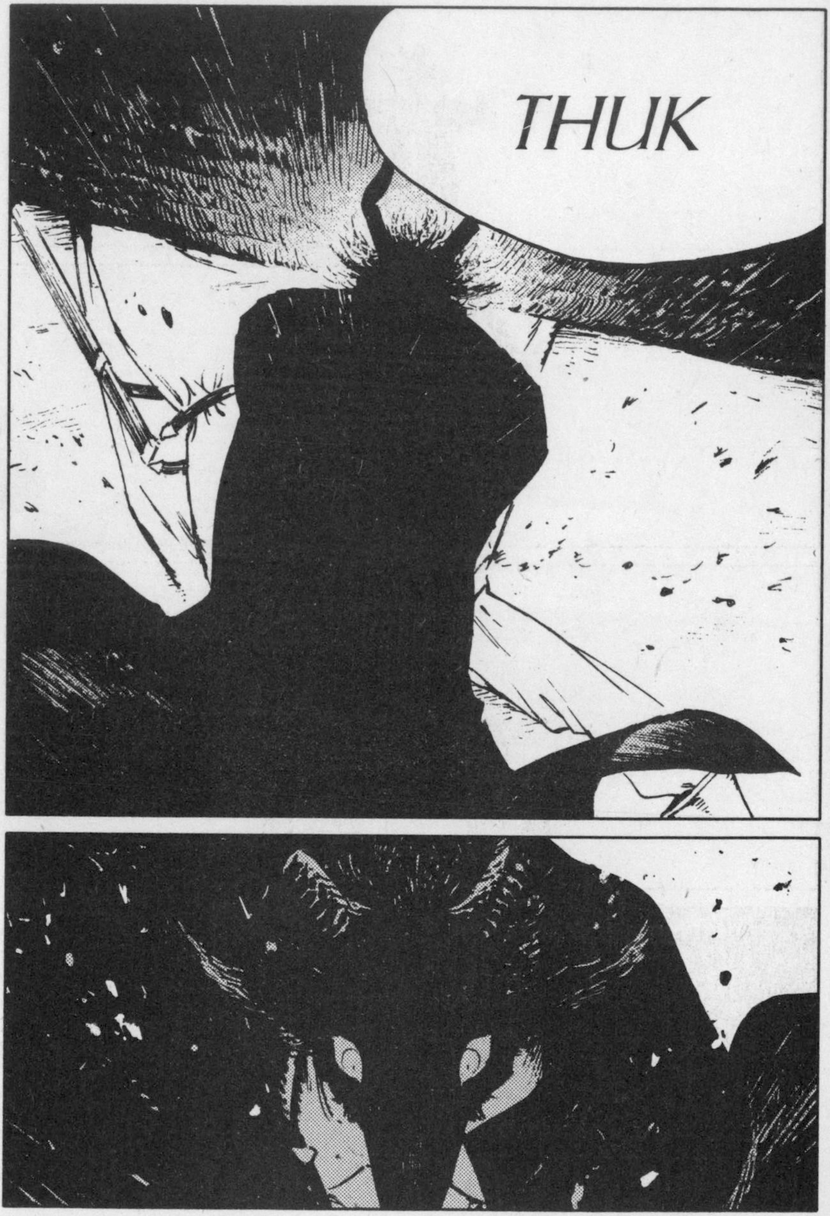
THUK

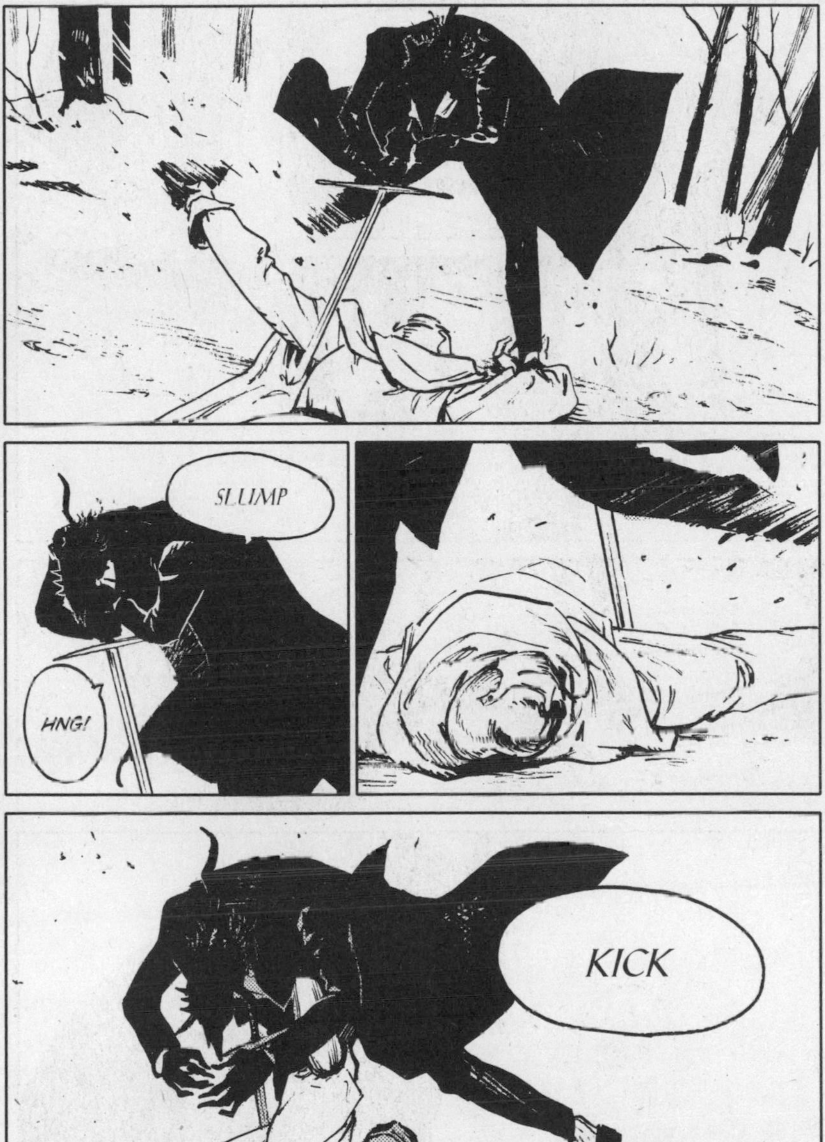
SLUMP
HNG!
KICK

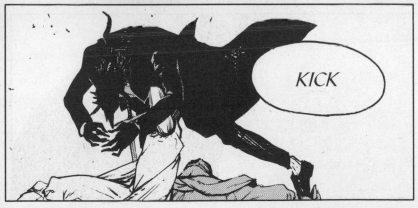

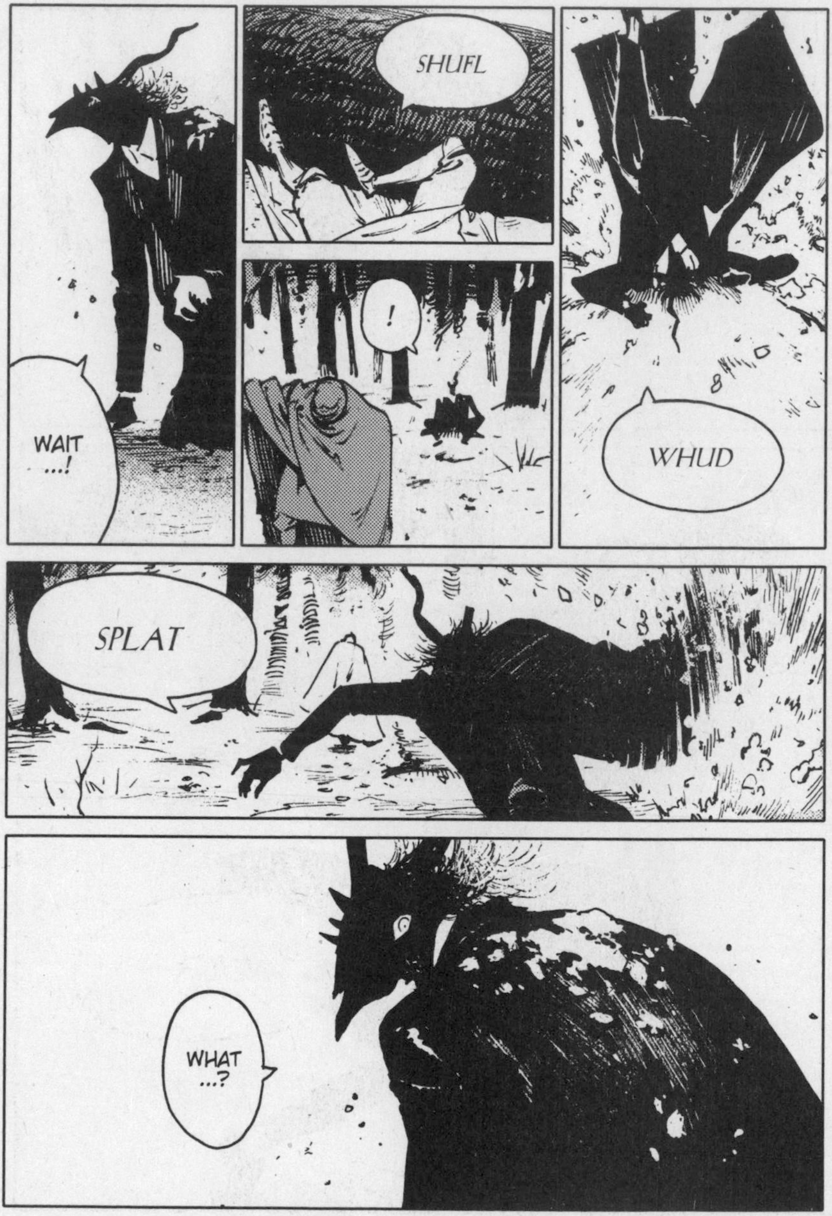
WHUD
SHUFL
!
WAIT ...!
SPLAT
WHAT ...?

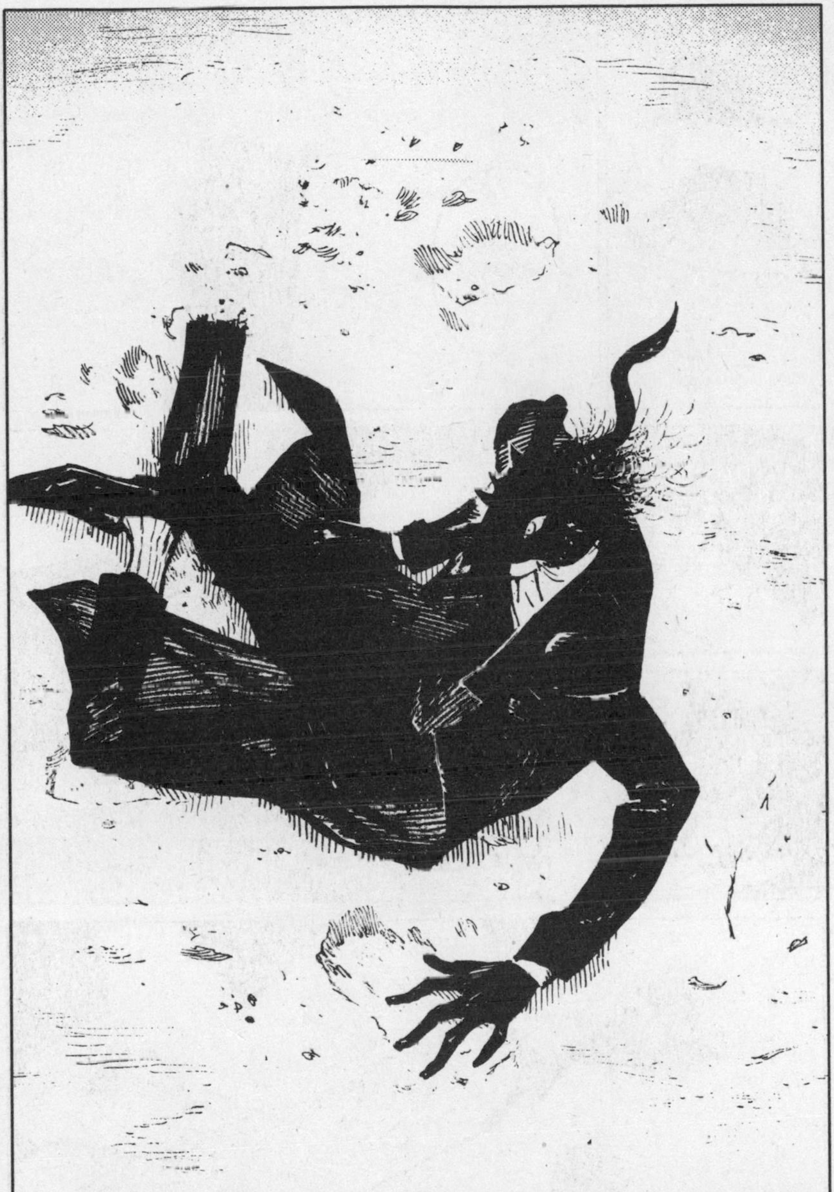

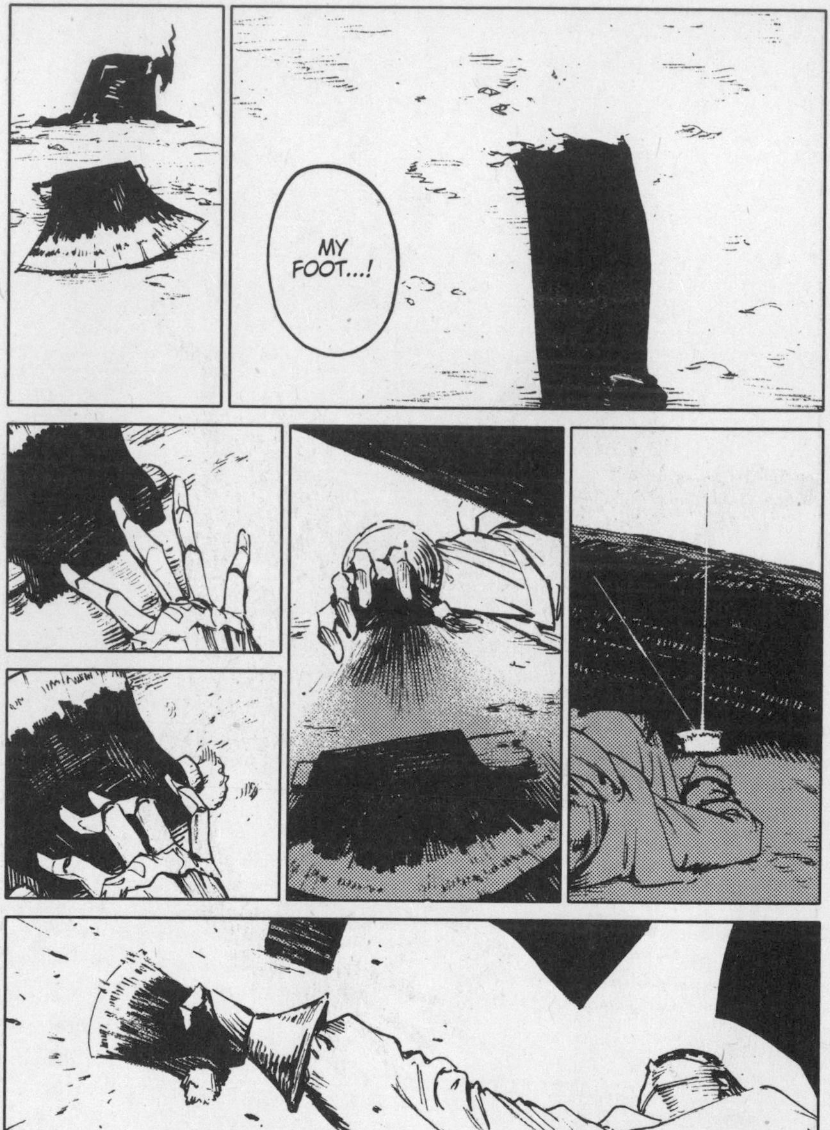
MY FOOT...!

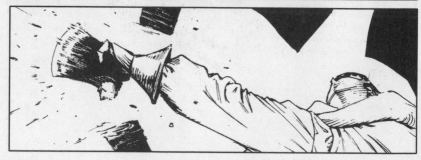

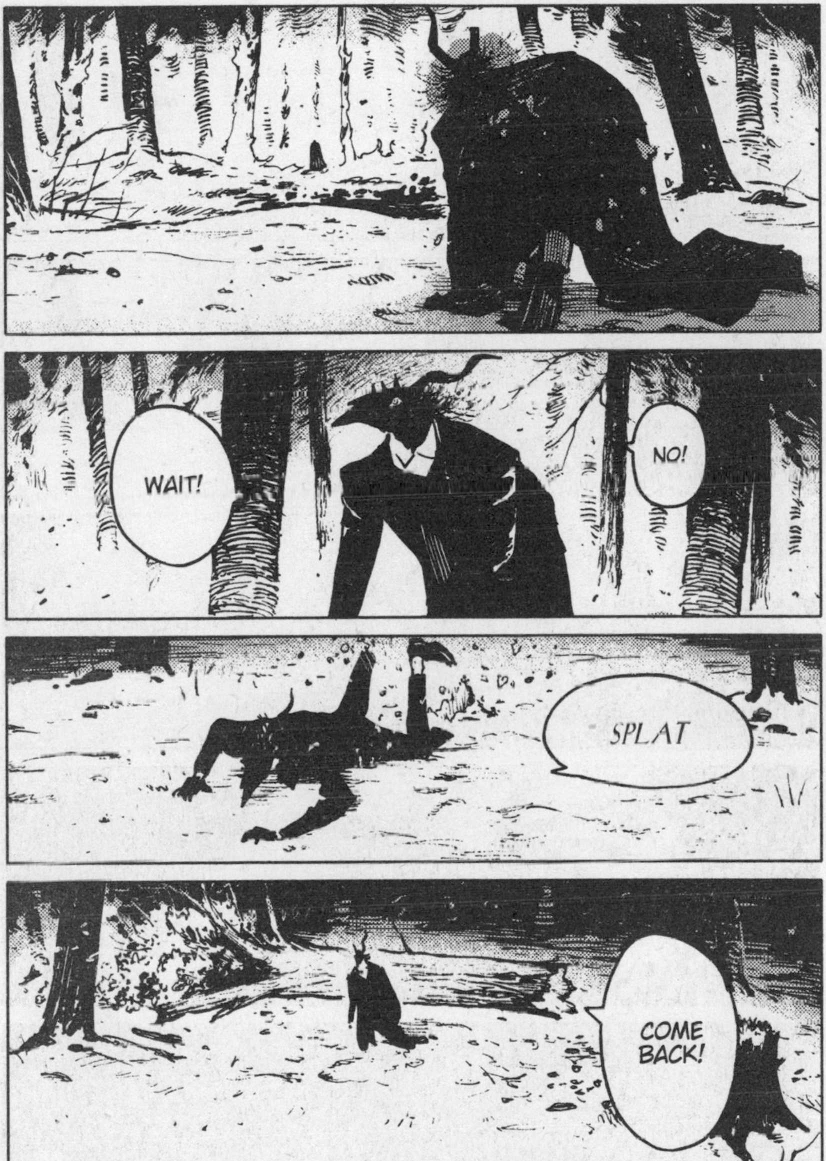
NO!
WAIT!
SPLAT
COME BACK!

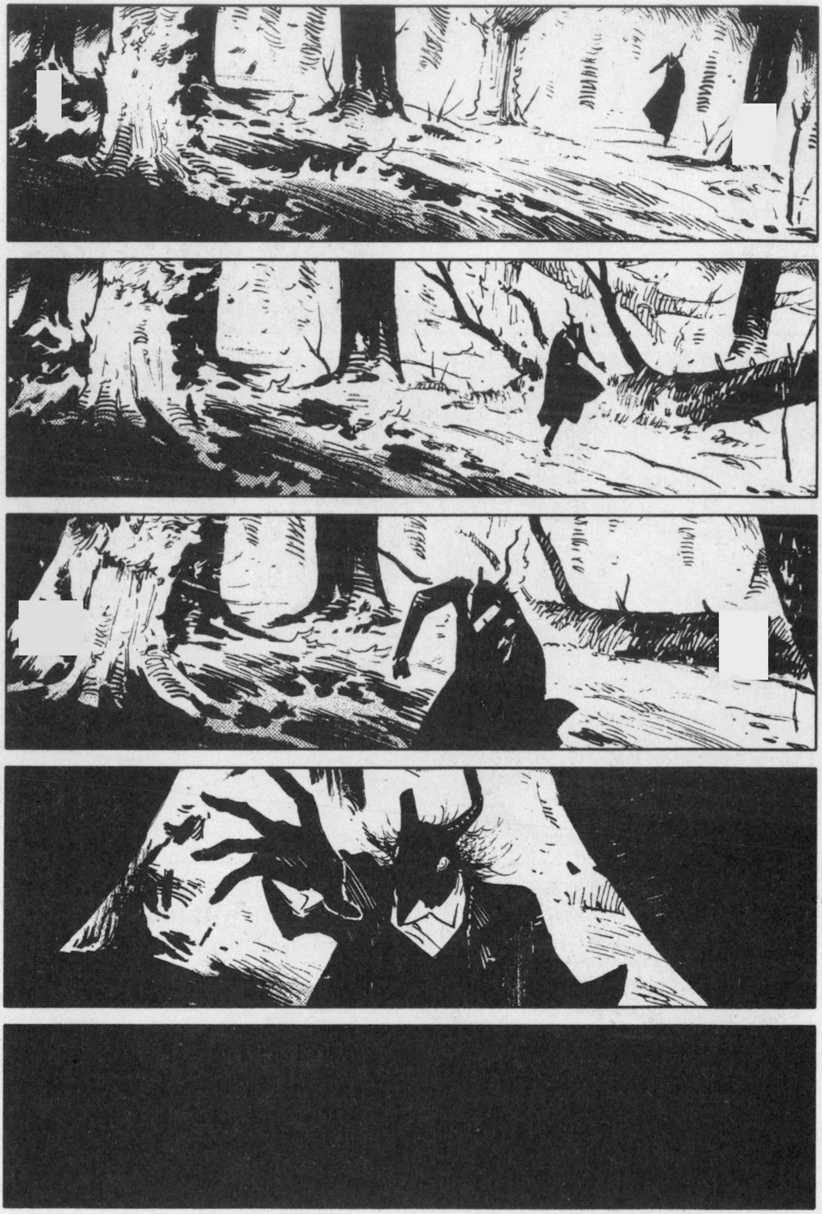

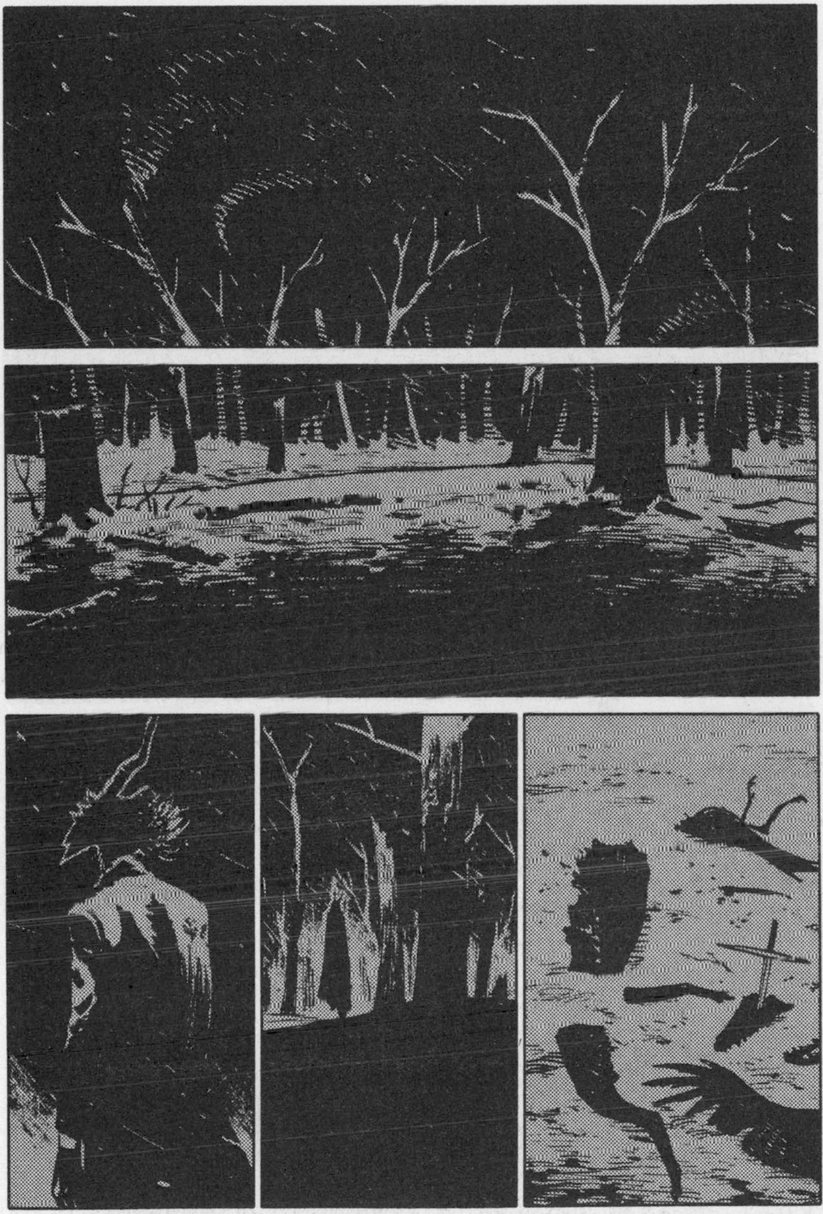

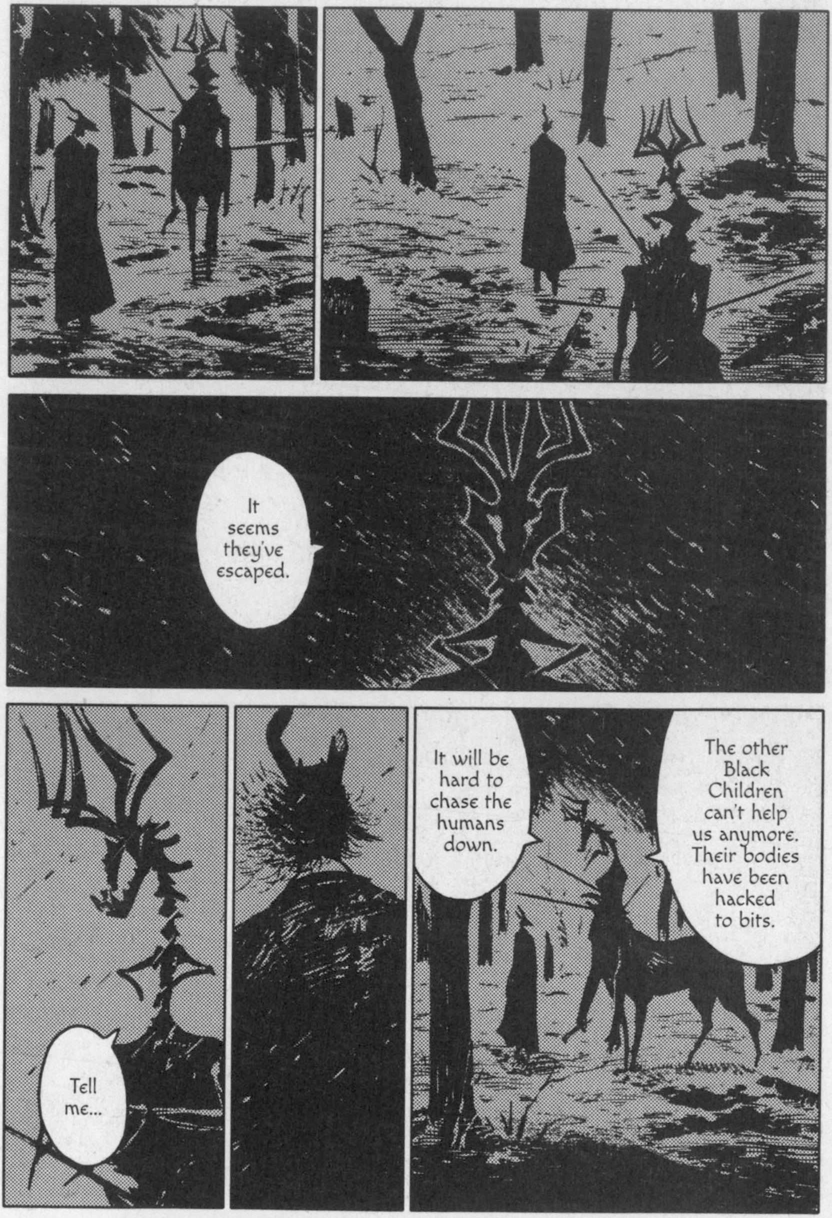
It seems they've escaped.
The other Black Children can't help us anymore. Their bodies have been hacked to bits.
It will be hard to chase the humans down.
Tell me...

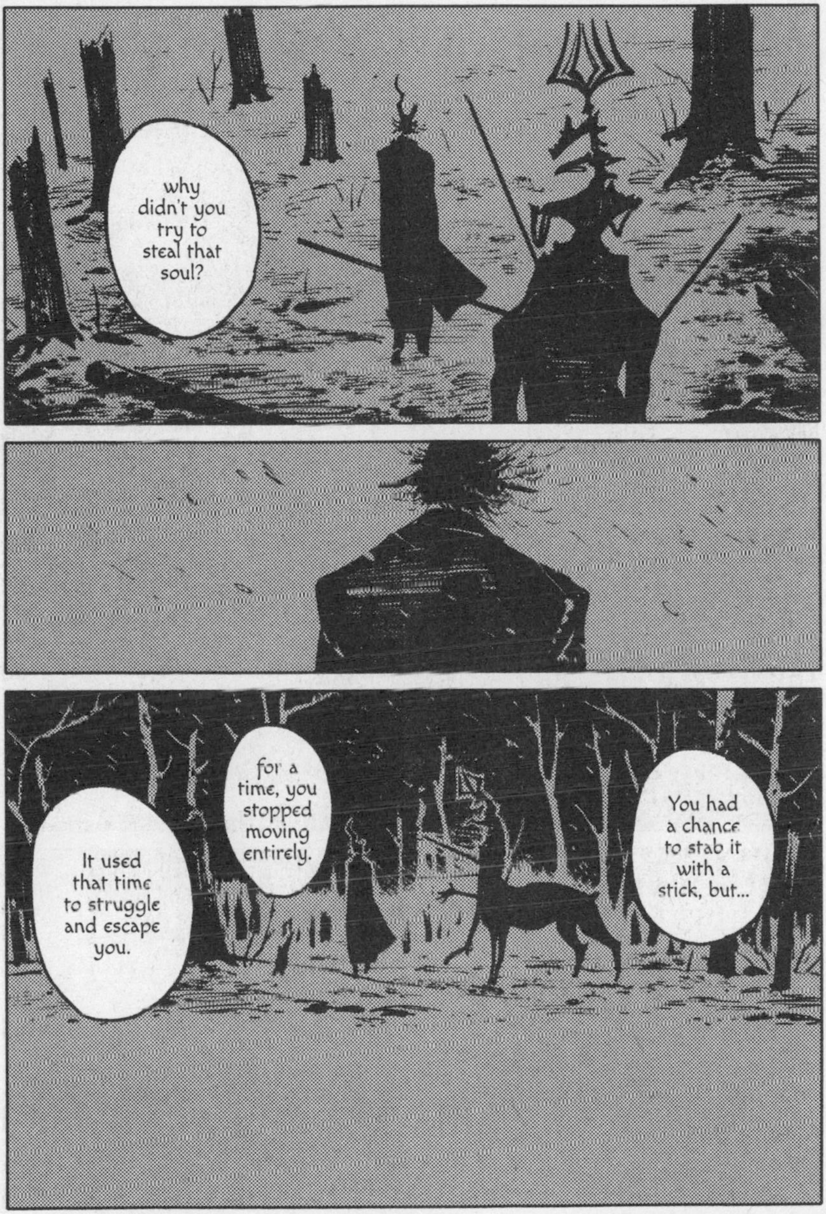
why didn't you try to steal that soul?
You had a chance to stab it with a stick, but...
for a time, you stopped moving entirely.
It used that time to struggle and escape you.

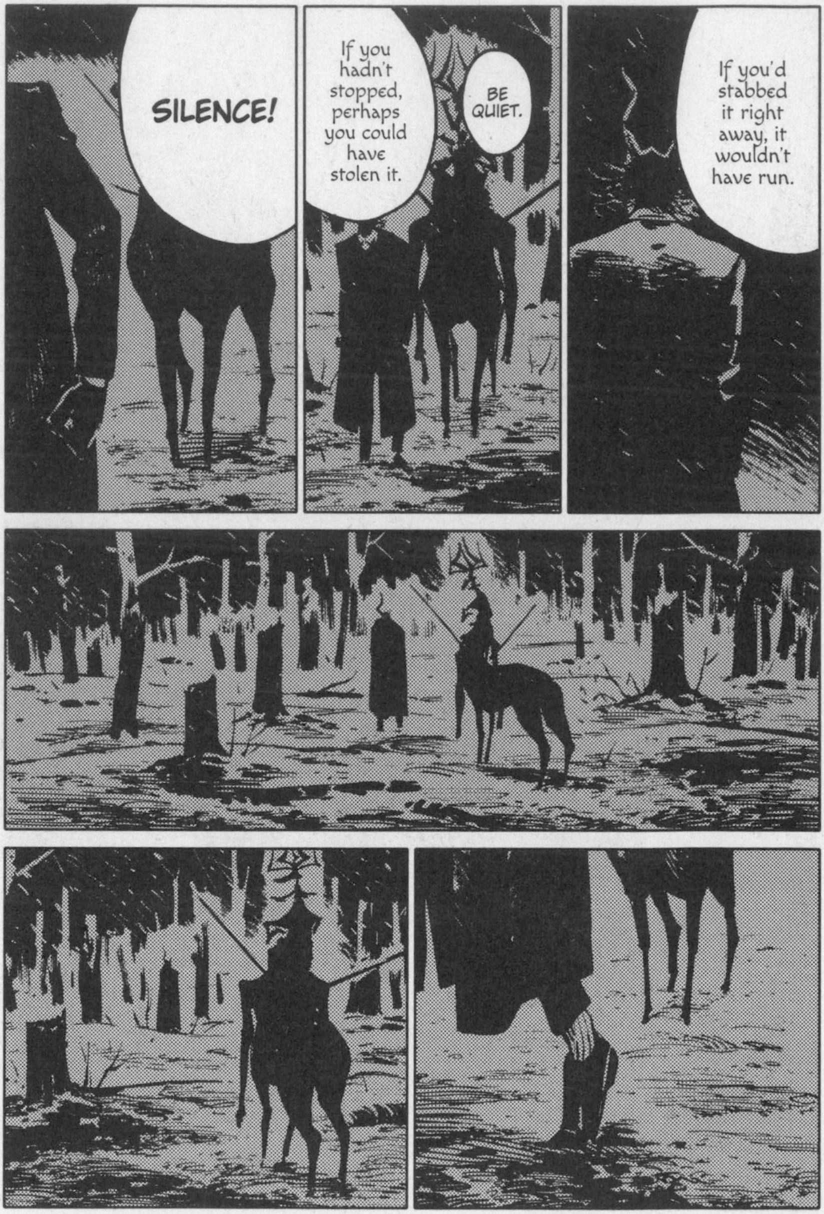
If you'd stabbed it right away, it wouldn't have run.
BE QUIET.
If you hadn't stopped, perhaps you could have stolen it.
SILENCE!

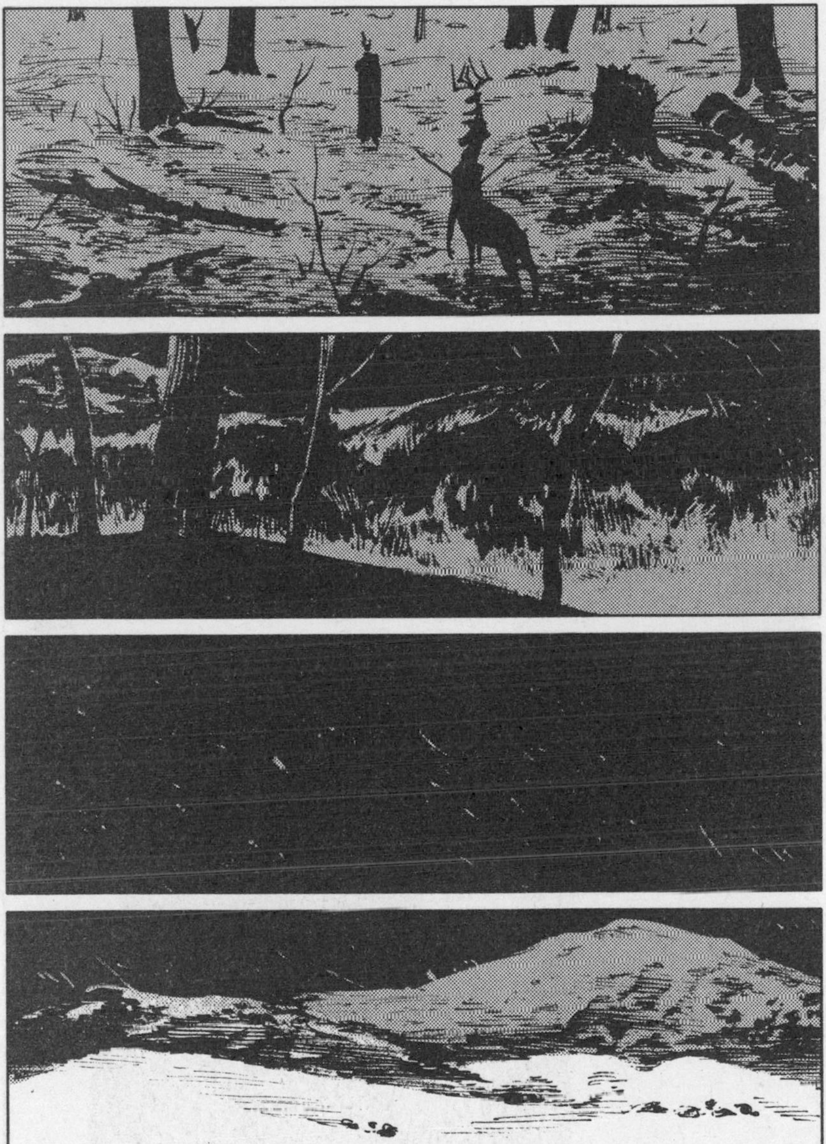

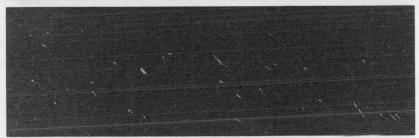

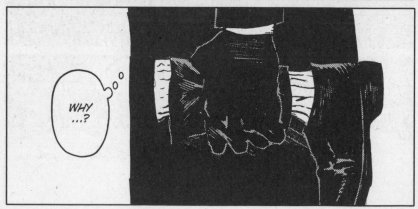

WHY
...?

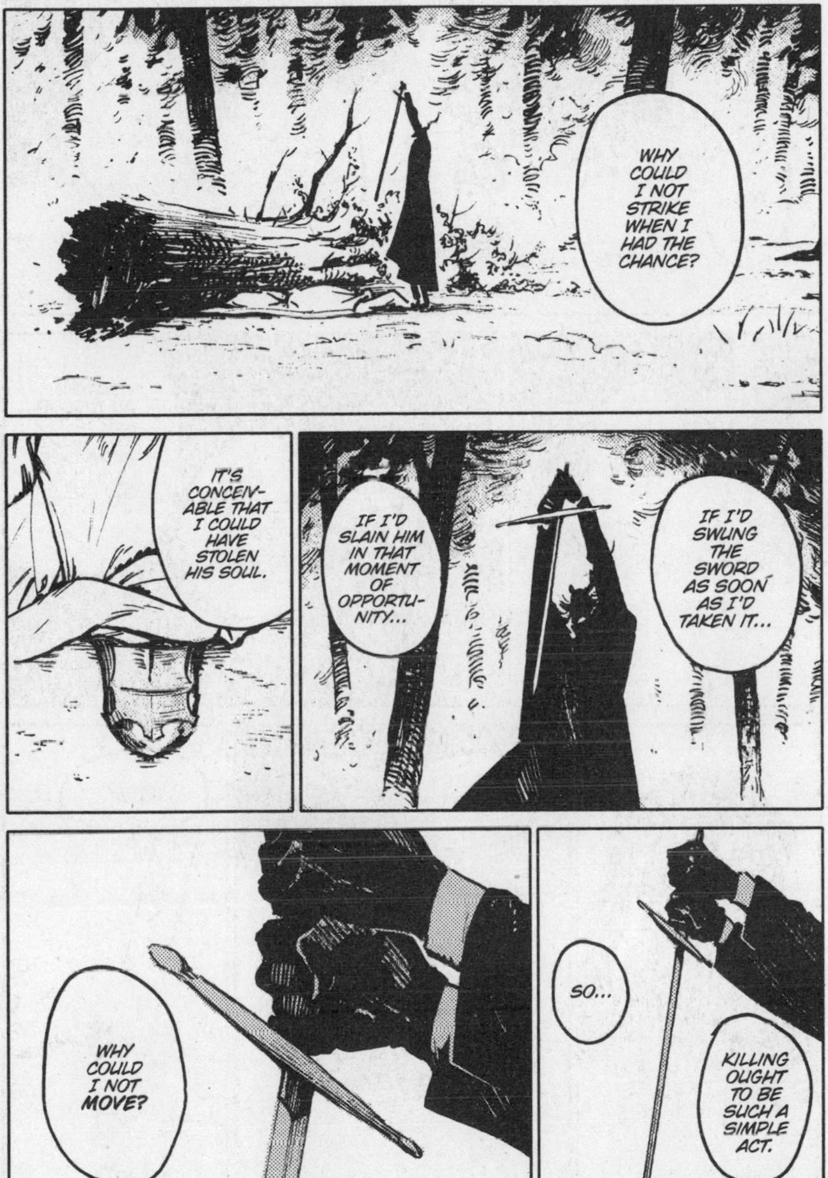
WHY COULD I NOT STRIKE WHEN I HAD THE CHANCE?
IF I'D SWUNG THE SWORD AS SOON AS I'D TAKEN IT...
IF I'D SLAIN HIM IN THAT MOMENT OF OPPORTUNITY...
IT'S CONCEIVABLE THAT I COULD HAVE STOLEN HIS SOUL.
SO...
KILLING OUGHT TO BE SUCH A SIMPLE ACT.
WHY COULD I NOT MOVE?

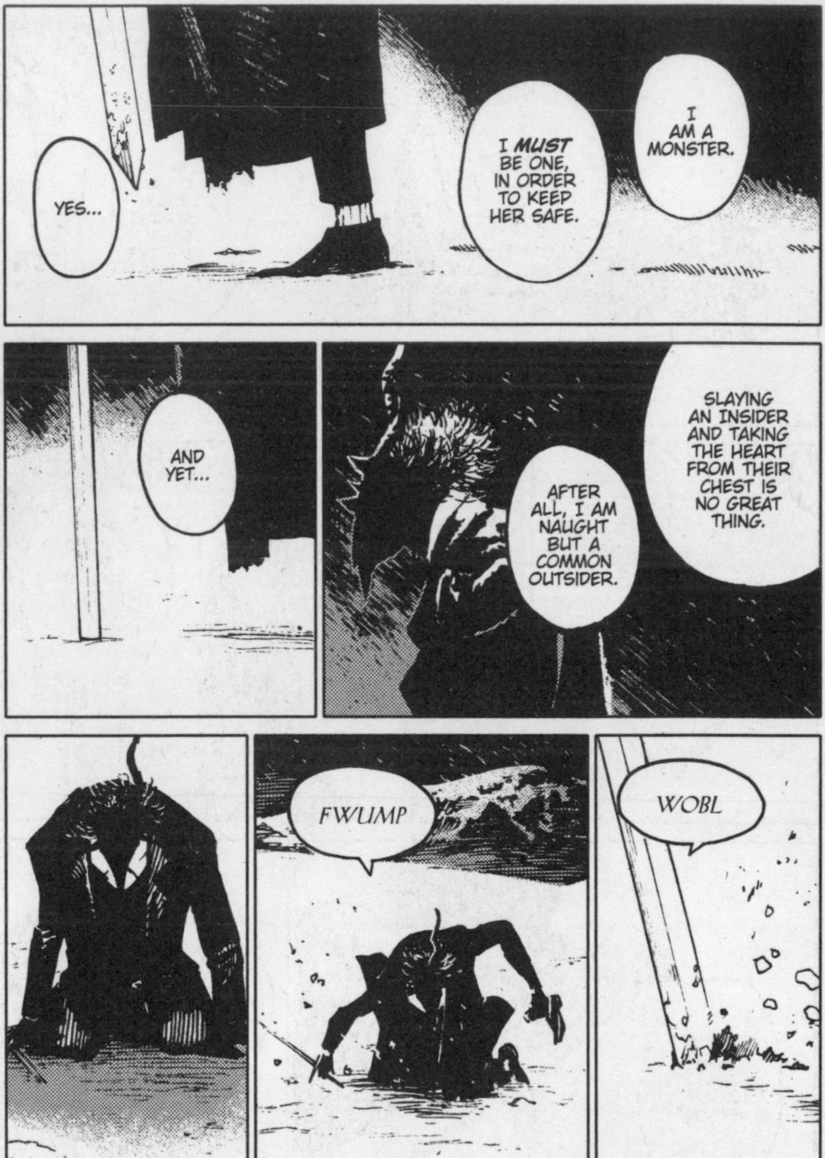
I AM A MONSTER.
I *MUST* BE ONE, IN ORDER TO KEEP HER SAFE.
YES...
SLAYING AN INSIDER AND TAKING THE HEART FROM THEIR CHEST IS NO GREAT THING.
AFTER ALL, I AM NAUGHT BUT A COMMON OUTSIDER.
AND YET...
WOBL
FWUMP

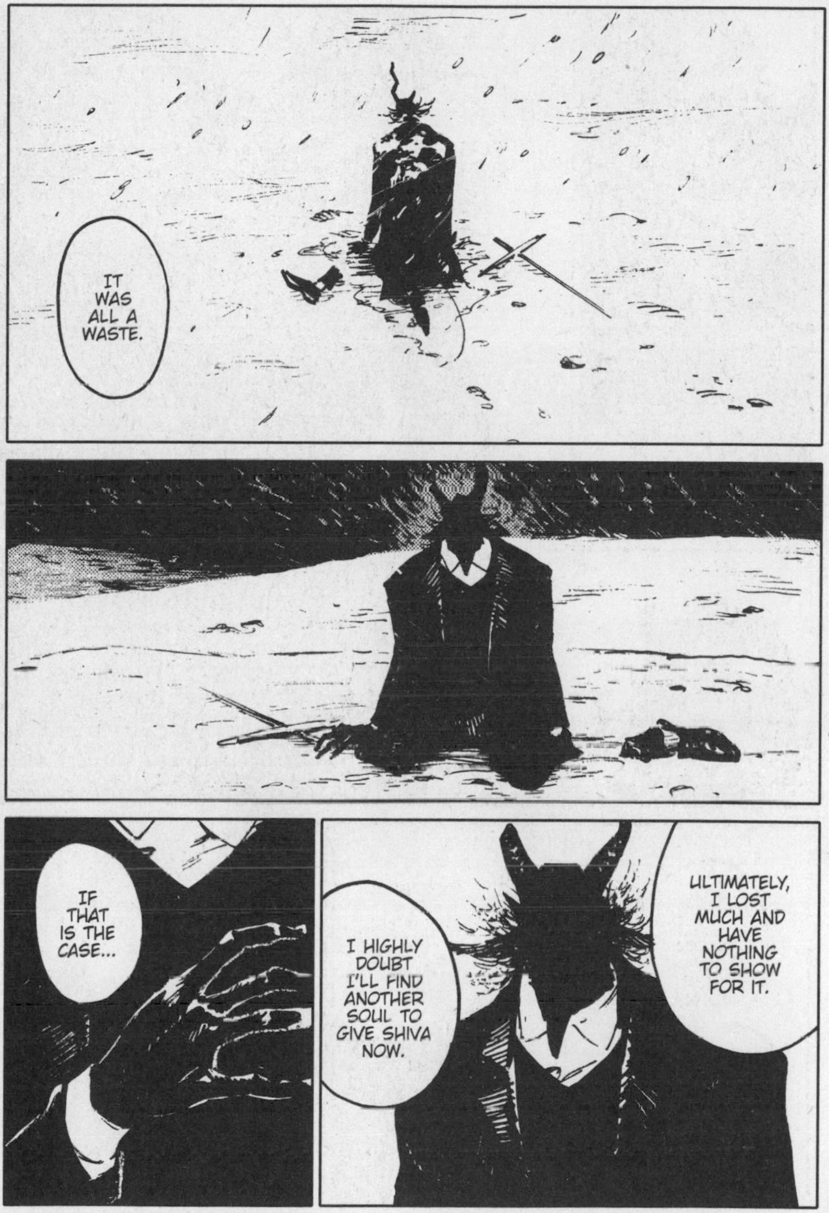
IT WAS ALL A WASTE.
ULTIMATELY, I LOST MUCH AND HAVE NOTHING TO SHOW FOR IT.
I HIGHLY DOUBT I'LL FIND ANOTHER SOUL TO GIVE SHIVA NOW.
IF THAT IS THE CASE...

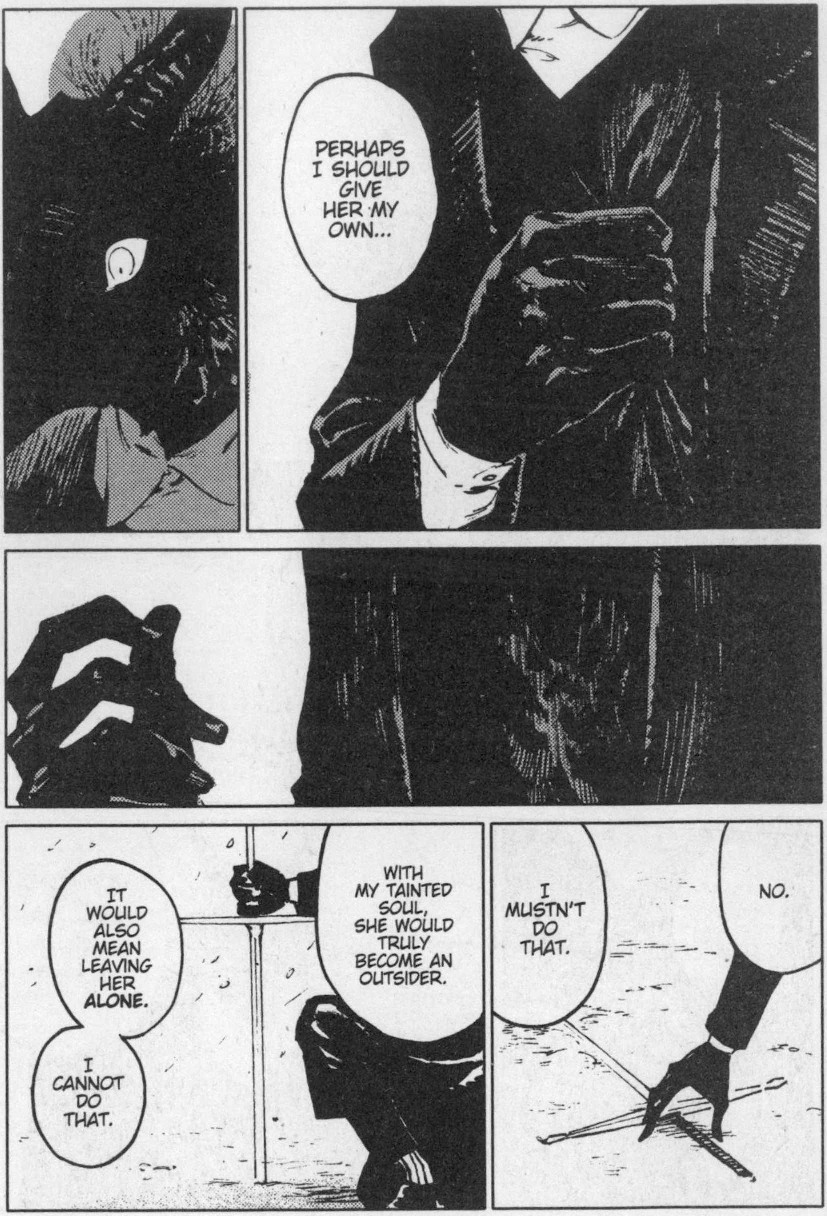
PERHAPS I SHOULD GIVE HER MY OWN...
NO.
I MUSTN'T DO THAT.
WITH MY TAINTED SOUL, SHE WOULD TRULY BECOME AN OUTSIDER.
IT WOULD ALSO MEAN LEAVING HER ALONE.
I CANNOT DO THAT.

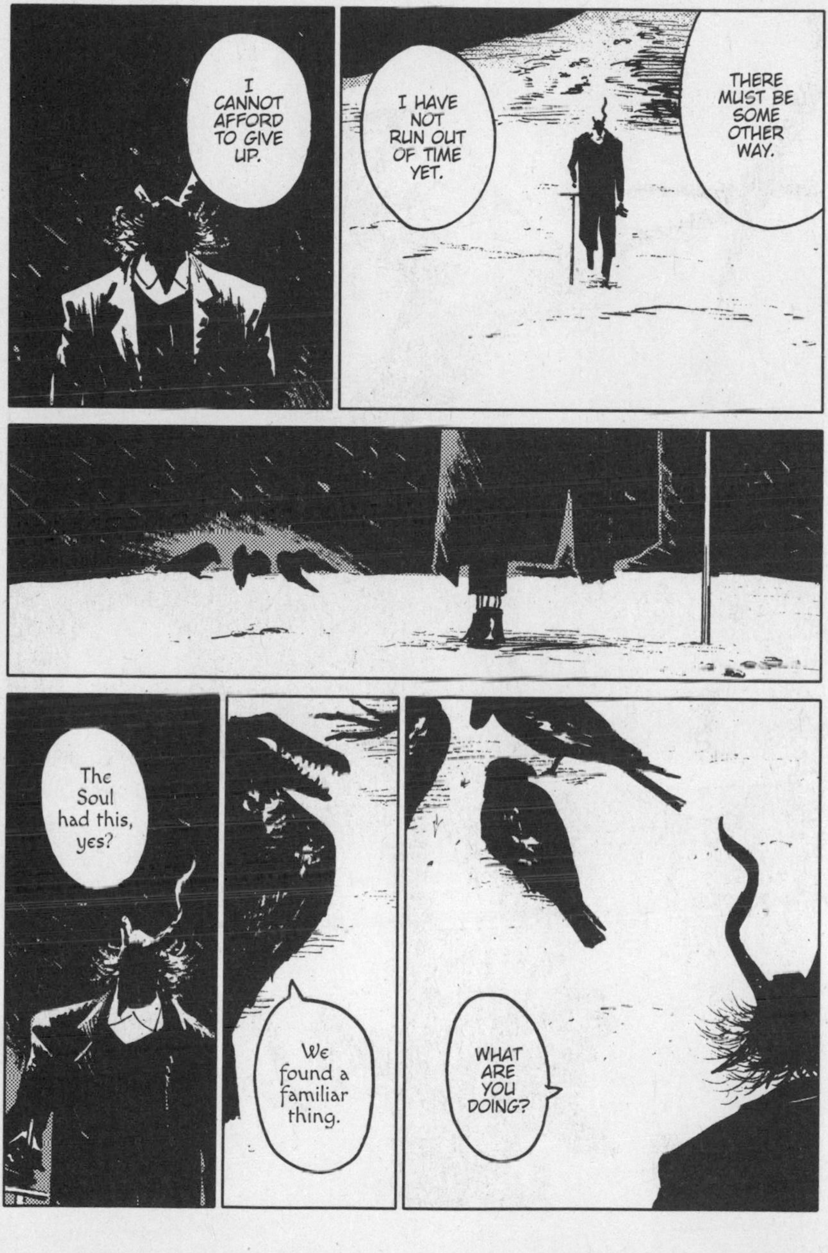
THERE MUST BE SOME OTHER WAY.
I HAVE NOT RUN OUT OF TIME YET.
I CANNOT AFFORD TO GIVE UP.
WHAT ARE YOU DOING?
We found a familiar thing.
The Soul had this, yes?

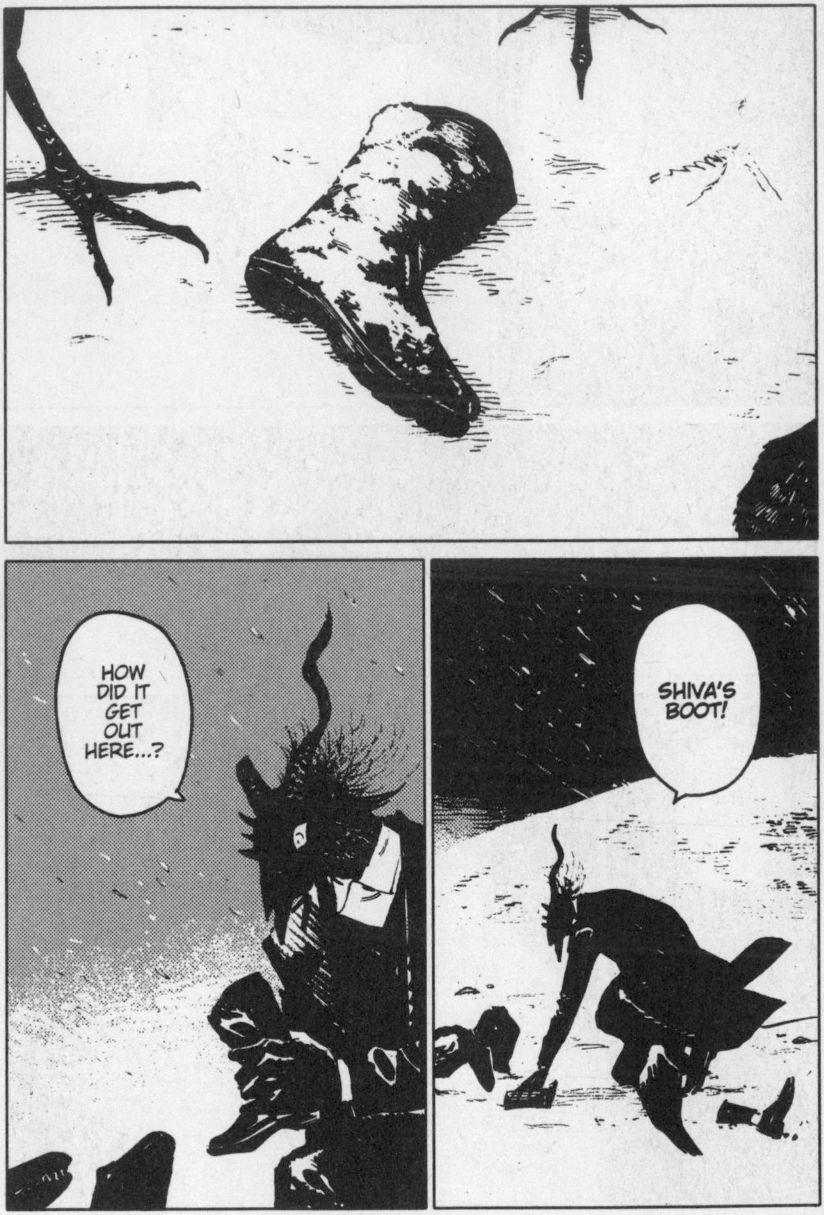
SHIVA'S BOOT!
HOW DID IT GET OUT HERE...?

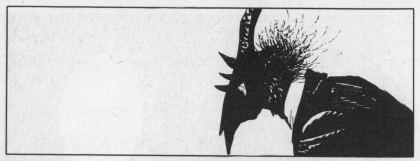

DASH

KREEK

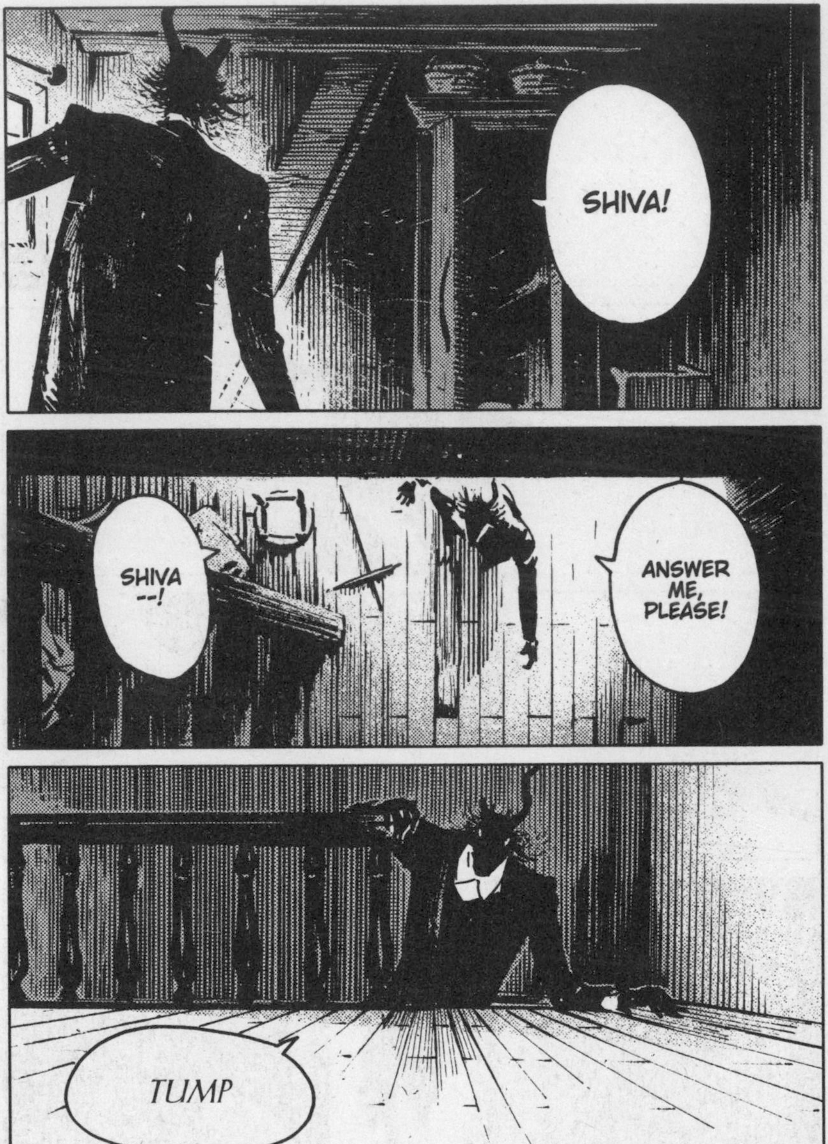
SHIVA!
ANSWER ME, PLEASE!
SHIVA --!
TUMP

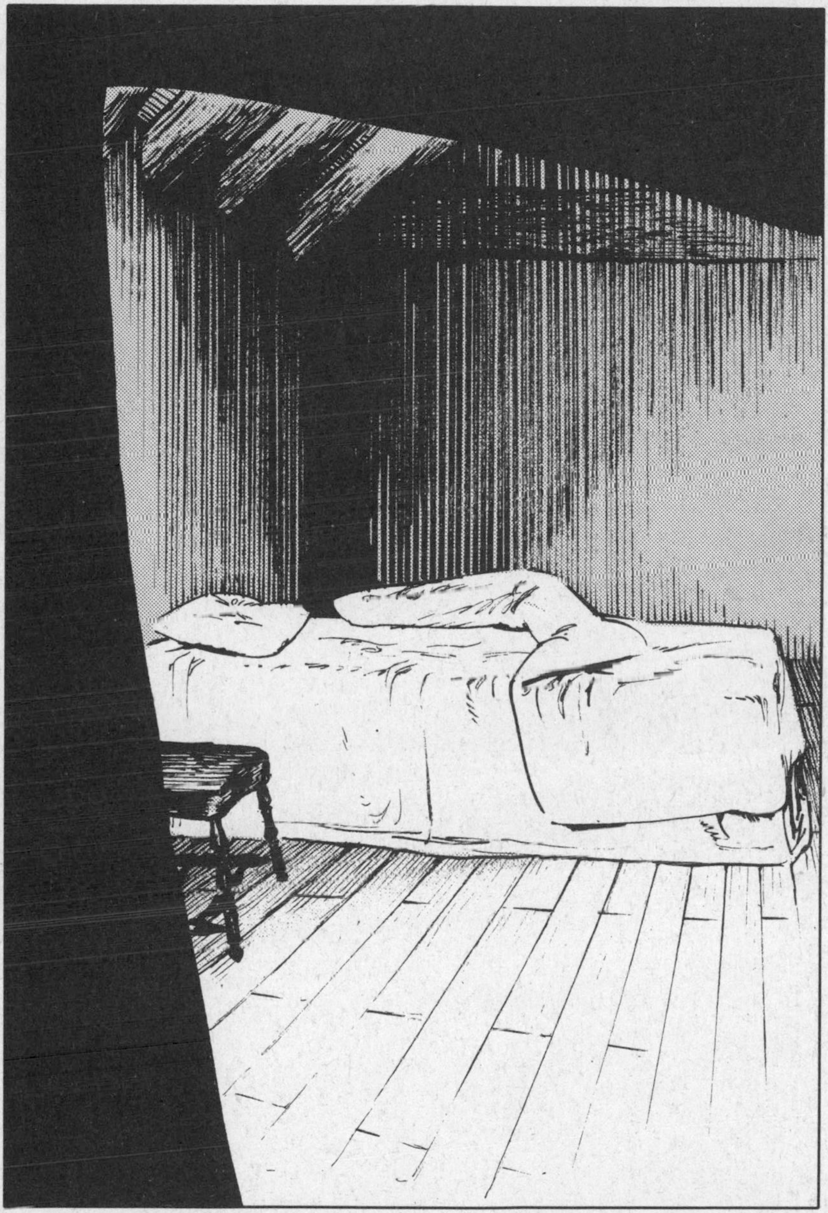

The Girl from the Other Side: Siúil a Rún Vol. 7 – END

A Bonus from the Other Side

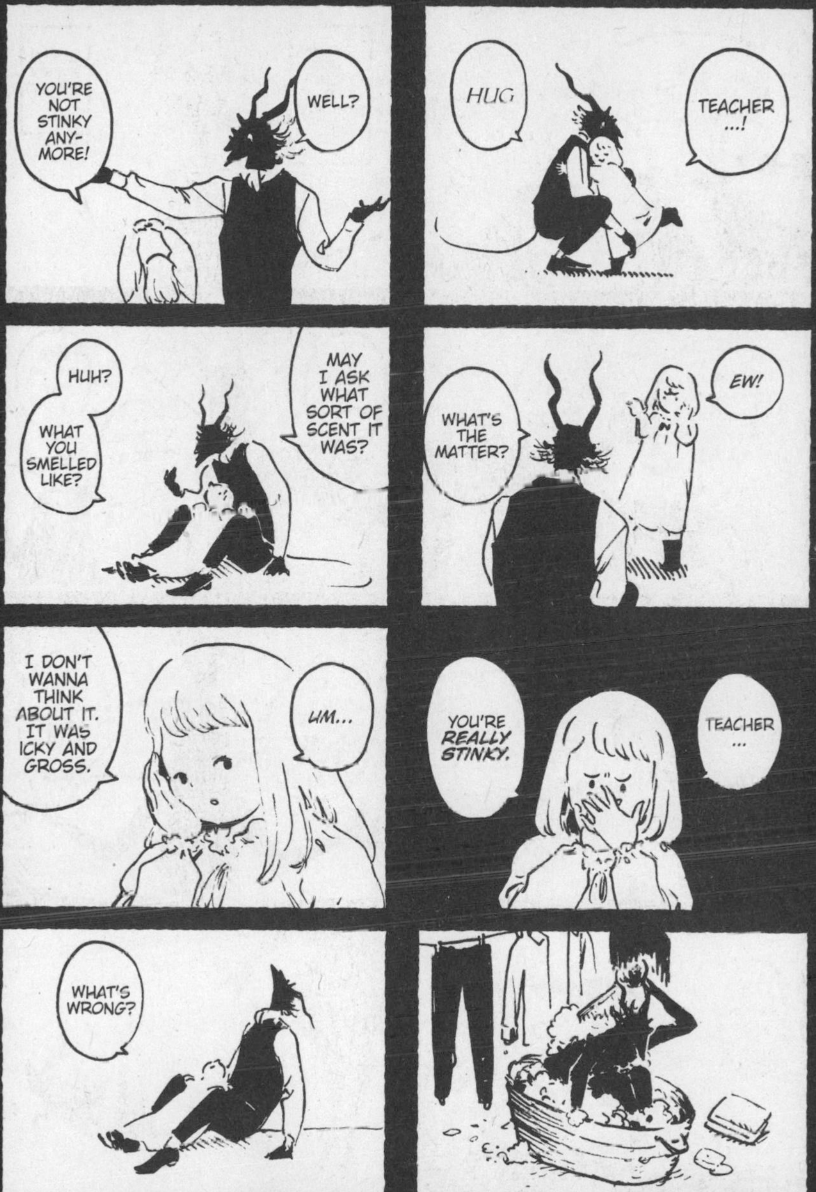
TEACHER ...!
HUG
WELL?
YOU'RE NOT STINKY ANYMORE!
EW!
WHAT'S THE MATTER?
MAY I ASK WHAT SORT OF SCENT IT WAS?
HUH?
WHAT YOU SMELLED LIKE?
TEACHER ...
YOU'RE REALLY STINKY.
UM...
I DON'T WANNA THINK ABOUT IT. IT WAS ICKY AND GROSS.
WHAT'S WRONG?